D1119025

Sounds

OF THE EARTH

ED HART

CLAY BRIDGES
PRESS

Sounds of the Earth

Copyright © 2021 by Ed Hart

Published by Clay Bridges in Houston, TX
www.ClayBridgesPress.com

ISBN: 978-1-953300-24-9
eISBN: 978-1-953300-25-6

Special Sales: Most Clay Bridges titles are available in special quantity discounts. Custom imprinting or excerpting can also be done to fit special needs. For standard bulk orders, go to www.claybridgesbulk.com. For specialty press or large orders, contact Clay Bridges at info@claybridgespress.com.

Table of Contents

Miners put an end to darkness,
and search out the farthest bound
the ore in gloom and deep darkness.
They open shafts in the valley away from human habitation;
they are forgotten by travelers,
they sway suspended, remote from people.
As for the earth, out of it comes bread;
but underneath it is turned up as by fire.

—Job 28:3–5

This book is about the gift of life, the reality of death,
hope, faith, doubt, love, laughter, romance . . .
and, of course, baseball.

I dedicate this book to Mrs. Iverson,
my second grade teacher at Factoria Elementary School in
Bellevue, Washington, because she taught me how to read.

Foreword

When I first read the title of this book, it jumped off the page at me. There are sounds down in a mine. The earth snaps and pops and groans. Sometimes, the hanging wall of a fault shifts and drives air through the drifts so fast that it rips out timbers, collapses everything in its path, and kills those unfortunate enough to be in its way. It's a tough way to spend your days and nights, but it pays well.

In the early 1960s, I was living in Wallace, Idaho, the home of the largest silver mines in the United States. I spent my summers earning money to put myself through the University of Idaho. Hourly salary and lots of overtime were critical considerations in earning maximum dollars in minimum time. Physically demanding jobs that involved a bit of risk were the best bet. At the time in Northern Idaho, logging, freeway construction, firefighting, installing natural gas pipelines, and underground mining filled the bill. I did them all.

Mining was high on the list if you were local and going to college. Being hired was automatic. It also meant you could work Christmas break and spring break—just show up with your mine boots and hard hat for the next shift. Until you had significant experience, you didn't actually mine; you did "grunt" work such as mucking the tracks in the drifts or maybe busting boulders on the grizzly. The shift foreman told you what and how much you were expected to do. If you did less or more than you were expected to, "You're fired!" On my first shift, I drove a small electric train engine pulling three ore cars— muck the tracks, fill three cars, and stop. I was to turn off my light and sleep if I could. "Someone will come and get you," I was told. It's dark—as in open your eyes wide and *nothing*. Many levels of a mine are hot and wet, and they have to pump air down to you. The deeper, the hotter. Many mines will have 50 or maybe 100 miles of tunnels.

Like logging, if you start young and you are still around by your 40s, you are most likely beat-to-hell and busted up. At the time, I had no idea that just 10 years later as a school principal on a spring day in 1972, a wide-eyed parent would enter my office to tell me there was a toxic fire in the Sunshine Mine.

My students had fathers, brothers, and uncles who worked in that mine. I said a quick prayer and turned on the news.

This excellent book was written by my pastor of several years and my good friend of what seems like a lifetime. It's fiction, but just barely. It's extremely well-constructed. The dialog is amazing and so real. It's an interesting book to read with wonderful insight into the human condition. Are there Bible references? He's a pastor, right? You do not have to be a Christian to enjoy it. It's a great and meaningful read for the individual. I would also recommend it for a book club. The questions at the end of the story are certainly thought-provoking. *Enjoy.*

Warren Bakes
Faculty, University of Idaho

Preface

In 1974, while traveling home from a funeral in the Silver Valley region of Idaho, I passed a monument of a miner standing tall and holding a drill. I asked the driver the story behind it. He began by saying, "I still dream of it some nights." He told me the story of 93 men trapped in a mine that was on fire and filled with smoke. It was the largest silver-producing mine in North America and the second-largest in the world. He told it from the perspective of a man who had driven many a hearse to help bury the 91 who died in the mine in May 1972.

I began asking others—people who had been around North Idaho at that time—what they remembered. The more I learned, the more the weight of it seeped into the recesses of my heart. Everyone had their perspective, just like, "What were you doing when Kennedy was shot?" It was these varied perspectives that caught my attention, and I decided to write a book—not nonfiction, but a novel where imagination could intersect life and perhaps make real life more real.

People, ideas, and events I had not planned in advance inserted themselves, coming both from my imagination and real-life stories. I found myself writing about things I knew people cared about, things that are as relevant today as they probably were in 1972. It is my hope that readers will take their own journey and see where it leads.

This book is not a historical novel that recreates events as accurately as possible. Rather, it is a novel—fiction, a creation of my imagination where the Sunshine Mine disaster of 1972, a real event, is the backdrop for my attempt to capture some of the human side. For an accurate nonfictional account of this disaster, read Gregg Olsen's *The Deep Dark,* for which I am very grateful. All the characters in this book are fictional with the exception of Gilbert Yates, Lorna and Chuck Sears, Bob Templin, Larry Frost, and, of course, public figures such as J. Edgar Hoover, Willie Mays, and others. The events at the J. C. Penney store in Coeur d'Alene actually happened and were relayed to me by the store's manager, Larry Frost. People who occupied real positions such as the mine superintendent and the Methodist pastor are creations of my imagination, and I apologize to the actual people who held those positions and whom I have demonized in my book. In my mind, many characters are conglomerates of people I have known. Mason Chalice represents a number of men who entered the ministry to avoid Vietnam and found themselves adrift when immersed in the lives of their flock.

I offer this book as a reminder that regardless of the statistics, in any disaster or tragedy, it is the people who are the real story. Lives are altered or ended, but regardless of our circumstances, God is forever creating hope and new life. I have seen many tragedies, not all as large as this mine disaster but no less heartbreaking. We are often forced to search for meaning when trust is broken and to decide whether forgiveness is a path worth taking and if trusting in God's faithfulness can bring healing. The unwelcome visitation of death ironically often puts us in touch with the intimacy of God and the preciousness of life. Characters in this book struggle with these things, and I hope the reader will be able to ponder them as well.

PART I

Hide and Seek

But so with all, from babes that play
At hide-and-seek to God afar,
So all who hide too well away
Must speak and tell us where they are.

—Robert Frost

CHAPTER ONE

Leaving

Pete took a last look around his apartment. The tattered, beige curtains covering the slider were closed, but then they usually were. In fact, he never opened them except when he barbecued on the Weber. He remembered the first time he had. He was watching a Huskies football game on TV. The game was tied, and Washington had the ball with less than a minute left. They were in field goal range with the best kicker in the conference, and Pete forgot he was cooking. The smoke was so bad that Mrs. Hutchins called the fire department, not that there was any need to, but that was Bertha Hutchins.

Pete looked at his magazines neatly displayed on the coffee table with the names staggered so all the banners could be read at once. Not that anyone would be reading them before he returned, but Pete had noticed the arrangement in a doctor's office, thought it looked classy, and knew he could use some class. *Field and Stream* was on top. It was Pete's attempt to prepare himself for his coming vacation. It seemed like the outdoors was becoming a growing trend. REI in Seattle was exceeding its dreams that had started in a garage in 1938.

Pete really hadn't read the magazine yet, but at least when Marcy and Max stopped by last night, they noticed it. "Maybe it will improve my image with them," Pete thought. "Why am I so self-conscious when Max isn't talking? Maybe it's the way he looks at me, like he's waiting for me to say something really revealing and personal. I should take the magazine with me, but it probably won't improve my chances of catching fish."

The orange ceramic bowl in the middle of the kitchen counter looked even larger when it was empty. Pete always kept fruit in it. And as always, Pete's eyes went right to the nick on the rim. "Another of life's imperfections," he thought. He knew it was a little extravagant to always have fresh fruit, especially during Seattle winters. "But one has to indulge themselves somewhere in life," Pete said out loud. "Though I'm no hedonist, I'm no aesthetic, either."

Pete was tempted to take one last swipe at the countertop, but he knew it would be silly. He could hear his father's voice: "Hurry up, Dear, or we will miss our train." And his mother would say deceptively as she wiped the kitchen countertop one more time, "I'm coming, I'm just now putting on my coat," and she and Pete would both glance at her coat on the chair by the door.

"I do need a vacation," Pete said to no one. "V-A-C-A-T-I-O-N, to vacate, to empty, to escape the ordinary. But how do you vacate something that is already empty? Isn't that the problem most of us have, trying to find something to fill the void?"

Before Pete closed the door, he picked up the picture of the cabin. The cedar shake porch seemed to be lower on the end away from the door. "I may have to do some repairs for the home team," he thought. "A little physical labor will do me good. The home team was always what Mom and Dad called us when we were at the cabin," he reminded himself.

The picture showed his mother standing on the porch with one arm around a post and the other around Pete's shoulder. He could almost remember the feel of her touch. Her hair was being blown by a breeze, which gave her a fresh, relaxed look. No one would have ever guessed the truth. Pete's father was leaning casually on the other side of the post with his hands in his pockets and his legs crossed at the ankles. Each had their most typical smile. Pete was grinning from one eight-year-old ear to the other. His father looked like he often did—confident—but also something Pete rarely saw—relaxed, a not-too-common state from what Pete could remember. "I remember that summer well. It was a summer to remember, a summer to wrap my childhood in and keep the other memories out," Pete smiled.

4

"I should have gone back long before now, but I just didn't want to face how much things have changed. Life is what happens while you're running away," Pete said to himself. "Well, I'll be there soon, thank goodness."

The sound of the door closing and Mrs. Hutchins's shuffling slippers obscured the sound of the falling picture and the shattering glass.

"Are you sure you need to leave just yet, Peter? You sure you have everything? Maybe you should take one last look."

Pete didn't need to look again, especially if Bertha Hutchins was leering over his shoulder. Bertha was dressed in her pink, terry cloth bathrobe with matching slippers. The white rubber soles had long ago turned black, and the pink had lost any brightness that made it colorful.

"Look, Mrs. Hutchins, everything will be fine. I'm only going to be gone two weeks. Nothing is going to happen. You'll be all right. And I'll be back before you have finished reading your latest *Ladies Home Journal*."

"Well, of course I will be fine, Dear. It's just that some things trouble me, you know."

Pete watched her pull at the edge of her worn robe. Her hands were small, knuckles enlarged from arthritis. The skin on her knuckles was as shiny as polished stone.

"I know only too well," Pete thought to himself. Bertha Hutchins's life, like the lives of most elderly, was a life of sustained anxiety and fear—the fear of falling, going hungry, not having enough money for the days left—all covered up by trivial, daily rituals. And there was the fear of being assaulted, living out the rest of their lives strapped in a wheelchair in a nursing home, and worst of all, being surrounded by people who know nothing of their past.

They would know nothing of the hardships Bertha Hutchins had endured in her time, the tears shed, or the laughter that carried her into the night as a young woman in love. If she tried to tell them, she would be dismissed as a prattling old woman. It always amazed Pete how quickly we dismiss the lives of the ordinary elderly. But he knew that, for them, their lives had been anything but ordinary. Pete knew Bertha feared the future in a strange place staring with shadowed vision and no one close to hear her cries. Ironically, time, our greatest gift, had become her enemy. Each day brought less hope and more fear. The golden years seemed to be more rust than glitter.

"What if something, you know, what if something . . . does . . . happen? What will I do?"

"Like what? Nothing ever happens here; that's why we live in this nice neighborhood, in these nice apartments." He tried to sound convincing, but being a reporter, he knew it wasn't true. Things happen everywhere, bad things all the time, and in places you would least expect it. You could live in one of the richest, safest communities, even gated ones with security guards and fancy alarm systems, and end up on the coroner's slab. That's the way life is, and you never know when the bad stuff is going to hit you in the face. But he also knew that his cynicism would not help Bertha. As annoying as she could be, Pete knew he really liked this old lady.

Bertha and her husband had owned a dairy farm near Carnation, and she had moved to Seattle after his death. Her only child, a son, was in Saudi Arabia working for Shell Oil. "Farms are for families," she had once told Pete. "Children have space to grow and be lost in the wonder and smells of plants and animals. Not that all the smells are wonderful, of course, but after a while, even the bad smells tell you you're home. You wonder about things longer when you grow up on a farm. You get to be a child longer."

Pete knew the little lady in the pink robe nervously standing in front of him was like many of her generation, a refugee from another time and place. She was a farm girl who now lived in a modern, American city, and she was alone. He had tried to make her feel not so alone, but that's hard to do when you're alone, too.

"Solos don't make couples," he thought to himself. "Maybe too much of the world is solo, and no one knows how to fit it together." He remembered hearing the term "married singles" and wondered if couples were an illusion, a slight of hand, not a reality.

"It's okay," Pete told her. "Max and Marcy said they would look in on you. Every morning, open your blinds when you get up, and they will know you're fine."

"But they both work, Peter. They can't watch out for me. Not that I need looking out for." Mrs. Hutchins was pulling at her robe as if she were a package that needed to be wrapped, and Pete found himself edging his way toward his yellow VW bug sitting at the curb like an impatient friend. Pete was beginning to feel a little impatient himself.

When you are trying to get out of town on a vacation, the first in several years, every obstacle, no matter how small, pushes up the blood pressure. He could feel his body heating up and the perspiration forming on his forehead, even in the cool of the morning. He was looking for a good exit strategy. "Look, Marcy doesn't work until noon and some days even later. And besides, Mr. Andrews would be happy to look in on you."

"Why, that . . . that . . . old lecher! He'd better not come snooping around my place," Bertha declared. "I'll call the police and have him arrested. He shouldn't be loose. He is a menace to us all."

Pete wasn't sure *menace* was the right word; *entertainer* would be more than appropriate. Mr. Andrews was best known for his daily martini and his recitations from Shakespeare. Mrs. Hutchins raved on about him, a man who was about as dangerous as a church organist, although much more colorful. Pete threw his bag into the bug and started the engine. He leaned out the window. "Mrs. Hutchins, I asked Gwen to look in on you when she picks up my mail. You will be fine." He tried to make his voice comforting and final.

"You didn't need to bother, Dear. I could pick up your mail and hold it for you. Is Gwen the one with the dark hair who drives that little red car?"

"Yep, that's her." *You know exactly who she is*, Pete thought. "It is no bother. She's going to water my plants, too. Bye!"

Mrs. Hutchins waved as Pete's yellow bug made its way out of the complex. She was nodding as if she agreed with the arrangement. The bug disappeared around the corner under the majestic dogwood tree near the complex's entrance. It suddenly occurred to her—Peter Webb has no plants, not even a cactus.

All his life, Peter Webb had wanted to go to the city, any city, and chase the big story, uncover the covered up, and be a recognized reporter—not famous, but appreciated. He was old-fashioned enough to believe in the Fourth Estate, and it concerned him that papers seemed to be more and more mouthpieces of political parties instead of the watchdogs they ought to be. He feared that the rise of television as the primary source of news for most would lead to a seductive relationship among politicians, media owners, and journalists. It would become an incestuous affair, corrupting impartial journalism. Cameras changed people's behaviors and perceptions. Pete turned on the radio to distract him from too much thinking. "That was Janis Joplin—'Me and Bobby McGee,'" the announcer said.

"Even those who read my byline wouldn't recognize me in a lineup," Pete thought. "Besides, what makes a big story? Its importance to the public? Its tantalizing content?" Pete wasn't sure anymore.

Pete pulled up to the curb and saw his passenger-to-be—his friend Darcy Jansen, or DJ as he had always called him—standing there chatting with Oscar, the newspaper vendor. Oscar sat on a short, green box with a Washington Huskies logo painted on the side. DJ's hair was long, '60s style, and his body was gyrating to whatever was coming through the small, handheld transistor radio in his hand. The hot dog stand behind him with its red-orange neon "Hot Dog" sign framed him like a picture from some pop art museum. "Andy Warhol would be ecstatic over this scene," Pete thought.

Oscar smiled and waved at Pete with the newspaper he held in the air. Pete nodded. Oscar yelled at DJ who was dancing around the newsstand, and then DJ grabbed the newspaper out of Oscar's hand. Pete rolled down the window and honked the bug's less-than-intimidating horn. "Morning, Oscar. And come on, DJ, I want to get going. The fish are getting impatient."

Darcy Jansen dropped the small radio into his pocket and opened the VW's passenger door. He waved to the hot dog vendor and to Oscar as if he were a performer casting his goodbyes to the audience. He hunched his six-foot frame into the bug and tried to find a place for his feet, the newspaper, his hot dog, and Pete's coffee.

"Thanks for the paper, Oscar," Pete yelled, leaning across DJ. "I'll see you in two weeks."

"Catch the big one for me," Pete heard faintly as he merged into Seattle's morning traffic.

"The fish aren't the only ones who are impatient," the long-hair said as he handed Pete a cup of black coffee whose steam temporarily clouded the windshield and blocked Pete's vision. "So how was Mrs. Hutchins? She try to tie you to a tree to keep you from leaving?"

"She was her usual worried self. She thinks some great catastrophe is going to happen at the apartments while I'm gone."

"Like what? A tsunami? An earthquake?"

"How do I know, DJ? Whatever she can conjure up, I suppose."

"You ready for the 'big empty,' Petie man?"

"There's that word *empty* again," Pete thought to himself. The bug was suddenly filled with an odorous mixture of onions, pickles, black coffee, and a wool shirt a few days past laundry.

"The big empty?"

"Yeah, you know, the big empty—vacate the brain and settle in, lost in the purity of nature and all that."

"Believe me, DJ, I'm more than ready for a vaca . . . the big empty."

A gray mist still covered Puget Sound, and all the buildings seemed more gray and damp than usual for the end of April. A large drop of water splattered on the windshield as they passed under an overpass. The entire city seemed to drip as if it had some strange kind of infection. Pete thought it needed to dry out from the long, wet winter. But to discuss the weather could make one's mood foul, and right now he felt especially susceptible. Besides, people who live in Seattle usually don't talk about the weather. It's people who live elsewhere who talk about Seattle's weather. DJ swallowed his last bite of the fragrant hot dog, belched, and said, "Are you ready for the challenge?"

"Sure. What's the score now?"

"You know darn well what the score is. It's 125 for you and 16 for me."

"Okay, give me your best shot," Pete said with a grin on his face.

"When was the first official baseball introduced into the game?"

"DJ, you're slipping. My first and final answer is 1876."

"I'm just warming you up with an easy one, but I'll bet you won't get the next one."

"The usual bet?"

"Absolutely, but I'm out of Indian head nickels. Here's the question: Who was the first player to burn his signature into a Louisville Slugger bat? You have 30 seconds."

"Honus Wagner, in 1900," Pete shouted. "You owe me five cents."

"I'll give it to you when you get back. Ask me one, and give me a chance to catch up." They both laughed and grinned at each other.

"Okay, DJ, the first ball's center was made of rubber. In 1910, it was changed to cork. In 1931, the cork was replaced with a mixture of cork and ground rubber. During World War II, rubber was not available. What was the center made of until it was replaced with synthetic rubber?"

"Jeez, did you stay up all night looking that up? I have no clue."

"We'll not count that one. It was something called *balata* that they just made from stuff. It was a lot like rubber but lacked elasticity. The ball never went anywhere when you hit it. Pitchers loved it; batters hated it. I don't think I'm really in the mood to play anymore, DJ. I still can't get over the fact that the best first baseman ever just died. He was my hero."

"You mean Gil Hodges? But he wasn't playing anymore, he was managing."

"Yeah, but he was still the best first baseman ever."

"Well, you can mourn ol' Gil, but last year we lost Louis Armstrong, then Mahalia Jackson. Boy, did that lady ever have pipes!"

"I thought you were a jazz man, DJ."

"Hey, a little gospel music never hurt anybody."

"Depends on what you mean by gospel music, I guess."

"Truth to that, Petie, but good music folks are disappearing fast. Remember, last month Phil King, the rock and roll guy, died."

"He didn't just die, DJ. He was shot in the head while gambling. Some folks take their games very seriously."

"My mom always said, 'Darcy, you'd better be careful about what your extracurricular activities are,' and she was right. What do you think the chances are for the Pirates to take the series again this year?"

"I don't know. Their pitching is still good, but you don't know with all the trades how strong they'll end up. It's not like the old days when a guy played for the same team for almost forever. Now they bounce around like balls in the batting cage."

"Have you seen the *French Connection* yet, Petie? I really want to see it, but if you haven't, I'll wait 'til you get back."

"Nah, Gwen and I were going to see it last week, but her folks came to town, so our plans got changed. It would be great to see it with you, probably better than with her."

"Ooh, that's a telling remark."

The radio saved Pete from an explanation.

Following the death of Supreme Court Justice James F. Byrnes last month, President Nixon is said to be screening a number of candidates for the court who may bring a more conservative influence, which experts say could affect the balance of the Warren Court.

"Do you think it will make a difference who Tricky Dicky puts on the court?" DJ asked.

"In the short run, no, but in the long run, DJ, it depends on how old they are, how long they last, and whether or not they change their stripes while they're on the court. Sometimes a justice drops one banner and picks up another. Remember, Eisenhower appointed Earl Warren who turned out to be the iconic liberal. I don't think that's what Ike had in mind at the time."

"Speaking of Tricky Dicky, what do you think will be the long-term effects of Nixon's visit to China?"

"Are you practicing to be a political commentator-slash-interviewer, DJ?"

"Nay, fair knight. Answer my question, and help supplement my thwarted education."

"Okay, I think the Chinese will get more out of it than we will. You watch; there will be a lot of imported goods from China in the future," Pete predicted.

"You think so, really?"

"Yeah, I do, and we will be able to thank Nixon and the American capitalist system."

"Why so, Pete?"

"How much of China's labor force do you think is unionized, DJ?"

"Oh yeah, I see what you mean."

"Now I have a question for you. Are your initials DJ because you are a disc jockey, or are you a disc jockey because you have those initials?" DJ smiled at Pete, knowing they had played this game before, and Pete never knew what DJ would come up with.

"You don't look like you're up for any heavy thinking this morning, Petie."

"Sure I am. I beat you at baseball quiz, didn't I?"

"On the subject of baseball, I don't think I've ever asked you who you think the greatest pitcher of all time is."

"Oh, that's easy," Pete said. "There are a lot of people who would disagree with me, but without any hesitation, I would say it has to be Satchel Paige. Did I ever tell you I was there the last time he pitched in the majors? So, DJ, you didn't answer my question. Did you become a disc jockey because your initials are DJ, or is it just a coincidence?"

"I'll say it again, Petie. I'm still not sure you're up for such heavy thinking this early in the morning."

"Sure I am. I've been up with my guru since dawn at the top of the mountain and back." Pete sipped his coffee and smiled. DJ gave him a scowl and cleared his throat.

"Well, as you know, Petie, since I'm a man with a deep appreciation for the mysteries of life, I'd have to say that it has something to do with the mystical power of names. It has been my destiny to be a disc jockey since my parents, with great fanfare, announced my name when I entered this aquatic-covered universe, or multi-verse as we may learn in the not-too-distant future. Names are very powerful, Petie, but most moderns don't realize it."

"Yeah, crystals are big, too. Besides, they didn't name you Disc Jockey. The title just matches your initials."

"The ancients believed that names shape our destiny," DJ added. "Native American names depicted events and characters. It's even in the Bible."

"Your name's in the Bible, DJ?"

"Ha ha. No, Petie, but yours is. Did you know the Hebrews had a whole bunch of names for God because they thought one alone wasn't enough? I'll bet they didn't teach you that in your old, stiff Presby Sunday school."

"You mean names like Her Essence?" Pete wiped the steam from the coffee fog on the windshield with the back of his sleeve and waited. DJ gave him a sideward glance and smiled.

"Petie, you talk like that, and your Calvinistic forefathers will come out of their graves and predestine something awful for you."

"Maybe my foremothers will come to my defense," Pete said as he turned up the volume on the radio.

"I've been wondering about something, Pete. Do you think they'll find D. B. Cooper?"

"I don't know. He jumped from the plane near the end of November, so . . ."

"November 24th," DJ was quick to add.

"Okay, so it's been about five months. I think if they don't find him by September, they never will. Anybody who has that sophisticated of a plan has prepared to disappear. Besides, rumor is that he knew things about the plane that are not common knowledge. So he's either a pilot, an aeronautical engineer, or a guy whose hobby is knowing everything about airplanes. Plus he knows how to parachute. So he may be ex-military or even present military. But if he is, he'd better not have left any fingerprints."

"But they must have the serial numbers of all the bills."

"DJ, where would you go to get rid of them if it were you?"

"Someplace where they're used to seeing hundred dollar bills and don't blink because they have so many customers. Casinos, I guess?"

"Exactly. Buy some chips in Vegas, play a little, cash in your chips, and now you have clean money. You do that with several casinos, and you have more than enough to get along quite well for awhile."

"This is what I think, Petie. He didn't get hurt, or he probably would have been found. He didn't hurt anyone, and this country has a history of glorifying bad guys. So I think it will make for an interesting book and a movie starring John Cassavetes. But I want to talk about your name."

"Okay, but you're the one who brought up D. B. Cooper."

"I know, but the stabilizers on my brain haven't engaged yet. It was a long night."

"Speaking of telling remarks," Pete grinned and DJ blushed. "My name? Let's see, my name is Peter, like petered out, worn down. You see, it's my destiny to wear out and die, but isn't that everyone's?"

"No, Pete. Be serious a second. Peter does come from the Bible."

"Yes, that's my Scottish Presbyterian heritage showing. Peter was the guy who walked out when the going got tough. That's my namesake for sure."

"Will you let me finish? Peter is from *petros,* meaning 'rock.' So your name means you're rock-like."

"Hardheaded, you mean?"

"No! And not to inflate your handsome head, but you are steady and rock-like. You are a dependable, grounded kind of guy."

"Not that I agree, DJ, but what do you do with Webb?"

"Easy. Webs are places of entanglement, connection, design, and gathering. You are an entangled rock, my friend." DJ smiled while jerking his head and flipping his hair out of his eyes.

"Webs are also places of death, DJ. But you're right, I'm pretty entangled. That's why I need a vacation. With the newspaper, Hitchcock, Gwen, and my normal mental imbalance, I'm pretty entangled. I just thought of something else. Rocks sink. Maybe that's my destiny."

"We all sink at one time or another," DJ said in a muted voice as he stared into his coffee as if beneath the dark, brown surface were some hidden secret.

His comment and tone concerned Pete, especially since DJ was on his way to visit his parents. But he decided to let it slide. "When you think about it, names do mean something. For example, did you know Jesus means 'savior'? Do you think it's a coincidence that the guy gets the name Jesus and then he's known as the savior of the world?"

"I think you have been spending too much time in the religious book section. There are a lot of guys named Jesus; most of them play baseball really well and come from Puerto Rico. The trouble with you, Petie man, is that you haven't tapped into your soul self, your feminine side," he said with a smile.

"Jeez, DJ, why would I want to do that? I'm having enough trouble with my masculine side. Hell, I've only been shaving for a year." They both grinned at the idea, given Pete's unshaven chin already casting its dark shadow. "What do you hear on the street, DJ? Anything?"

Darcy Jansen was a talented disc jockey whose brain had recorded almost every piece of music written in the 20th century outside of classical, though he knew more classical music than he cared to admit. He had a late-night gig and then spent most of his days on the streets. He knew every wino and runaway in or near Pioneer Square by name. He was without a doubt the best source Pete had. DJ knew about nighttime encampments at the arboretum and secret places adjacent to Woodland Park Zoo. But best of all, he never lied, and he was Pete's best friend. He was exceptionally loyal. Pete knew DJ would do anything for him short of being tortured. DJ despised pain even in the smallest quantities. He considered stepping on an ant an act of terrorism.

"I thought you were on vacation."

"I am, but I'm a reporter. I have to keep my tools sharp like any craftsman. So have you heard anything?"

Glancing up from the newspaper, DJ asked, "Who do you think will be the Democratic nominee for president? McGovern or Muskie?"

"Muskie will have to expand his base beyond college kids and white intellectuals. The last intellectual candidate, Adlai Stevenson, went down in flames, and right now I don't think intellect is driving the country. Besides,

McGovern has more political capital to draw on, but he hasn't officially declared yet. I don't think it really matters who the Demos put up because Tricky D will play dirty. It's in his nature, more than most."

DJ stared at the newspaper and shook his head. He looked out the window and took a deep breath. "The folks in India must be reading German history books. They killed up to 3 million people and raped between 200,000 and 400,000 Bangladeshi women. A systematic campaign of genocidal rape, the sources coming out of India say. Some even put the numbers higher. You just have to love those peace-loving Hindus and the Islamists who've got their backs," DJ said sarcastically.

For some reason, the tunnel lights were out. DJ craned his neck out the window and looked upward just before they entered the tunnel and darkness engulfed them. "Probably those Californians. Seems like the more of them that come up here, the more things get screwed up." They both laughed. It was becoming a common Pacific Northwest mantra. "Tell me, Petie, why would anyone leave the Golden State of sunshine, bikinis, and hot tubs for this cold, damp state? When people move to this soggy place by choice, you have to wonder about their senses or their criminal past."

"Max said he moved here because people who live in wet damp much of the year are prone to depression, so there's a need for good shrinks."

"Humble of him to consider himself a good shrink," DJ remarked. "Is that an oxymoron, by the way?"

"There are a lot of good psychiatrists in Seattle, DJ. I know some myself."

DJ glanced at Pete with an inquiring look, but it was clear that no more information was to be expected. Pete's thinking often went beyond conventional boundaries. His mother said he was creative, but his father said creativity was not in the interest of good reporting. "You have to stick to the facts," his father said. "Don't wander into feelings. Tell what happened, maybe why and to whom, but not what you feel—unless, of course, you're the editor. Then it's your responsibility to shape the opinions of others."

Pete's father—Charles Webb—had been the editor of the *Bellingham Herald*, and every night he came home with the latest edition tucked under his arm. Pete could remember his father nodding at the neighbors sitting on their porches as if he had just arrived from a long journey and they were all waiting for him. It was as if he thought they had nothing else to do. Pete remembered how surprised he was when he found out that Mrs. Bentley across the street never read his father's editorials.

Charles Webb was a definitive man who often ridiculed reporters from the East who called themselves journalists. "Journalists," he had said, "are people who want to make things up or stir up trouble so they have something to write about. They're either talking about journalistic objectivity or about creativity, which means they probably have neither. Someday, those journalists will be more annoying and do real harm. Reporters tell the story of who, what, why, when, and where. That's news. The rest is pedantic rubbish, political propaganda, and Ivy League snobbishness. Elitists are those who have never had blisters on their hands and only tell the hardworking people of this country how to live and, even worse, how to think." So went Charles Webb's analytical, prophetic pronouncement on the state of journalism in America, and there were many more, Pete thought to himself.

"There isn't much talk about anything, Pete. Just the usual stuff like who's selling what to whom, nothing much except . . ."

"Except what, DJ?"

"Remember my friend Betsy from Portland?"

"Is she the one who's studying economics at U dub?"

"That's her. She's working for a company that handles credit cards to help pay for school. If people don't use the cards often enough, the company looks into it and tells them how convenient it is to use their card. Well, it seems there's a sudden increase in credit card activity."

"So it's spring, DJ. People feel good. They're hoping to dry out from winter, and they're spending."

"Wrong, Petie. Betsy says the problem is that most of these cards were unknown until they got used and someone was billed."

"So some pickpocket is trying to cash in. No big deal. Wait a minute. What do you mean they were unknown until used? How could people not know they have a credit card? They send those stupid statements even if you don't use the darn thing. They're mailing those cards to every college kid who has made it to their senior year. Supposedly, they are the wave of the future, the path to a cashless society."

"I think your reporter's instincts are already in Idaho, Pete. That's the problem. As I said, a significant number of these cards weren't even known to exist. They belonged to dead people, deceased, passed on, and the cards are being used *after* their last hurrah. I always thought the Big Guy provided everything when you got to the great beyond—you can't take it with you and all that jazz. The cards were unknown because the relatives of the dearly departed who owned the cards didn't realize they existed until the deceased's estate started getting billed for purchases made after the person who owned the card is dead and presumably unable to sign their name. Get it?"

"You mean someone has started using the cards after the owner is dead?"

"Now you're catching on, Petie man."

"DJ, maybe you're right and my instincts are on vacation already."

"Yeah, well, there is more than one kind of 'empty.'"

"Very funny, DJ."

"That's okay. Sometimes I'm ahead of myself, too."

For a moment Pete considered responding, but he wasn't sure where to start. He was distracted by the tunnel they had just gone through, which brought back the memory of one of his first assignments. It was about a man crushed by a diesel Cat while working on a tunnel project. The man had forgotten his lunch, and his wife walked up to the work site with her husband's lunch pail in her hand, doing a special thing for the man she loved because she knew how hard he worked and didn't want him to be hungry and get too tired. She wondered why there was an ambulance there and then suddenly realized that everyone was looking at her. They were big, burly guys with hard hats looking at her like she was their little sister. Then it hit her, and she dropped his metal lunch pail and folded to the ground like a wilting flower. Every man Pete interviewed kept saying the same thing. "I can still hear that lunch pail hitting the ground." One man who was standing on a grader blade said, "It looked like slow motion. She let go of his lunch pail, and it seemed like it fell forever. It bounced once, and I could see the inside was white. The stuff just fell out. An orange rolled onto the ground a few feet away, and then she was on her way down, too."

Pete was never surprised by what he could remember, like the first time his father took him into the press room and he watched the chaotic yet purposeful busyness. He loved the energy of the place, how the smoke hung in the air just under the lights, how the arguments heated up over what stories should take what space in the layout and whether there should be a byline. There were the strategy sessions over editorials and how story emphasis was all calculated to mold public opinion and, according to Charles Webb, build a better community. It was a wonderful, unpredictable world that changed every day before your eyes. One time, Pete had compared it to war. Each day is the same but different; people die, and you wonder what your role will be in it all. You wonder if anyone ever wins. Does all the energy and information go to anyone's brain? Does it make a difference anywhere? Or does it all end up around someone's fish and then in the trash can?

No, he knew there was something you couldn't see on the surface, but it was real. It shaped people's ideas about themselves and the world. It shaped history. Newspapers were more than a business, more than a way of life. They were life. It was a recording of witnesses, however flawed, and the voices of free people. They were an echo of the lives lived yesterday and a window into tomorrow. A good newspaper throbbed and pulsated with its own life and the life of its community or nation.

Pete had to admit that he shared his father's distaste for journalists, especially those slick pompadours who called themselves TV journalists. They were becoming as abundant as rabbits. Ever since the Kennedy assassination, every city with a TV station had two pompadours and a pretty female face staring at the camera saying inane twitter to one another. The thoughtful and important news lasted as long as the camera person could hold his breath. Print media, the press, was where news was still news and not amateurish entertainment. But Pete was beginning to wonder if even the *Times* might be shirking its duty to the public with Winston Hitchcock at the helm.

DJ sat quietly looking at the paper, leaving Pete to ponder Betsy's information about the credit cards. But Pete's thoughts were elsewhere. The tunnel darkness had also reminded him of the time some neighborhood toughs locked him in the trunk of his dad's Plymouth. It was quiet in the trunk. The quiet was heavy and pushed down on his chest, and he couldn't breathe. Even worse, for a long time, he couldn't yell for help. He was afraid that if he opened his mouth, the darkness would fill it and force its way down his throat, and then he would choke to death. His stomach was feeling a little unsettled.

The brightness of the morning sun coming off the lake forced Pete to squint. But as he did, he could see the beauty of Lake Washington and to the south the crown of Mt. Rainer—all 14,000 feet of it—still snow-covered in all its winter glory. The sun was warming the mountain, and a mist surrounded the summit like a veiled maiden not yet ready to reveal herself. Crossing the old floating bridge, Pete could see a patchwork of weather. To his left, from the city circling east into the Cascades, were fog and dampness with the water of the lake a dull gray color. But to the south, the sun was reflecting off the water, bright and shiny. Pete thought about the air, the shining water, the sunlight—the greatest inventions of God. But then he remembered there is no God.

Don't say that, Peter!

"Damn! Why can't parents stay out of my head?" Pete muttered under his breath.

"What did you say, Pete?"

"Nothing, DJ, nothing, I was just thinking out loud."

It seemed strange that they could cross on a bridge held up by floating concrete blocks. It took a real paradigm shift to believe that concrete could float. Pete had heard the first pontoon was put in place by a man who lost a bet that you could build a bridge out of floating concrete pontoons. He wondered how many people were willing to make a complete shift in their thinking with the new and unknown or whether they would stay stuck in one place all their lives. Then the question snuck in the back door, and Pete found himself asking, "Am I stuck?"

The dark clouds seemed to arrive from nowhere. Closing in like a silent shutter, the entire sky was gray again. Having heard his mother's voice in his head, Pete's thoughts traveled toward her memory. He remembered her as a believer. She believed in the world, in purpose, and, of course, in God. Her Scottish roots ran deep into the old country when there was less separation of church and life. The world was filled with simple folk with simple faith. But *simple* didn't mean they lacked courage. It meant they faced life with a combination of determination and acceptance. The sovereignty of God was a hopeful gift or a heavy curse, depending on the events that marked your life. But there was a melody in the air in these simple folks' hearts, even in hard times. It bound them to the ends of the earth, to all of creation, and to God.

Mom saw good things in the worst of people, even old Mr. Murphy who fell down drunk by lunch most days. Good old Mom would feed him on the porch and clean him up. She would tell him the good Lord loved him and that he could still make something of himself, but he never did. Pete remembered the scene. Old Murphy died one day at the end of the street. The mailman, Mr. Carlyle, noticed a gathering of dogs huddled together under an old maple tree, and there was Murph, lying dead in the middle of them.

Just as they were loading Murph's body into the ambulance and the policeman was picking up Murph's backpack to put in the trunk of his patrol car, Mr. Carlyle stopped the policeman. "Officer, there is something in there that belongs to this boy," and he pointed at Pete. "Murph told me if I was around when he died to give it to this boy." The policeman nodded, and Mr. Carlyle reached into the backpack, pulled out something wrapped in red tissue paper, and handed it to Pete.

"I carefully unwrapped the paper," Pete remembered. "I could feel the light weight of the object in my hand, whatever it was. After I pulled off the last piece of paper, I saw a beautiful compass with a glass face encased in a brass ring. It looked a lot like a pocket watch. The points of the compass were written in a fine scroll, and if you held it up to the sun, the glass face magnified the lettering and points of the compass. When I turned it over, there was an engraving on the back. 'Find your way,' it said. I had lost my compass somewhere years ago, being a dumb kid. I wished I had been more careful."

Pete thought about the time he said something judgmental and caustic about old Murph to his mother. She had looked him in the eye and stood like a prize fighter ready to do battle. "You don't know anything about him, Peter Andrew Webb. You don't know his story or the pain that has washed over his life, so don't be playing God. People who play the judgment game rarely wait to be the one judged. But unless you're willing, don't step out there and judge anyone else."

Pete remembered how red her cheeks were, the veins in her neck pulsating as she spoke. Years later, he watched some women shun and make fun of another woman in a laundromat, and his mother's words came back to him. He realized then that she probably wasn't speaking theoretically but rather from her own experience as one who had been falsely judged. Behind her words was a history of a hurt unknown to him. Children, Pete realized, rarely understand the life their parents lived, especially the undercurrents.

"What are you thinking so hard about, Pete? Are you sitting by a river in Idaho?"

"No, DJ, I was just thinking about my mom."

"Oh. I'm sorry I never met her."

"She would have liked you, DJ, especially because you love music. Above everything else, she always believed people could change, that the worst of them could become good. It was both her strength and her weakness."

Pete thought, "I'm sorry Mom, but for me there is no God. The world is just too screwed up, too much pain piled upon itself, generation after generation, and the change in most people is phony."

As they passed through Factoria and climbed the hill toward Eastgate, DJ looked up from the paper and belched an invisible cloud of onions, pickles, and mustard. Pete gave him a disparaging look and pulled over just before the next exit.

"I appreciate the ride, Petie. Hope you catch lots of those slimy swimmers," DJ said with a laugh.

"They're called fish, DJ, mountain trout." Pete caught a breath of fresh air as DJ opened the door. I'll do my best, and keep your ears up about this credit card thing. Maybe when I come back, we can take Betsy to lunch and find out more."

"You mean *you* can take Betsy and me on your expense account," DJ yelled over the sound of traffic.

"Sure thing. You sure this is okay, DJ?"

"Petie, I've walked from this exit a thousand times. It's safe."

"You know what I mean, DJ, and it's not about traffic."

"Yeah, I know, Pete. I'll be okay. Honest."

Pete watched as DJ's slim form seemed to sway from some hidden source as he made his way up the road toward the suburban enclave where house after house was built close to the other to shelter the World War II vets and their baby-making families. Most of those babies had left the nest by now. Pete realized this suburban pearl was beginning to fade, and he thought about the marks of time people carry.

Rain clouds are expected in the north Cascades, moving southeasterly as the day progresses. Some rain with periods of sunshine through-out the day, and a high of 60 degrees with perhaps a slight warming trend as cloudy skies and rain move farther east. The Puget Sound area should see scattered showers with intermittent sunshine and clearing tomorrow. Eastern Washington, if you're traveling that way, may see more rain as the day progresses, and showers are expected in the foothills of Idaho. That's your morning weather update. Have a good day.

"You can't ruin my vacation with rain," Pete shouted at the radio as he looked down the highway at the clouds lingering above the Cascade peaks.

While he always enjoyed DJ, Pete admitted to himself that it was finally good to be alone. He could feel the tension leave his shoulders. It was as if the weight of Seattle and the problems and questions it carried were sinking into the dark, gray water of Puget Sound behind him as he drove east. It felt exhilarating to have nothing in front of him but the quiet of the unsuspecting fish of North Idaho. He could easily imagine the feel of the cool air by the river's edge. He turned the radio up. Truth was that he could only endure so much quiet, and he knew it would be a long drive.

Unnamed sources say President Nixon is planning to announce a major new development in the war against North Vietnam. The same source indicated there may be a major shift related to the policy of restricted bombing . . .

"Yeah, drop bombs on palm trees and grass huts, like it will make a difference or something," Pete said to no one as he thought about the lunacy driving American policy in Vietnam. Eisenhower started it with his well-meaning "military advisors." Then Kennedy, ignoring the advice of those who knew history, expanded it. Then there was the inept Johnson who wanted to prove he had balls, and now Tricky Dicky. The New Nixon was at the helm and about to get his ass whipped by a bunch of peasants. Pete felt a tinge of guilt when he thought of the boys he knew were there. "Life is strange," he thought. "I'm on my way to go fishing, and some guy is probably scared to death in a firefight somewhere, just praying to stay alive. It makes no sense, but then what does?" He turned the radio off.

Pete admired his small bug. It was his first new car. He knew that in 1949, two little Volkswagens were offloaded onto dockside in New York Harbor when there were no VW dealerships anywhere in America. He could imagine the sneers from the longshoremen. But those two little "beetles" were like revolutionaries sent to overtake the oversized monsters Detroit belched out. In the first years, fewer than 500 bugs were sold. Yet by the end of 1957, sales exceeded 50,000, and VW had not produced a single advertisement. He felt himself fitting comfortably into the seat as he scanned the road ahead. He sensed his quiet, peaceful vacation was finally beginning.

But Pete's mind couldn't say goodbye to DJ just yet. He remembered when he learned about DJ's family. He and DJ were in an all-night pizza joint. He remembered it well.

"Can we have another pitcher, please?" DJ said as he glanced at the coed serving the tables.

"Coming right up, gentlemen," said the waitress, who looked like a poster girl for the University of Washington.

"Well, Pete, it is not a fun story to tell, but seeing as you have bared your soul and all your Calvinistic paranoia, I guess I should, too. My dad worked for Boeing. He was one of their chief engineers and was in on the testing of all new planes and prototypes. He is a very smart man."

"Here's your pitcher, guys," the cute coed—the one with her hair pulled up in some sort of bun and a Huskies T-shirt on that flattered the dog—announced as she put the pitcher next to the remaining pieces of pizza that looked like bait for a man trap. They each poured themselves a fresh glass and took a sip. DJ rubbed the table with his finger a few times. He took another sip, cleared his throat, and picked up where he left off.

"Anyway, he worked for Boeing, and my folks loved to dance. Every Friday night, they went dancing. They usually weren't into the drinking and that stuff; they just loved to dance, and they were good. Sometimes, a song would come on the TV, and my folks would look at one another and stand up and start dancing. I loved it. It made me laugh. I got my love for music from them."

"But something happened?" Pete asked. "Did they get a divorce?"

"No, nothing like that. Much worse," DJ said as he took two big gulps of the beer and wiped his mouth with his sleeve. "They were coming home from dancing in Renton, and it was raining horribly. Well, that night my dad had one too many because it was some kind of a party, and Mom drove home. This was before 405 was the big road it is now. They hit a flooded spot, and my mom lost control. They slid into oncoming traffic. Another car rammed into the passenger side. The driver was drunk, doing 80 miles per hour. The only thing between his car and my dad was the door. My dad's legs took the brunt of the crash, and he would never walk again." DJ paused and stared through his glass. "The other driver went through his windshield and onto my folks' car. He was dead at the scene."

"That must have been horrible. Were you at home with a babysitter?"

"Yeah, her name was Carolyn LeGrande. She was 16, and I was 10 and in love with her, but of course, she never knew it. Anyway, my dad also had some brain damage, and he couldn't do process calculations or problem-solve anymore. So he couldn't keep his job. He hit the bottle and has never stopped."

"What about your mom? Was she hurt bad?"

"No, she came through with only a couple of bruises. Her damage all came later. My dad blamed her and said if he had been driving, he would not have lost control and been on the wrong side of the road. He reminds her every day one way or another. Now, if some peppy tune comes on the radio or TV, he yells at her to turn it off and shouts, 'I can't dance! I don't want to hear it!' So most of the time, she tiptoes around hoping something she does will please him, but it never does."

"You got any brothers or sisters, DJ?"

"Nah, so they're stuck with a disappointment of a son, a college dropout who is a disc jockey. It doesn't matter that I am a good one. To my dad, I am just a loser, and maybe he is right."

"You don't seem like a loser to me. You're smart, talented, mildly good looking," Pete said with a smile, "and the way that waitress keeps eyeballing you, I would say women find you attractive, which is more than I can say for myself."

"I doubt that, but thanks for the compliment. Your words warm my heart, or maybe that's the beer," DJ said, grinning.

"It makes my Calvinistic paranoia look pretty petty and small."

"You're a reporter, Pete. You know bad things happen. Hell, look at the Addisons. Nice people living their lives doing well, and then the gate to hell is left unlatched. The devils creep out, and hell breaks into their lives. Bad things happen to good people. This is a messed up world, but there will always be music." DJ smiled as he took several long swallows of his beer and pantomimed the playing of a trumpet.

Pete remembered when he and DJ first met. Amazingly, it was all tied to this crazy war and a young man named James Addison, Jr. Like most of the graduating class at Garfield High School, James received his draft notice the week of graduation. But unlike the others who marched down to the Kings County Draft Board on Fourth Avenue, he marched instead to the bus depot in downtown Seattle and rode the dog north to join the community of young men in exile in Vancouver, British Columbia. But James soon found that neither his new community nor the nation of Canada was particularly hospitable to young black men, especially those who chose not to fight for their country. White boys were principled, but blacks who ran from the draft were considered cowards.

James also had the legacy of a decorated father whose service in the Marine Corps was legendary in the black community of Seattle, and it worked on his conscience. Pete didn't know if it was a moment of clarity or grand delusion, but one day in Vancouver, James Addison, Jr. decided to come home and stand on his principles. Maybe he was encouraged by the fact that 58 percent of the American public was now wanting to get out of Vietnam and bring the boys home. As he explained it to the judge, he wasn't against war and would have fought the likes of Hitler. But this war was "unnecessary, unjust, and immoral" and, he added, "historically stupid." Having been a straight A student, he might have known something about history. The judge however, only saw a young black man who didn't want to fight, had run to Canada, and, frankly, was now stupid enough to come back and face the music.

It was Walter Beach, DJ's uncle (his mother's brother), a mediocre attorney with a big heart and a bigger appetite for booze, who took James Addison, Jr.'s case. It would be his last. The judge, rather than sentencing James to community service for the duration of his military service after a token period in county jail, sentenced him to two years in Walla Walla, the state penitentiary. Two years in Walla Walla would be sentence enough for most adults, Pete mused, but the penitentiary for an 18-year-old kid was a sentence to hell.

Mr. Walter Beach, attorney at law, went off to a Seattle pub to drown his sense of despair at not being able to save the youth. After several hours of pumping down a glass of scotch decorated with a minimal amount of ice, Walter made the mistake of wanting to do penance. He wanted to spread his remorse upon the already grieving Addisons. Unfortunately, only Mrs. Addison was home, at least for the moment.

James Addison, Sr. had cashed in his World War II honors for a cup of coffee and a job at Boeing. He was now a small cog in Eisenhower's infamous Military Industrial Complex. He worked graveyard that night, a shift he had taken only because he could not stand to be home while his wife mourned, and he grew more and more angry over his shameful son he had always been so proud of. But two comets were about to collide, or at least one comet and a falling star.

Walter had awakened the very attractive Mrs. Addison, who was sobbing on her couch. When a tired James Addison, Sr. came home, he found what he thought was the white lawyer who had failed to protect his son now pawing at his scantily robed wife. The black raging bull almost killed Walter, but instead, he sentenced him to a life of imprisonment, if you can call it a life. Walter would spend the rest of his days at a nursing home drooling in his lap, unable to speak or walk. Addison, Sr. went to live with his son in Walla Walla.

Pete had been doing a story on possible inequities in the draft system of Kings County and how the war was spending the lives of the young, especially the poor, when he came across Addison's story and met Darcy Jansen—DJ, the nephew of the drooling Walter Beach. It was more than an amazing story; it was a modern tragedy. But just as amazing was DJ's own story. When DJ told the story of his family tragedy, Pete couldn't understand how DJ could be so upbeat all the time. He knew music was DJ's great escape, as it is for many, but so was the distance between the two cities. Seattle and Bellevue might as well have been different countries because it kept the pain of the Jansen clan from being DJ's daily diet.

CHAPTER TWO

Home, Sweet Home

As DJ turned the corner onto his parents' street, he found himself walking down memory lane and revisiting his childhood. He remembered the time he and Bobby Anderson both had measles and strung a wire between their bedroom windows and talked into a tin can. They thought they were the Alexander Graham Bells of the east side. Vicki Hunt's house was now blue and had a flag of Mexico in one of the bedroom windows. He guessed this was no longer "wasps only" territory and considered it a good thing. The tree where he and all the kids used to gather before they played kick the can or hide-and-seek until it got dark and their mothers started calling them in, was now a stump with a ceramic pot on it. He stopped for a moment and looked across the street at a beige split level.

We were celebrating Fitz's birthday. Which was it? Seventh? No, it was his eighth. The party was really over, and we were all joking around with balloons. Suddenly, Fitz fell on the ground. He was turning blue and couldn't breathe. He remembered the mothers screaming and his mother running to the phone to call an ambulance, but by the time they got there, he was already dead. Fitz had aspirated a balloon, and it had cut off the air to his lungs. "We missed you," DJ said to the street as he turned toward his folks' house.

At the end of the block, leaning up against the county's chain link fence, was an old rusted bicycle with bent fenders and one wheel missing. The chain hung down like a man hangs his head in defeat or shame. DJ thought it was a fitting symbol for this street that had seen better days.

Turning up his parents' driveway, he noticed the two flower planters on either side of the sidewalk that marked the entrance to his folks' home. They used to be bursting with flowers befitting each season of the year. Both were filled with dirt now with no sign of either past or future vegetation. He could see his mother standing at the kitchen window, but she hadn't noticed him yet. "She's always at the sink when she is not cooking," he thought. "It's as if she thinks washing her hands enough times will perform absolution. But guilt isn't easily washed away by empty rituals, especially if the reminder of your supposed grievous sin is in the next room."

As DJ opened the door, the aroma of seasoned pot roast rushed to greet him. He turned toward the kitchen where his mother was drying her hands and moving toward him. DJ noticed how nervous and small his mother appeared, like a fragile, fearful bird always watching for unseen danger. For some reason, the kitchen seemed to get smaller each time he visited. He could remember sitting at the table on Saturday mornings watching his mother make pancakes or waffles. She always warmed up the syrup in a pan of water. He could still taste it and feel its heat on his tongue, despite the power of the pot roast.

"Your father's asleep. We'll let him sleep. I think he was awake most of the night. The pot roast isn't ready yet, and he should be awake before it's done. You look so, so thin, Honey. Are you getting enough to eat?"

"Mom, you say that every time I come."

"Well, Darcy, you always look so thin," she whispered.

Sounds like the pot calling the kettle black, DJ thought. "I'm fine, Mom, really. I eat plenty, all five food groups." *Well, eventually five,* he said to himself, *sometime within a month. Besides, a combination pizza must cover at least three food groups.* But he didn't share the thought.

When he entered the living room, DJ could smell the acrid odor of stale cigarettes and beer. The once gold shag carpet was a dull mustard color, and the curtains were a deep beige, but DJ didn't think it was their original color. He wondered if the cigarettes had taken their toll. It seems no one here was paying attention to the surgeon general's report released last January on the hazards of smoking. The couch was covered with some floral patterned cover, which looked like it could use its own cover. The television was on, but there was no sound. A very animated sales person was silently selling cars to a deaf room. DJ could see the red TV tray that once had a bright white lily in the center. Now, two beer bottles, an ash tray, and a pack of Camels sat on it. He presumed that at least one of the beers was empty and the other had been recently invested in. Maybe it, too, was empty. The round ash tray was full of butts, and some had fallen onto the tray. DJ thought they looked like small paper maggots resting from a feast.

His father's head was laid back against the headrest attached to the wheelchair. With his mouth wide open, a slow guttural sound periodically escaped. His hair was thin and matted, and he looked like he had been sleeping in his clothes for a few days. DJ noticed that his father's stomach had grown since his last visit. There were cigarette burns on his sweater, connected by small trails of ash. If all he does is sit, eat, and drink beer, it shouldn't be any surprise he has gained weight, DJ thought. He quietly turned and went back to the kitchen where his mother was washing her hands.

"How are you, Mom? I mean really, how are you?"

"I'm okay. I manage to keep myself busy."

"I know that, but how is your heart? That's what you used to ask me. Remember how you used to quote Thoreau? 'The heart is a deep well.' So how is . . ."

"Helen! Come move this crap out of my way. I gotta pee!"

DJ turned back into the living room. "Here, I'll help you, Dad."

"Well, look who's here. My loser boy, Mr. Music Man. Have you been asked to replace Dick Clark yet?"

DJ ignored the comment and moved the TV tray and its contents so his father could manipulate his wheelchair into the bathroom. When he moved the tray, he confirmed what he suspected: one empty beer bottle, one two-thirds gone. When DJ heard the bathroom door shut, he cleaned up the TV tray, emptying all its contents into the kitchen trash and putting it where it would be out of the way when his father returned.

"Well, have you come out to the 'burbs for the weekend to feast on your mother's good cooking and remind me of what a loser I raised?" his father shouted through the bathroom door.

"Howard! Please don't talk like that."

A few minutes later, his father wheeled himself out of the bathroom, scraping one wall as he went. "I'll talk any way I damn well please, thank you. DJ, put the tray back and get me another beer. And Helen, don't bother to tell me I've had enough already. I can see the look on your face." DJ's mom turned toward the kitchen, and DJ put the TV tray back in its dutiful place. His mother handed him the beer and went back to the sink to wash her hands again.

"You didn't answer my question, Music Man. Have you come for the weekend?"

"No, Dad, I just popped in to say hi and see how you two are. Here's your beer."

"We're fine, just fine. Can't you tell? Turn up the sound on the TV. I want to watch *Days of Our Lives*. I have to see what kind of mischief they're into today."

DJ walked toward the kitchen and glanced back at his father. He felt pity inside. He used to feel anger, but no more. He had seen folks manage who had suffered far worse than his father. They had not only managed, but they had bettered themselves.

"Um, I think I'm going to go, Mom. I've got things to do. It's a really busy time at the station."

"Oh, DJ, aren't you even going to stay for lunch? You just walked in the door. Your dad didn't mean what he said, and we can all have a family time like we used to."

"No, Mom, it's never going to be like it used to, and that's the problem. This is our life. If I stay, he takes me down, and I've been down because of him too many times." DJ put his arms around his mother, gave her a peck on the cheek, and reached for the door.

"Helen! Come turn up the TV," Howard thundered from the other room.

Outside, DJ shook his head and sighed. He sensed the hint of rain. He took a deep breath and told himself he would never be a smoker regardless of what any surgeon general said. He reached into his pocket and looked at a torn piece of paper with a phone number on it and wondered how long it would take him to get back to Seattle. He knew Betsy hadn't seen *The French Connection*, and she loved Gene Hackman.

CHAPTER THREE

The Gift

Pete's mind shifted to fish and the hope of a relaxing drive all the way to Idaho. He was glad to have nothing in front of him but quiet and the unsuspecting fish of North Idaho. He could almost feel the cool air by the river's edge. He was even looking forward to the long, boring drive across the Columbia Plateau. He knew he would give in and turn the radio on now and then, but he could also turn it off. You couldn't do the same with people. Pete noticed the needle was kissing the red mark, and he realized he had been so busy finalizing things yesterday that he forgot to fill the tank. He needed to fill up before climbing the hills toward the pass. "Just another obstacle in the way of my vacation," he thought. He could push toward North Bend, but his gas tank had never been this low before, and if he were wrong, it would mean a hike, and he only wanted to do that with a fishing rod in his hand.

He saw her standing there on the side of the road as he exited at Issaquah. Blonde hair, cut short, a brown leather jacket a size too large for her frame. It was probably her boyfriend's. Jeans that accentuated the particularly female curve of her hips. "Girls shouldn't hitchhike. They're likely to get mugged, raped, or worse. Dumb blonde," Pete said out loud to no one.

He pulled into an old Texaco station with the round-top pumps. All he wanted to do was get away from Seattle and out from under the insipid glare of Winston Hitchcock—owner and managing editor of the *Seattle Times*, esteemed member of the Bellevue Country Club on the east side, member of the Longacres Racetrack Golden Card Club, and, of course, member and past president of the Seattle Yacht Club. Old family, old money, and one pain in the ass. Winston had connections but little else. He sent reporters after the ridiculous and then ridiculed them for the outcome. Subscriptions were falling off, the typesetters were threatening to strike, and the paper's reputation was on the skids. The shadow of a commercial disaster made Winston look for a scapegoat in every department, and lately the favorite goat's name was Peter Webb.

At the gas station, a pimple-faced kid with grease all over his baseball cap, which may have once been a Yankees cap, filled up the tank and took Pete's money.

"Ya goin' east or west?"

"East, toward Spokane."

"I hope your little German bubble can make it over the pass. It's pretty steep from Denny Creek to the summit, a hard climb for trucks and toy cars," he said, grinning. "Me, I'll stick with American, *real* horsepower." He turned and pointed to a maroon Chevy Malibu with the back end raised too high and spinner hub caps that were the rage in the '50s. Pete could tell the boy thought this was a gem, but it had already gone too many miles and probably suffered from some bad driving as well. Anyone putting money into that car was throwing it away. The car with its rear end pointed to the sky made Pete think of an old man waiting for the doctor to goose him during a prostate exam.

"Herb owns the place," the boy went on. "Says foreign cars are made from melted down beer cans, and the steel ain't worth squat. If anyone hits you, your guts will be everywhere."

Pete didn't feel like getting into a philosophical debate on international trade or the propriety of gas station attendants getting into anatomical descriptions of hypothetical accidents with their customers. He was certain this grease-stained, adolescent Dennis the Menace look-alike wouldn't understand. Pete didn't think NASA had recently released any of its top hands to pump gas in western Washington.

"Your Chevy is *real* cherry," Pete replied, with an emphasis on *real* just as the kid had said it.

As Pete climbed into his bug, he glanced at the newspaper Oscar had given him, and his thoughts went back to Winston Hitchcock. When Winston's father managed the paper, things went well, but when the old man died, Winston decided to make his mark and bring the paper into the modern era. That's when the problems began.

Leaving the gas station and cradling the remains of his coffee between his thighs, Pete shifted into third and wondered for a second what a real race car would feel like: "Power shift, grace, shift, power thrust, like a mechanical ballet. Speed and power, timing and grace. The crowd cheers as Peter Webb crosses the finish line at Indy and gets the checkered flag."

She was still standing there, just beyond the corner near the on-ramp. She didn't have her hand out, and she didn't look frustrated or dejected. She was just there, as if she had always been there. Pete could see that she had a pretty face. She looked at the bug and smiled. Her right hand came up, but not with the hitchhiker's salute with her thumb up. Instead, she waved like she had been expecting him, and for a second, Pete felt like he was coming to meet an old friend. But Pete Webb was on his vacation, the "big empty" as DJ called it, and he was not interested in filling it up with a messed up kid so dumb that she hitchhikes. There already had been enough delays. It was time to move on. *But Peter, you don't know her story,* echoed somewhere in the catacombs of his mind. The blonde also piqued his reporter's sense of curiosity and played tug-of-war with the desire to just not bother. But it was his mom's voice he had heard, and you're supposed to listen to your mother.

Pete drove by her without even looking in her direction, but then his right foot almost involuntarily went to the brake pedal while his left hit the clutch. He pulled over and glanced back. He expected to see her running anxiously to get her long-awaited ride, but she strolled up to the car like he wasn't even there. She opened the door but didn't get in, and stood leaning down.

"Why did you stop?"

He could see a pink T-shirt under the jacket, a crew neck type. She had blue eyes and perfect teeth. "Some orthodontist somewhere was building a second home on this mouth," Pete thought to himself.

"I thought you wanted a ride. You're hitchhiking, aren't you?"

She stood there not moving. She scanned the back seat, looked into his green eyes, and asked, "Are you safe? What do you do for a living? You going to Spokane?"

Gripping the wheel, Pete took a deep breath. "Why do I feel like I'm being interrogated? I'm a serial killer, and yes, I am going to Spokane, but I'll never get there if . . ."

She slid into the seat beside him and threw one of those hippie bag purses that look like they're made from carpet scraps onto the back seat. She pulled the seat belt across her chest and, looking straight ahead down the highway, said, "The serial killer stuff isn't funny. What do you really do?"

Pete began easing back onto the highway thinking, "This never happens to real Indy drivers," he mused.

"I'm a reporter for the *Seattle Times*, and I'm on vacation. What about you?"

"Do you have a name, or do they just say, 'Hey, reporter guy'?"

Pete was beginning to long for the brief solitude he had only temporarily experienced. He was wondering what kind of confused person he had admitted to his traveling sanctuary, but she had a warm voice, and she was pretty. It was obvious that this was a girl who was determined to hold her own. There was something appealing about her abruptness, her confidence, and, of course, her beauty.

"The name is Pete Webb, and I'm an entangled rock. Do you always interrogate everyone when you first meet them?"

"I hadn't met you until you told me your name. Didn't your mother warn you about strangers and the importance of being polite and introducing yourself? What do you mean, 'entangled rock'? How come it smells like onions in here?"

"Never mind the rock stuff. It's an inside joke. My last passenger had a breakfast of hot dog well-oiled in onions."

"Your last passenger had to be a guy because no woman would eat a concoction smelling like that, at least not for breakfast."

"You don't know some of the women I know," Pete said, smiling.

"And what kind of women are they? And what happened to your last passenger?"

"I dropped him off at his destination back in Eastgate, and I'll pass on the women, thank you. If you're so concerned about strangers, what in Sam

Hill are you doing hitchhiking? And yes, my mother taught me all of that, but . . ."

"My name is Faith," she interrupted. "Faith Marks, and the expression 'what in the Sam Hill' is allegedly attributed to a land surveyor in the 1850s whose language was so profane that locals used the descriptive expression instead of swearing."

"What are you, a human encyclopedia?"

"No, I was just a curious girl who spent a lot of time in the library by myself reading books."

"Nice to meet you, Faith Marks." *I wonder what insights DJ would have on her name*, Pete thought. Putting more attention to the road, Pete realized he was going to be stuck behind a semi belching diesel fuel and not be able to pass because of a pea green station wagon on his left with what looked like someone's nursery school. There were kids everywhere, and seat belts were obviously not required. The one on the passenger side had his nose and mouth pressed against the window and looked like some kind of deformed jellyfish.

"The little brat will probably be mooning people in a few years," Pete said. Then he glanced over to see her reaction.

Faith had turned her head toward the window and closed her eyes. Pete could tell by the way her body surrendered to the seat and the rhythm of her breathing that she was already asleep. It was a gift he had long envied in others. The interview was over for now.

All the questioning made Pete think of the time the Tacoma police wanted to know what he was doing in a known drug dealer's apartment from 1:00 in the morning until dawn. It was a simple question, but the answer was too complex for any of them to understand because they only saw "drug dealer," not the only brother of a buddy who died in his arms alongside a muddy river in the jungles of Vietnam. Ironic that an investigative reporter should hate interrogation so much.

Pete glanced over and noticed how soft her cheeks looked. She was no adolescent, as he had first thought. Maybe in her late 20s, but no more than 30. Her frame was small, and he could tell from the grasp of the seat belt that she was small busted. "At least I've given a ride to a pretty girl, even if she is nuts," he told himself. "Keep your eyes on the road, and think of fish. You're after fish, big mountain trout swimming in a deep, swirling emerald green pool on the North Fork of the Coeur d'Alene."

His eyes were again drawn to her. As she slept, he had an image of a small girl curled up on a sofa somewhere, a blanket over her, lost in sleep, suspended in time. He remembered the coffee between his legs and took a long drink. It was cooler and mostly cold caffeine at this point, but going down, it was still a small pleasure. Pete looked out at the springtime growth, layer upon layer of green leaves in blended shades on the many trees covering the foothills that separate Seattle from the Cascades. He found himself thinking not of solitude but of a comfort that comes from the presence of someone else, even a person who is still new to you yet a mystery—only a name. "Maybe DJ is right," he thought. "Maybe there is power in a name." "Faith," he repeated to himself under his breath. He felt for the first time in a long time that the world was alive and the beautiful and strange life next to him might perhaps be a gift.

The steady hum of the bug's engine had met up with Faith's tension-filled exhaustion and lulled her to sleep. A thousand scenes burst forth from somewhere in her memory and flashed before the screen of her consciousness. She saw herself getting ready for Hope's funeral with tears in her eyes, eyeliner running down her cheeks. The sight of the small, white casket. The wrenching, mourning wails of Hope's mom. The busted radiator hose. Her need to see her father. The moment they realized Hope had breathed her last. The tubes. The smell of the ward. A bump jostled Faith back to the present and her traveling companion, a handsome guy in a yellow VW. Then more sleep.

She could see black button eyes of the puppet, feel her hand inside the sock. She held it before Hope's face, spoke in her squirrely puppet voice. She watched the child smile while emitting a giggle that took on a life of its own the more the puppet spoke—a giggle that defied the context of her circumstances. They were in the hospital courtyard, the sun was shining, the rain had stopped, the plants were wet and fresh, reaching for the life-giving sky. Hope, watching for birds when she wasn't engrossed in puppet silliness. One sparrow carefully drinking from a birdbath, glancing about. Hope saw it, called it Mr. Tweets. After getting its fill, Mr. Tweets flew to the ground and began hopping toward Faith and Hope. Both were startled when Mr. Tweets flew briefly to Hope's shoulder and then off and out of sight. Hope giggled and said, "Mr. Tweets says he'll be back later." The scene of her last night with blood transfusions, her failing body, life seeping out of it. Faith remembered locking herself in a small, women's restroom and sitting on the toilet seat crying. There was a knock at the door. "Are you all right in there?" one of the nurses asked. *How can anything be all right when a child dies?* she asked herself. "I'm fine," she lied. Traveling with a serial killer? She laughed in her dream.

Stained glass windows telling the story of the disciples . . . hid before . . . locked . . . slept near an exit. The rose window . . . sun shining through the next morning. The window . . . redder and redder . . . blood red. She sat up, rubbed the sleep out of her eyes, curled her knees to her chest. Tears came . . . she shuddered as she gazed at the blood-red window.

She remembered wondering if her dad would bother looking for her. If he did, others would ask why she ran away. He could always say, "Just some troubled teen, never got over her mother's death." Most people would believe him, but some would wonder if there was something else going on. Before Faith closed her memory door, she thought of her discovery—*the grace of forgiveness.*

She imagined her dad standing on the front porch, tears in his eyes, a smile on his face. She saw herself coming up the road, a long, hard journey. She imagined the father in Jesus's parable the same way, except she wasn't the prodigal—her father was. Both had tears because of what would never be. Forever lost. They were now together again, not in some dark, evil alienation. "Yes, my prodigal father, I forgive you," she dreamed herself saying.

The hum of the engine was the first sign of consciousness, and then she opened her eyes. Faith felt the weight of her bladder and knew she must act soon.

"I have to pee," Faith announced as she stretched her arms above her head, arching back to clear the bug's roof and turning to smile at Pete. "You hungry?" she asked. "I'd be happy to buy you a donut or something. It's too early for lunch, and you probably had breakfast, and I really, really do need to pee."

"It's a common occurrence," Pete muttered as he pulled into the parking lot of a roadside coffee shop.

"Yes, it's pretty normal, but I didn't bring my emergency container," she said as she pointed at the empty coffee cup between Pete's legs. With that, Faith grabbed her purse, leaped from the bug, and ran into the coffee shop. Pete followed several paces behind at a slow walk. Surveying the lot, he noticed one RV, a couple of cars, and a pickup with two fishing rods in the cab's gun rack.

Inside, an emaciated fellow sat at the counter, and it looked like this was probably his home away from home by the mountain of butts in the ashtray in front of him. An elderly couple (Pete decided they belonged to the RV) sat in one corner nursing what looked like oatmeal and orange juice. He noticed an army of pill bottles decorating the table. Two guys in a booth, one with a Black & Decker cap and the other with long, stringy hair that hung over his shoulders and probably hadn't seen soap for some time, were mumbling in their untrimmed beards and throwing glances in syncopation at the peroxide-headed waitress. The place had the delightful aroma of fresh-baked cinnamon rolls. Pete could see a guy in the kitchen lifting a tray from the oven, and all his senses cried, "Yes!"

When Faith emerged from the back, the guy at the counter gave her a detached once-over, turned back, took a long drag on his cigarette, and temporarily disappeared in a cloud of smoke. When he exhaled, it sounded like his insides were coming out. The beards in the booth transferred their adolescent leers to Faith, but it was obvious to them that she was attached to the guy who had come in right after her, and they returned their attention to the manufactured blonde once again.

"Pete, did you order?"

"No, you didn't say what you wanted, and the service seems a tad slow here. You feel better?"

"Yeah, thanks for stopping." Faith glanced around at the empty booths. "The help's probably slow because it's so crowded," she laughed, and Pete enjoyed her smile and the sound of her voice.

"Coffee for the two of you?" The bottled-blonde suddenly appeared from nowhere.

"Please. What about you, Pete?" The way she said his name made it sound like they had known each other long and well. The name *Gwen* suddenly came and went through his mind like a rocket without a landing place.

"Me, too, and I think we want two of those cinnamon rolls, don't we?"

"Sure," Faith said. "If the fat starts to grow, we can run beside the car. Does your bug have a name?"

"No, it doesn't need a name. It's a machine."

"Why not? I thought guys always named their cars."

"Not this guy. Besides what would you name a yellow bug? Lemon Drop? It's hardly a hot car."

"I don't know, but I'll work on it. It may not be hot, but it's cute."

"So back to our original conversation. Why are you going to Spokane. Is it home?"

"No, I'm not going home," Faith explained. "Seattle is home, and I'm not going to Spokane. I'm only stopping off there for a few days." She turned, looked out the window, and sighed. Her body seemed to collapse in upon itself, and she was no longer smiling. "I'm going to Kellogg. It's where I'm from."

"Hitchhiking isn't very smart, especially for a woman. You could find yourself in a bad situation."

"You don't hitchhike much, do you Pete?"

"Never. Well, once when I had a flat without a jack, but otherwise no, never. No offense, but it's a dumb thing to do."

"It's only dumb if you are not careful and ride with serial killers," she said, grinning. "You have to be careful. When you hitchhike, it's dangerous to give your real destination. You can always get someone to pull over sooner than they expect and get out."

"How in the world do you accomplish that? Do you pull a gun?"

"No!" Faith shouted, and heads turned in the near-empty coffee shop.

"What if they won't stop when you want them to? Then what do you do? Panic?" Pete whispered with his head down and eyes darting around.

"Never panic, Pete. Just get sick," she whispered back and smiled. "No one wants you to throw up in their car."

"Here ya go. If you need more butter, holler." The waitress started to walk away.

"Why are you telling this to a serial killer?" Pete said to Faith, louder than he intended.

The waitress, who seemed oblivious to the world a moment ago, abruptly stopped and without completely turning gave Pete a hardened but quizzical stare. Faith laughed and started waving her arms like a football ref signaling an incomplete pass.

39

"It's okay," she assured the waitress. "It's a private joke. Besides, he's on vacation, so he's safe for now."

Pete spit a little coffee on some of his cinnamon roll and found himself laughing and choking. It was obvious the waitress now considered them both suspect. Faith and Pete looked at one another and became very occupied with their cinnamon rolls.

"I told you that wasn't funny," Faith mumbled without looking up.

"I'll try to behave, but it isn't my nature," and he toasted her with hot, black coffee.

Later, as he pulled onto the highway, Pete said, "Do you realize that on this highway there are only two stoplights left? Theoretically, we could drive all the way to Boston without stopping. I wonder if we could hit the one in Post Falls on green."

"That's in Idaho, Pete. I thought you were going to Spokane." Faith looked puzzled.

"I am, but I'm not stopping there unless someone has to pee. I'm going to North Idaho to go fishing. A driver shouldn't give away his real destination when picking up hitchhikers." Pete looked at her and grinned. Faith took in Pete's playful smile and pondered this new information.

She opened her purse and pulled out a book. Pete could tell it was serious reading, especially when Faith pulled out a pen from inside her jacket and began underlining and writing in the margins.

"What are you reading? Is that a textbook?"

"Oh, it's a book I have to read for work. Not very exciting, but you have to keep up or you might not be able to do enough when it counts."

"Sounds like you're chasing a money career."

"Ha! If you call pediatric oncology a money career. About the only time I think about money is when I'm on my way to the laundromat or the rent is due."

"You a doctor?"

"Hardly. I'm a nurse. I work with an oncology team at Children's Hospital. It's great work. I love the kids, but sometimes it can get real tense. I like it because it isn't just cold, clinical treatment. You're treating the person consistently, not just seeing a one-time patient. The kids draw you in because they need strength from wherever they can find it. But sometimes . . ." She looked out the window away from Pete so he couldn't see her eyes, but he knew there were tears there. She sucked in and swallowed a breath. "Sometimes . . . you . . . lose them," she said as she took an empty breath and wiped a tear from her cheek. It's like losing a piece of yourself after you've spent a lot of time with them, cared for them, played with them, and even cried with them.

"People use the expression 'a broken heart,' but the pieces are never quite the same. When I was a little girl, my mother had an antique porcelain cream pitcher that had been her mother's. It was the only thing of her mother's she had left. One day, I accidentally knocked it on the floor, and it broke in so many pieces. We glued it back together as best we could, but it was never the same. Every once in a while, I caught my mother touching it gently with a sad look on her face. When a child dies, the world is altered forever; the cracks are always there. Parents may go on living, but it will never be the same. Somebody once said, 'Death is the only corner we can't turn back around.'" Her face was flushed, and tears began to roll down her cheeks in a steady stream.

Pete found himself wanting to ease her pain, so he pulled over near a farm gate and reached his arm around her. To his surprise, she buried her head in his chest and sobbed. He held her gently, and he could feel her body throb as she cried. Her hair had a slight perfume, like from a shampoo. He didn't know how long they sat there, but it didn't seem to matter to either of them. In fact, the thought occurred to him that this might be the highlight of his vacation. The truth was, he wasn't a very good fisherman. The cabin gave solitude, but he knew it could also be very lonely, and he had never been there without his family. After a while, she looked up and began wiping the tears from her eyes and cheeks.

"This is crazy. I don't even know you, and I'm blubbering all over you."

"Sometimes, we're more ourselves with strangers. They're safer because we'll never see them again. They can't mess up our life."

Pete put his hands back on the wheel as Faith settled back into her seat and took a deep breath. He looked at the mountains ahead, and his thoughts seem to pass over them. "My mother used to say, 'We don't give enough attention to the baptism of tears, and it may be our truest sacrament.'"

"Your mother sounds like a wise woman, but I still feel like a fool." Neither one said anything as Pete pulled back onto the road.

CHAPTER FOUR

Moving On

One year earlier . . . Mason Chalice looked out upon the manicured green bordered by ivy-covered walls. Now, it was finally coming to an end. He would no longer parse Greek verbs or memorize Hebrew roots or argue over Aquinas's proofs for the existence of God. He would enter a time-honored and respected profession that could lead to many arenas of recognition. "Yes, arenas of recognition," he thought to himself. He knew humility above recognition was a Christian virtue, but even Jesus said, "Let your light shine before men." He knew the Chalices were good at getting light to shine on themselves, and they all seemed to thrive on recognition. "Perhaps it's genetic," he thought to himself. Chalices have always been among the recognized and influential. His own father was an economic advisor to more than one occupant of the White House, both publicly and, more significantly, very quietly and privately. While most of the American public know that presidents place their holdings in blind trusts until their term of office ends, what they don't know is that *blind* refers to the public, not the president.

"At least my draft board in Virginia recognized that I'm significant enough not to put me in some stinking jungle with people trying to kill me," Mason said to himself. It had never occurred to him before, but he suddenly realized there were no war heroes among the Chalice lineage.

"I wonder how many of these future pastors and theologians believe in God," he contemplated as he glanced down the row of classmates in their black robes and multicolored hoods. "We all believe to some degree in something we call God, I suppose. But I wonder how many really have faith, whatever it is. It's only another word for superstition. The human species hasn't evolved as much as we'd like to think, but one doesn't say that too loudly, even here in one of the more liberated gardens of academia. People, even educated ones, still cling to the old myths, especially if cancer has ravaged their body and their next matriculation is death. We cling to them as a way of coping with the ambiguities of life, but anyone who thinks for themselves knows differently." Mason lifted his chin and looked toward the dais with a look of quiet but reverent certitude, hoping others would notice. He could hear Dr. R. B. Terroid begin to bring his typically too long and too boring commencement speech to a conclusion. "Why couldn't we have gotten someone famous?" Mason thought. "We might have been featured on some news broadcast."

Mason had always been particularly enamored with the idea of being on television. For him, it had a somewhat seductive quality. "It expands one's potential of recognition by geometric proportions," he thought to himself. "Besides, the media is the message, and Marshall McLuhan had proved it. It didn't matter so much what one said or did on TV, but your presence there said you were significant, beyond the common crowd. "Air time" was becoming "real time" and the most important media of exchange, even more important than any content. The church of the future would be a worldwide television extravaganza, and if Mason had his way, he would be its most important star.

"So, graduates, remember," Dr. Terroid intoned, "as the German theologian Hemult Thielecke has reminded us, 'The question why God permits this or does that, or whether he exists at all, shows that faith thrusts us out into open country. . . . Faith bears witness here that God cannot be imprisoned in a world-view in which everything is easy.'[1]"

Mason's mind drifted to a visit to his mentor's home on Long Island. Dr. A. L. Morgan, pastor of one of the largest and oldest Methodist churches in New York City, lived in a white, colonial style home on three acres. It had been a gift from a congregation whose heart dwelt more with Wall Street than his pew in the Methodist church. Mason could easily imagine himself in such a home. His mother would approve. She had wanted him to enlist in the Navy, but there is always the risk you might see combat, and the thought of it sent chills up his spine. Death wasn't something Mason was comfortable contemplating, let alone visiting. Unlike most people, the 23rd Psalm was a threatening, not comforting, scripture for him.

He had chosen the ministry as a clean profession that could keep him from harm and also provide recognition and an income for a comfortable station in life. The risk of going to Vietnam and the chance of returning maimed or not at all had shaped his "call to ministry." "Yes, the call to ministry was loud and clear when one considered the alternatives," he had said to himself. "Someday, when I have my own church or am president of a college or seminary, I will have a grand house set apart from others. Maybe one day, I will be the bishop of the entire church. I will sit at my desk and give my weekly television address to thousands, no, millions."

"It will be a few years yet," his thoughts continued. "First, I have to spend some time at that entry level church out West, but before long, Father will have arranged something with the Bishop, perhaps an endowment somewhere for the church's holdings, and then I will be placed in a parish more suitable to my talents. For the life of me, I cannot understand why they are sending me to Idaho. And a mining town. My God! People living like moles, digging their sustenance out of the ground. The place is probably covered with dirt. What am I supposed to do with a town full of uneducated miners? There probably isn't a theater or art gallery within a hundred miles that performs something besides *Annie Oakley* or shows cowboy art. Oh well, Mason, even Jesus had his time in the wilderness; this will be mine. Perhaps I can learn to fish. It's supposed to be therapeutic, and I may need some therapy after a few months among miners in the wild. I wonder how one prepares fish for eating."

"Hey, Mason," a whispered voice said, "Do you think this will end before Jesus comes back?"

Mason knew the whispered voice behind him without even looking. Douglas Applegate, a skinny fella from Louisiana, was affectionately known as God's Clown by his classmates and a scandal to his professors.

"It may be a long time before we can get drunk again," Applegate whispered in Mason's ear. "Our every move will be watched by someone. We'll have to be respectable preachers. I can hardly wait for the church teas."

Mason couldn't help but laugh, choking it down. He had a vision of Applegate with a small cup of tea balanced on his knee with his forever messy hair nodding to bland comments such as, "I understand Mabel Hogendale isn't entering her roses in the fair this year. Poor dear. She tried so hard for so many years, but they are for some strange reason without fragrance, although Helen Alden tells me they are quite colorful."

"The class of 1971 will now rise and receive their diplomas." As Mason crossed the dais, he glanced at the anxious, proud parents, perky faces all, but he knew his were not there. They were never there when it mattered to him. His father was in Geneva working on some international trade negotiation. His mother was sailing somewhere between Australia and Tahiti with her latest, 20 years her junior. Ever since she turned 50, Mason's mother seems to have preferred men who are bodies with no brains, endowed more with testosterone than intelligence.

"Mason, congratulations. I hear you are going to North Idaho. I envy you. I'm going to Chicago. There are worse places, I admit, but I'm just not a city guy."

Mason stared at John Bankfield for a moment. "Yes, I'm going out West where the buffalo roam, but I hope they don't make too much noise on Sundays. It might disturb my concentration."

"I think you'll even be west of the buffalo, Mason. Last I heard, they were pretty much confined to Montana and Wyoming."

"I can see I will have to brush up on my geography and Western culture, if that isn't an oxymoron," Mason said with a dour look.

"Don't be so sour, Mason. You'll enjoy it. My uncle spent his entire ministry in the West and loved it."

"I'm sure it's wonderful, John, but I was hoping for a multiple staff church in the mid-Atlantic region or the Northeast. I'm not sure I want a small church of my own, especially in such a remote and primitive locale. It doesn't seem to fit me somehow."

Bankfield, who was already slipping out of his robe, said, "Well, my father always said, 'Ministry is not just talking about God but learning how to be like Christ in the lives of others, in the midst of their pain. And it's not always the preacher who fulfills that role. It might be the custodian.' From what I know about ministry, we all do our share of grunt work no matter

45

what size church. If I had a dollar for every chair I ever moved for my dad at potlucks, I'd be a rich preacher. And that, my friend, is an oxymoron. Take care. My folks are waiting."

Mason cringed and found himself coughing. "Custodian. Grunt work. What did he think I was learning from Dr. Morgan, contemporary mop techniques?"

"I have to go, too, John. My parents are waiting, and Dr. Morgan is throwing a little celebration for me at his place." Mason hoped his voice had not betrayed the lie, but he could see in Bankfield's eyes an awareness that went unspoken.

Mason moved away quickly, wondering to himself how he would really celebrate his degree in the mastery of the divine. And why hadn't the good Rev. Dr. Morgan planned anything for his favorite intern? The auditorium was filled with graduates who had shed their robes and were posing for pictures with friends and relatives. Mason felt distinctly out of place having neither. He headed out the door only to find that the sun had vanished, and it was beginning to sprinkle. "Go ahead. Rain on my parade, on my graduation party," he said to no one in particular. His new black BMW sat by the curb, and as soon as he heard the engine sing, he popped the clutch and swerved into the street without looking for traffic. His mind was filled with pictures of happy parents and graduates, and he hoped that if he drove fast enough, he could lose the image.

But other images came to mind. He remembered when his parents got into a fight that exceeded the bounds of normal marital propriety. His mother went to the neighbors and then to the emergency room. His father fled to an apartment he had in Washington, DC. Mason knew he was baggage from a failed marriage. He was not going to waste his energy like so many of his peers, rebelling through self-destructive behavior in a vain attempt to get his parents' attention and, hopefully, love. He told himself he could look out for himself. He had been doing it for some time now.

By the time he reached the freeway, it was raining hard. He drove until he was hungry and pulled over at a roadside cafe. It was Thursday night, so the place was empty. He liked it that way; he felt he deserved to be alone. "Suffering should have its own reward," he thought to himself. "It's not true that misery loves company; misery loves to be alone."

The sound system was emitting *Sergeant Pepper's Lonely Hearts Club Band*, and a dark-skinned waitress who could have been from almost anywhere but Sweden approached Mason with a menu and a glass of water. As she handed him the menu, a large man with tattoos on both arms began putting clean cups under the counter. He was balding, and Mason could see the perspiration on the top of his head. He wondered if the tattooed man had a thing for the waitress. No, she was probably married to a tailor who was trying to learn how to sew polyester instead of real cloth, like in the old country. "Man, I hate polyester," he said to himself. He watched the sweat on the man's head. "I wonder how much sweat is mixed with American cuisine." Before he could speculate an answer, a group of noisy collegians filed in and took over most of the counter. The tattoo man didn't look pleased, but the waitress gave them the nod, meaning, "I'll get to you in a minute."

Mason wondered if they taught that in waitress school somewhere. "All right, ladies, this is how to nod so the customer will know you see them." The waitress took Mason's dinner order, and to his surprise, she didn't have an accent. Mason looked around for a discarded newspaper and spotted one on the counter by the students. When he went for the paper, he realized that the girl on the end nearest the paper was attractive.

"Excuse me, Miss, is this your paper?" Of course he knew it wasn't. She had brown eyes, long shiny hair, expensive clothes, and nice full lips accented with Marilyn Monroe red lipstick. Mason watched her eyes check him out. Then she looked into his eyes and smiled; he smiled back.

"No, it's not mine. Help yourself." She continued to smile and drew out the words somewhat invitingly. As Mason sat down, he glanced back, and she was still watching him; she was still smiling. He smiled and raised his beer, but the others gathered her in with their noisy chatter.

Mason was surprised at how hungry he was. He realized that in the excitement of getting to graduation, he had skipped lunch. "Here I am in some no-name place all by myself," he thought, "while my classmates are out celebrating with friends and family." For Mason, loneliness was not a new companion. The two of them had spent a lot of time together. Mason knew his hunger was deeper than his stomach and more intense, but maybe he could satiate it with enough beer, for tonight anyway.

"Mind if I join you?" She didn't wait for an answer. She had caught him at just the right moment, hamburger in his mouth and ketchup on his chin. Mason chewed without trying to appear frantic and discovered the napkin holder was empty. "Damn," he thought, "here I am looking like a slob."

Brown eyes passed him a couple of napkins she snatched from the adjacent booth. Mason realized the other girls had gone, only to be replaced by a number of new customers all busy with petty conversations about nothing. She sat across from him, smiling, waiting patiently, dangling another napkin from her slim fingers like a crisp apple.

When Mason left a few weeks later on his trip to Idaho, he took a two-lane road because he had heard someone in the diner say it would "save you hours." Mason believed in shortcuts, but now he wasn't so sure. He stared at his flat tire and began to walk.

"Maybe there will be a gas station around the corner," he said to no one, and even if anyone had been there, the wind was strong enough that his voice would have been carried away. "I haven't seen a car in any direction for hours." He wrapped himself up in his coat, bent to the wind, and kept walking. "At least it's not raining. What was that?"

The rain began slowly with large drops seemingly spaced apart, but then it came in a torrent. Mason grabbed his coat more tightly and looked for cover, but there was none, not a bush or a tree in sight. Small rivulets were forming, and the ditch alongside the road was rapidly filling with water. He began to run. He was in good shape despite the occasional cigarette because he had played Lacrosse both at boarding school and seminary. In a way, it felt good to run. There was something exhilarating about it, but he wasn't sure if anything would change as he approached a bend in the road.

"If I were a praying man, I would ask that there be an open gas station around the corner, but it either is, or it isn't. Prayer changes nothing but the one praying, despite what the superstitious think. And there *is* a gas station. Thank goodness I am saved," he said through the rain and his heavy breathing.

The gas station looked like a stage prop for a 1930s movie, and Mason wasn't sure it was operational, let alone open. He glanced at the old pumps as he walked by and noticed that neither one of them was locked, but then who would be around to steal gas? It was dark inside. He tried the door, but it was locked. The wind was pounding on his back. "At least I'm under cover here," he thought to himself. He could see a slightly open door on the far wall with a dim light coming through the doorway. Somebody must be in there. "Can't you hear me knocking?"

"Help! Is there anyone in here? I'm stranded on the highway and need some help." He shouted as loudly as he could, but his voice seemed to leave with each gust of wind. The door didn't move, and he felt defeated. He put his back to the door, slipped to the ground, and grabbed his knees. He felt miserably alone.

"What the...!" Suddenly the door behind him broke away, and Mason fell backward, almost hitting his head on the floor. He found himself looking up at a tall, thin man in coveralls who was holding an oily rag in his hand and staring down at him.

"Did you want somethin', Fella?"

"Why am I cursed with idiots?" Mason thought to himself. "Just once, could I encounter someone with intelligence when I need help?"

"Yes, I have a flat tire down the road and need some help."

"Do you have a spare?" the man asked.

"Probably, yes. It's a brand new car."

"Do you have a jack?"

"I guess so."

"Do you have a tire iron?"

"It's a brand new BMW. I am sure it has everything *we* need."

"Except it doesn't have four round tires, and if it has all *you* need, what do you want from me?" the man said in a rather curious but not insolent tone.

"I want you to come and change it, of course," Mason said with the superior tone he used on those he thought inferior.

"Well, Fella, this is a gas station, and when people come in here with problems, we try to help them, but you forgot to bring your car. I don't know any men and only a few women for that matter who don't know how to change a tire. Maybe you should just trot back there and see if you can change it, and if you have trouble, come on back, and I'll see what I can do. But I have a bigger problem right now."

"You mean you are refusing to help me?"

"No, I'm just telling you how you can fix the problem yourself because it's your problem. And according to you, you have all you need to fix it. That's all most people need, but when you do it, get the lug nuts right."

Mason stared with a simmering anger. "Okay, I know how this works. I can pay. How much?"

"Like I said, I have a bigger problem right now. Widow McKelsey's car broke down, and it's an old car, and she doesn't have much money on account of her son has all sorts of big-named medical problems, and she needs the car to get medicine and go to doctors and the like. So it's pretty important that I fix it as soon as I can. She's out there on a ranch about 10 miles up the gulch that you haven't come to yet 'cause your car stopped rolling. So I don't care about your money. I care more about widow McKelsey and her son, and my wife says if I don't get the widow's car running today, I better not come home to supper."

"You don't understand. I am on my way to Idaho to take charge of a church there, and it is important that I do not miss my first Sunday."

"You look awful young to be a preacher."

"Well, it's my first church, and it is important that I make the right impression."

The mechanic rubbed his chin, "Impression, huh?" Then he reached down and extended a hand to Mason who was still on the floor. "That explains a lot. Is your daddy a preacher, too?"

"No, he is the personal financial advisor to the President." Mason smiled for the first time.

"Woo wee! He must know a lot of important folk. You, too."

"That's right. Now go fix my tire. I'll pay you $50."

The man glanced out the window at the rain and shook his head no.

"Okay, this is robbery, but I will pay you $100."

This time, the man glanced at the back door and shook his head no again. "Like I said, Preacher, I got a more important problem. So you go fix your tire, and you may want to fill up when I repair the flat for you, if it can be fixed, 'cause it's 103 miles to the next gas station. Or you could go back 53 miles and get gas, but you probably don't need any 'cause you filled up then."

"No, I didn't." Mason turned to look down the long road, and when he turned back, the man was gone, the back room door was closed, and he was standing in the dark.

"Damn," he mumbled to himself and headed toward his car. The wind had died down some, and the journey back was not as uncomfortable. As he got to the car, the rain stopped, and the water in the ditch seemed to disappear as fast as it had appeared. He opened the trunk, took his suitcase out, put it in the front seat, and began dragging out the spare. He found himself getting warm despite the cold and quickly shed his coat. He surprised himself that he could change the tire. He almost got the lug nuts reversed, but he remembered the man's warning and was careful to put them back exactly the same. The knees on his pants were muddy, and his shirt was filthy from lifting the wounded tire back into the trunk. He had worked up a sweat, and his body was chilled before he could get the heater going.

As he drove toward the gas station, Mason thought about passing it by, but he knew he needed gas, and he wanted to at least wash his hands. As he drove up, all the lights were on, and the place looked like an oasis in the darkness. When he stopped, he noticed the door to the back was wide open, and before he could turn off the car, the mechanic came bounding through it and outside.

"You drink coffee, Pastor? I just made a fresh pot. I see you got her all fixed up. Do you want me to see if I can repair the flat? You can wash up in the men's room." Mason was a little taken aback by the mechanic's sudden friendliness, but he figured he had a change of mind after he thought about the importance of Mason's father.

When Mason emerged from the restroom, the mechanic was standing over a tire clamped by some machine. When he heard Mason enter, he turned.

"You're lucky. It was a small nail, and it didn't tear up the tire. I plugged it, and it's good as new. Drive your car around to the bay door, and I'll put it back on for you."

Mason was about to say something but decided not to and headed for his car. When the repaired tire was on the car, the mechanic stood up, looked at his watch, and said, "It's time for supper. The Missus will be expecting us."

"I thought you had to get Widow What's Her Name's car fixed before you could have supper."

"I finished it while you were putting on your spare. So now we can eat."

"You're inviting me to dinner?"

"Sure, Preacher. There ain't no place to eat around here, and unless that fancy car of yours is also a catering truck, I reckon it will be another couple of hours before you eat. Besides, this is Friday, and we always have grilled pork chops on Friday night."

"What do I owe you for fixing the tire?"

"Ah, nothing. Anyone who has to change a tire in the rain shouldn't have to pay to get it fixed."

"But I can afford it," Mason said indignantly.

"You made that clear, but I don't want your money. I'm a rich man."

"Yeah, sure," Mason thought. "If you were a rich man, you wouldn't be working in this dump in the middle of nowhere."

"How long does it take to get to your house?" Mason asked.

"Well, my slowest time was three minutes, but I had a kink in my leg. It's right behind us."

Mason walked into a kitchen made warm by a wood stove and filled with the aroma of sizzling pork chops, homemade bread, and warm cider. He couldn't remember ever experiencing so many wonderful smells in one place. The mechanic's wife would win no beauty contest, but she was a poised woman. She seemed to exude confidence, and before Mason could say a word, she embraced him with a bear-like hug that made him very uncomfortable. Mason's family didn't hug.

"I'm Emily, and I am so glad my Richard brought a guest. It is always a joy to share with others."

"A joy to share with others," Mason thought. "I'll bet he told her about my father, and they're planning to hit me up for some kind of gift of money. That's what he meant by being a rich man. Won't they be surprised? My father wouldn't spring for a nickel. He's not very giving."

"Come stand by the stove and dry off. Here's a towel to wipe your pants off," Emily said cheerfully.

Minutes later, Emily placed the pork chops on the plates and sat down. Mason started to reach for his fork when he realized they were both looking at him. "Am I in some kind of Stephen King book?" he wondered. "These folks are odd."

"Would you give thanks?" Emily asked, with her rosy cheeks lifted by her smile.

"I would, but my throat got a little something out in the rain," Mason said, although it sounded feeble even to him.

"Richard?"

Mason closed his eyes and then realized that Emily and Richard had each grabbed one of his hands, and both had a firm grip. He hadn't seen anyone do that except a few radicals at seminary who were always praying and holding hands.

"Lord we are grateful for all the bounty you provide us," Richard began. "For the clean air, the refreshing rains, the wind like your breath, this abundance of food we are about to eat, and for this guest you have guided safely to our home. We pray for Margaret McKelsey and her young son, David. Lord, please heal him so that both their lives might be easier, and give us wisdom to provide what support we can. Please be with this young preacher, your servant, as he tends his first flock, sharing with them your joy and mercies. Amen."

Mason was somewhat stunned as he looked around the small kitchen. He could see through the door what he assumed was the living room, which looked like a museum of old furniture and worn carpet. This is not the home of a rich man, he thought.

"I have to admit, Mrs...."

"Emily."

"These are the best pork chops I have ever eaten, Emily."

"My Richard loves his pork chops, but we had to give up Sally Jo to have them. Sally Jo was our pig, of course, and a cute one, too. But we all have our place in God's design, don't we, Preacher? Oh, excuse me. I don't know your name."

"It's Mason. Mason Chalice. You have probably heard the name. My father is a presidential advisor."

"Can't say as I have," the mechanic said as he forked some mashed potatoes. But then we don't have a TV, and nobody delivers a paper out here. We get one when we go into town for supplies and the sort."

"No TV. What do you do for entertainment? I mean, there is nothing to do out here. Aren't you bored to death?"

"Emily, are you bored to death?"

"Of course not. I don't have time to do all the things I need to do. Between my reading and Bible study, cooking, sewing, baking, and errands, there is no time for TV."

Mason looked at the couple and thought, "These folks are Luddites. They're against modern conveniences."

"I'll show you my shortwave if you like," Richard offered. "That's how I keep up with the world. I can talk to folks anywhere. Because my folks came from Kiev, I speak Russian and talk weekly with a Christian in Moscow, several in Cuba, and three in Kenya."

"What do you talk about with all these people?"

"The blessings people are receiving and the obstacles they need prayer for to cope with what is happening in their countries that the news people never talk about."

Mason, like many of his generation, had seen seminary as a way to avoid Vietnam, and it had worked. But now, he was discovering there was a world of faithful people unlike anything he had experienced in his family's large church in New York. He glanced at Richard and Emily who had far less than his family and wondered about the nature of happiness.

After dinner, Richard invited Mason into a small bedroom where he kept his shortwave radio. As Richard was tuning the radio, Mason saw pictures on the wall of a young boy on a young man's shoulders, and he knew the man was Richard. There were pictures of the boy with a bat and glove, with ice cream at what looked like a fair, at a high school graduation, on a college baseball team, and in a Marine officer's uniform. Beneath the picture in the uniform, Mason saw an American flag encased in a walnut, triangular-shaped box.

Their son is dead? No, they are too happy. The flag is probably from his Marine officer's graduation.

"Are these pictures of your son?"

"Yes, this was Dennis's room."

"How long has he been a Marine?"

"Dennis graduated from Annapolis near the top of his class, and then he joined the Corps and served two tours in Vietnam before he was killed."

"I'm so sorry."

Richard turned around to face Mason, and his entire face and demeanor seemed to soften. "It hurt us both hard; still does in some unexpected moments. He was our only child. How could God allow such a thing? That was all I could think. I can even remember standing outside yelling at God to take my cattle, too, like Job. But the funny thing is that I didn't have any. But I know how Job felt. When we heard the details of Dennis's death, it helped some, but only God heals the broken heart. It's funny. People are always asking for miracles, but God heals broken hearts all the time, and no one thinks of it as a miracle. The Lord brings comfort even in our sorrow. He lifts us up from our brokenness and calls us into life."

"I hesitate to ask, but what were the details?"

"The short version is that three men were cut off from their platoon and wounded, and Dennis carried them each to safety, receiving wounds of his own with each trip. He dragged the last man to safety before he bled to death."

Mason noticed a tear easing its way out of Richard's eye before he wiped it away.

"Fresh blackberry pie for any who want it," Emily called from the other room.

"Oh, you don't want to miss this. Do we get ice cream on it tonight, Em?"

They both wanted Mason to stay, but he wanted to get on the road, not that he was anxious about getting to Idaho. He knew he would make it in plenty of time, but he wanted to be alone. Being in this couple's home had been both pleasurable and disturbing. He needed to escape the anxiety it was causing him and the questions it raised in his mind.

CHAPTER FIVE

The Back Pew

That winter, in early 1972, Lou had gone to replenish the wood box by the stove. He went to the back of the house and laid his carrying strap on the ground where he could easily reach it. The pile of wood was wet on top with moisture underneath the first layers of the pile, but further down, Lou could see that the wood was dry. He pulled at a few pieces near the top and lifted them so he could reach below and pull out the dry ones. He put one small bundle on the strap and tried to wrestle more out. He had just put his hand in to grab what looked like an end cut of a two-by-four when he felt a sharp pain in his hand. He jerked it back immediately.

"Damn you, varmint!" Lou looked at his hand and knew immediately he had not been bitten but had put his hand on a nail. His grasp and the weight of the wood above had actually driven the nail into his hand. "You got to be rusty, damn you anyway." He grabbed his bundle of wood and headed for the house. Lou dropped the wood near the stove and looked carefully at his hand. "Damn, damn, damn! This is when a fella could use some help," he said to no one.

The thought catapulted him into a dark place, and he cast it aside as quickly as it had come. He washed his hand and inspected it closely. It was bleeding and reddening around the puncture. Reaching into the medicine cabinet, Lou pulled out some rubbing alcohol, a razor blade, and some gauze bandaging. He slowly but carefully cut the tough skin around the hole. "I could use some medicinal whiskey about now." But Lou knew he had purged the house of all alcohol for drinking. He turned his hand over and realized for the first time that the nail had gone all the way through. His hand seemed normal except for the hole, but it was all he could do to keep it from shaking. After trimming off the skin, he poured the rubbing alcohol into the hole from the palm side. He waved his arm in the air, hoping to take out some of the sting, but it didn't help. He looked at the back side and the blue vein coursing across the landscape of his hand. He took a breath and realized he had been holding it. The nail had just missed the ligaments. He could still bend his fingers and move his thumb. "Thank you," he whispered but not to himself. He repeated the procedure, pouring the alcohol into the wound on the back side of his hand but without cutting any skin for fear he would cut a vein and be in a worse situation.

Lou sat there for a moment looking at his hand, turning it over and over. There were heavy calluses on his fingers and the palm of his hand. He thought of the years chopping wood, carrying ore, handling drills, lifting stulls. How many miles or years can a hand take before its tread is worn out? How quickly things can change. You think you know what you're doing. Things are under your control, and blam! The whole damn world is turned upside down.

"We were happy once," he said to himself, "or maybe we just thought we were. Maybe it's something I've just made up to make myself feel better about the evil I rode with and harbored in my soul. So dark, oh God, so dark." He took a deep breath and resisted the urge to purge himself with tears again. He finally wrapped the gauze bandage around his hand and went to the phone. He lifted the black receiver, put his large finger into the holes and dialed the number.

"Hello, Twila? This is Lou Marks. Is Doc there? . . . With someone? Well, you can probably tell me. I poked myself with a nail. . . . No, nothing serious if putting it all the way through your hand isn't serious. But I wanted . . . yeah, when was my last tetanus shot? . . . Okay, I'll wait. Thanks. . . . So I don't need another one? . . . Yeah, I know, keep it clean. Tell Doc I said hi. . . . Goodbye. . . . You, too." Lou did as he was told and spent the rest of the day resting and periodically cleaning his puncture wound. He gathered up his dishes, cleaned things up, and decided to go to bed early, thinking tomorrow it would feel better.

Lou thumbed through his copy of *Outdoor Life* before he reached over and turned out the light. He thought maybe he might do a little fly fishing on the Clear Water. It amazed him how you could actually see through the river to its bottom. He needed to get away. There were too many ghosts haunting him around here. But Lou knew there were no ghosts, only his conscience, which he thought had died a long time ago. He lay there for a moment and then got up and took two Tylenol because his hand had begun to hurt. There was more throbbing with each beat of his heart. He lay in the dark, staring at the ceiling—and thinking.

Will things just go on like this, and then one day I'll die, or worse? I'll be too old to take care of myself, and they'll ship me off to some nursing home, and I'll lay there in my piss with spit drooling down my unshaved chin. He thought for a moment about the loaded pistol in the drawer next to his bed. It would be quick and easy, and it would save a lot of hurt. "Nope," he thought, "that's the coward's way out, and I may be a lot of things, but I ain't no coward. Besides, maybe Faith will come back. Nah, ain't gonna happen."

Lord, you got no reason to hear me, but you said you would forgive. You spent time with those prostitutes and other sinners, so you must have loved them some. You didn't condemn the adultery lady, so I guess it may not be asking too much if you could bring my Faith home again. Even if she hates me, which, as you know, she should. I would just like to see her one more time. I know I deserve no blessings, but you seem like the blessing type. Amen.

He turned and tried to sleep, but his hand continued to throb with his pulse. He found himself counting the beats, and then he felt himself riding the wave of his pulse. Despite the pain, he drifted into the land where up is down and down is up, and his mental gyroscope was lost in non-space. The drill vibrated too much, and then it morphed into one of the pumps in a mine with its beat pulling water out from deep within the earth. He drifted to the sump pump his dad used to pull the water out of their basement every spring. He could hear the sucking, gurgling of the dirty water as it was lifted from the basement floor. He found himself standing in an unfamiliar grocery store. All the floors were carpeted, and it was quiet and peaceful. He was all alone. Lou was in the dream and outside of the dream at the same time, the actor and the audience, but he didn't know which he was or which he was supposed to be. The vegetables were playing checkers, and the soup cans were having a pyramid contest in Aisle 3. The ice cream containers were all open; they had big spoons and were sampling each other and giggling. That made him smile.

He went to the meat section and found a hand with a bent rusty nail piercing through it. Lou turned quickly away. The store was now empty and dark, not normal dark but a heavy, solid, weighty dark that he knew he could not lift, and even if he had his flashlight, the light would bounce back or be swallowed up. Lou knew he should be frightened, but part of him knew he was watching a dream; the other part was more curious than scared. In a far corner stood a door half open with light coming through. Rather than a solid stream of light, it was formless like a morning mist or campfire smoke. Despite its seeming frailty, it penetrated the darkness like a phalanx penetrating a rugged stone fortress. The light had power.

Lou looked to the front of the store. It was so dark he couldn't see it. He felt a pain in his hand and held it close to his chest. He looked back across the store at the door and began walking toward it. The carpet was gone and had become sharp, penetrating stones that pierced his feet. Lou realized he was barefoot. "Dumb fool!" the audience (Lou) said to him as he moved toward the door. The floor had become a hill, and he was climbing up it.

He cautiously peeked through the door and saw nothing—no dark, no light, no floor, no sky, nothing. He couldn't describe it to the audience (Lou) because nothing is nothing, but he heard music. He thought it was music, but it was like none he had ever heard. The music without voice told him to step through the door. As he watched himself from outside of somewhere, he knew he was dying. A shadow crossed before the door, and he knew it was Faith; a deeper darkness penetrated the light. Lou felt himself swallow; his throat was raw. The music grew louder and continued to beckon him through the door. He could hear voices that said, "Don't go, you will die!" Others softly encouraged him on. "There is nowhere to step," he muttered. But the music kept insisting, and the beat got louder and louder. It vibrated over and over . . . again . . . again. He could feel it in his feet as if he were walking on fire. Despite its intensity, it felt inviting at the same time. So Lou raised his left foot and stepped through the door.

He felt the throbbing in his hand grow more and more intense, and he saw himself hanging on a cross with both hands nailed to raw timber. His head was covered with perspiration, and then he felt the pain in his feet, the tightness in his lungs, and he gasped for air. Suddenly, he couldn't breathe. His chest convulsed, and his lungs reached out and grabbed for air like a drowning man desperately trying to put a gasp of life-saving air into his lungs.

Just as quickly, he knew he was no longer on the cross. He turned and looked back where he had just been; it was someone else hanging there. He couldn't see the man's face, but he could see the muscles of his arms twitching uncontrollably and his bloody feet. Lou watched as the man's chest heaved, and suddenly he felt an increased pain in his hand. Then there was silence . . . more silence . . . just silence. Time could not measure the length of the silence because it was outside of time. It was longer than any silence he had ever known, and he felt the weight of it. It seemed to press down upon his heart. His hand throbbed all the more as the silence seeped into his pores.

He wondered if he should speak. The silence remained, but Lou sensed now the silence had a voice. It wasn't a voice yet; it was a coming voice, and Lou knew it was coming . . . for him. He knew it would speak to him . . . only to him . . . it would speak . . . truth. He could feel it coming, and his body became hot and flushed. His hand, which he didn't think could hurt any more, was hurting with even more intensity, and with each beat of his heart, he thought it would burst open into the silence.

When he heard it, he wanted to flee both the audience-Lou and the dream-Lou, but there was nowhere to go. There was no fleeing this voice—this truth.

> *You are a thief. You stole the love she had for you, the joy of being a child. When she was in pain, you brought her no comfort; you brought her more pain. You listened to the voice of evil instead of my voice. You trampled on her childhood trust. You brought fear, not love. When she needed you the most, you cast aside your opportunity to be a healing soul—the gift, the gift of being a father was trampled by your blackened heart.*

Lou's head fell to his chest as the perspiration seeped into his eyes and made them burn. His heart felt like a dead rock, and it did not beat with any rhythm now. It, too, was silent. It felt like someone was standing on his hand. "Oh God, it hurts!" he cried out to no one, for there was no one there. There were no more words, not a sound. Silence covered all truth, hanging like a heavy blanket of fog blocking out all light, going nowhere. He was alone. He turned back toward the crucified man, but he was gone. Only silence. Lou awoke in a cold sweat, his red hand dangling at the bedside. It was dark—quiet.

One morning about a month later, Lou stared at the buttermilk residue that clung to the inside of the glass. A yellow film hung there like the trail of a long ago intruder. Lou stared at the glass. The dirty emptiness of it filled him with a dark sense of regret, and he felt as though the emptiness and filth were somehow inside of him. He knew he had not always been this way, but it was hard to remember the days when he was a hopeful young man, when he and Claire were young and in love. It was hard to remember the days before Claire died and Faith left him, the days before booze was his daily lifeline.

He remembered the day Faith was born. It was the first day of sunshine for nearly a month after the rain and flooding down at Cataldo and most of the creeks. He had wanted to name his daughter Sunshine, but Claire said no. She said people would think we named her after the mine, but he knew she would always be his Sunshine.

The sour aroma of the glass began to fill his nostrils, and he remembered those nights in the darkness. He didn't feel the tear as it traveled down his cheek, but he watched it spread when it hit the bottom of the glass. Slowly, it turned milky white, and he pushed the glass away and wept. Parts of the dream raced in and out of his mind.

Lou wasn't aware of the time. He had stopped keeping track of it the day Faith left. He managed to get to work, but there was nothing else he cared about. He wiped his nose, rubbed the tears from his eyes, and rinsed out the glass. Glasses clean so easily, he thought to himself. He glanced around the kitchen and thought how surprised Claire would be if she could see how clean he kept the place. It wasn't next to godliness, but it was much better than the dark chaos he had been living in those first years. He could feel the regret and self-hatred welling up again somewhere between his stomach and his heart.

He looked out the window at the Thorsons' wash hanging on the back porch. John Thorson's union suit was dancing with the breeze between two sheets that looked like they would soon be in Sally's rag pile. Lou knew the

Thorsons would save them as long as they could. New sheets cost money, and God knows there was little of that to spare. The rain hadn't started yet, but he knew it was on its way and it wouldn't be long. The clouds were probably gathering between Fourth of July Pass and the other side of Graham Mountain and getting ready to drench the valley.

"Sally, you'd better bring John's suit in or he'll have a cold ass tonight. Spring hasn't come to these hills yet," he said to the empty room and found himself laughing at the idea. The hollow sound of his words seemed to expand the emptiness. He stepped out onto the enclosed porch and carefully put his slippers in the old tin breadbox that sat against the wood stove chimney. Lou thought this was one of the best ideas he had ever had as he pulled on his old leather boots and tugged at the laces. He couldn't help but remember the trip the three of them had made to Spokane to White's to get his boots. For some reason, Faith was mesmerized by the clock tower by the Spokane train station.

When Lou stood, he could feel the strain on his knees. He wondered if he could make it until August when he planned to walk from his shift for the last time. Lou knew he could help Angus McFarlin at the hardware store in the winters and maybe lead some fishing tours for some of those pink-skinned tourists from the East or the loud ones from California in the summer.

As he turned the corner of the house, he looked at his mailbox. He could barely make out the rainbow design Claire and Faith had painted on it years ago. It pulled at him like a seductress that you knew would only break your heart. "I never get any mail except for those damned life insurance ads. Those dumb jerks sure don't know much about mining if they're offering insurance to every soul in the valley." The box rattled on the post as he opened the door, and the faded red flag dangled from a rusty bolt, but to Lou's surprise there was mail. He tried to remember if he had checked yesterday, but he couldn't remember. There was a sheet of coupons for bargains around town. He could get 10 percent off a perm at Mar-Dee's and a free gift from All Star Safe and Lock—probably a cheap key ring, he said to himself. Another ad told of the social pleasure of drinking at the Longshot Saloon. Hell, the Longshot had been sitting on Railroad Avenue for almost a hundred years, and everyone knew about it. Lou certainly did. He had been one of their best customers, but no more. There was an ad for a "free" credit card. Just fill in the information and return it, no postage required. "Yeah, then you'll charge interest on a pair of gloves or a new fishing pole and own my ass 'til the day I die."

He ripped all the mail into a few pieces and dumped them into a rusted, three-gallon can he kept beneath the mailbox for that purpose. When it was full of damp, moldy paper and some unidentifiable sludge, he would dump it into the trash or throw it beneath the juniper bush on the side of the house. It was his private vengeance against the postal service and the people who were destroying all those trees. He never let mail get into the house, but then again, he never got any real mail.

Lou looked across the street at a pair of boots sticking out from under an old Dodge pickup that had so many different colors of replacement fenders, doors, and rust that Lou couldn't remember the original color.

"What's wrong with that rig now, Jason?" Lou shouted across the street.

"Nuthun much," the boots shouted back. "Just the starter is all, and I changed the oil. I'm almost done" was the reply from beneath the color-confused truck.

"If you need any help, I'll be back in an hour," Lou said as he stared toward the boots.

"Thanks, but I'll be finished by then. I have to get it ready because we have a family gathering in St. Maries. We get together the last weekend of every month," the boots commented.

"You'd better make sure you're back for your shift on Monday, or Nims will have your ass down an abandoned mine shaft or out the door."

"I'll be back, but I got Monday off, so I won't be there 'til Tuesday. So I'll be back, but not because of that little number cruncher. Did I tell you what Gordy Hawkins said?"

Lou was staring at the bottom of the boots and wondering if this tidbit of mountain gossip was worth a walk across the street. But curiosity is a powerful instinct, and he couldn't resist. "What did that ornery cuss say?"

"Well, it seems he was in Reno last month cuz some relative died, and he and some cousins went to the casinos after the funeral stuff and all, and guess who they saw?"

"So who did they see? Some movie star?"

"No, dummy. The number cruncher himself."

"So what's wrong with Nims being in a casino? Gordy was there," Lou asked somewhat indignantly.

"No, Lou, that's not the good part. Seems Mr. Nims, the upright citizen and super of one of the richest silver mines in the world, had a young lady with him who wasn't Mrs. Nims, if you know what I mean."

"Nims with a prostitute?"

The boots slid out from under the truck, and an oil-stained, red-bearded man in his 20s lay on the trolley looking up at Lou. "I guess the local whores in Wallace ain't good enough for him. He has to go all the way to Nevada to get his kicks."

"I'll be damned!" Lou said under his breath. "Did he see Gordy?"

"No, Gordy said Nims was too busy putting his eyes all over this Reno rent-a-gal to see anything else. Besides, he wouldn't know one of his own miners if the guy sat on his lap. He could care less about us. To him, it's all about numbers and money. It just goes to show, you never know about people."

Lou pulled at his jacket and turned away, "Yeah, you never know." He began walking down the hill. There wasn't much activity with the coming rain.

A couple days passed, and Lou figured it was Sunday. Yes, it was Sunday, and he was getting it right for a change. He knew for certain it was Sunday because he heard the bells of St. Rita's Catholic Church over on Maple Street.

He had been in St. Rita's twice. The first time was when a friend of Claire's was having her baby christened and Claire insisted they take Faith and go. Lou didn't remember much about it except some proud parents, a grandpa he knew who worked as a mechanic, and everyone crisscrossing themselves every time the priest said something. He got so drunk later that he couldn't even remember leaving or how he got home. Suddenly, he felt a burning sensation in his eyes, and he wasn't sure if it was the wind or the thought of the embarrassment he must have caused Claire and Faith.

The second time he was there, he was stone sober until afterward. It was Bob Caufield's funeral, and he was a pallbearer. He couldn't remember anything the priest said that day. He could remember sitting behind Bob's brothers with their fresh haircuts, staring at the back of their heads and wondering if he would die before any of them. How many people would come to stare at the back of heads while someone tried their hardest to say something good about him? The fellow would probably have a sleepless night the night before and break into a sweat straining to find some goodness to tell. He could say what a good miner Lou Marks had been and how he never missed a shift except when he had that illness that time. In the end, he would have to lie.

"I wonder if God has some special kind of forgiveness for priests and preachers who have to lie at funerals," he thought to himself. "What can you say about a drunk who killed his wife with neglect and drove away the most beautiful daughter in the world after he made her hate him? Folks only knew she ran away, but not why. Most just thought she was a crazy teenager. They could only guess and gossip like they had been since that day. But they would never really know." He watched his own boots move beneath his sullen frame. He knew some of them would get it right, but they would be too ashamed to ever speak it out loud, even in gossip.

He hesitated when he got to the steps of the Methodist Church. He wasn't sure why he'd been coming other than his horrible dream, but he was grateful to be a little late. Everyone had already gone inside. He wondered if he was doing the right thing like he had every Sunday these past couple of months, but how could it not be the right thing? Maybe God got sick to his stomach every time he walked in the door and was just waiting for the time when he would puke all over him. But Lou didn't figure God could do anything worse than the hell he had already created for himself. "Hell," he thought. "Dying would be a relief." He knew he didn't deserve to be in a holy place, but he could name a few others who didn't either, and they were even members. But then, maybe they were like him; maybe they hated themselves, too, and were hungry for some tiny piece of goodness. "Oh, God, yes, if you could just give me a tiny drop of goodness, please," Lou whispered as he climbed the steps.

The congregation was singing the last verse of "Blessed Assurance, Jesus Is Mine"[2] as he entered, but Lou was looking for a seat and paid no attention to the faltering singing of the small congregation and sparse choir.

Perfect submission, perfect delight,
Visions of rapture now burst on my sight;
Angels descending, bring from above
Echoes of mercy, whispers of love.

There was no one in the back pew, so Lou didn't have to climb over anyone to find a seat. He was glad it was not like it was in his grandpa's day when they kept the front pews empty and made the latecomers march to the front before the eyes of everyone. When the hymn ended, the minister began praying, and Lou caught a phrase or two but didn't feel like joining in the thoughts offered. He knew the words were good, comforting words, the kind that live in a holy place. Lou remembered the phrase from a few weeks before—"and the Word became flesh and dwelt among us."[3] "Yeah," he thought, "these kinds of words need to be in the flesh or they're just words." Lou could hear the words, but he felt the man's voice was not in the spirit of the words. "If they never get out of this place, they probably wander among the pews like ghosts. Maybe *Holy Ghost* are words that never got out the door." The words were good, but it seemed to Lou as if the man's voice was carrying a different message. It was as if the man was a machine, saying what he was manufactured to say, but the words did not live in him. The preacher reminded Lou of a used car salesmen he had met in Spokane.

It was hard for Lou to sit in church. It always had been, even when he was a little boy. He spent more time counting window panes and how many times the preacher said things like "the Almighty expects us to . . . and every day we fight demons without and within." He wasn't sure about the demons without, but he sure knew he had the demons within. He heard the preacher say, "What regrets did the prodigal have on his way home? What terrible things was he remembering?" The memories were welling up within him, and he wanted to flee, but he couldn't move. Lou could hardly feel the pew beneath him. The darkness residing in his soul was too heavy.

Then he heard it. He didn't know if it was in the prayer or if the preacher was reading from the Bible, but he knew he had never heard it before. He felt like someone very strong had sat down and put their arms around him like his mother had done when he was a small boy. He could remember sitting by the wood stove on their ragged, brown couch, and she would sit and put her soft fleshy arm around him and pull him close. He could remember feeling the heat from the wood stove as it filled the room and the warmth of his mother's body as she held him close. He remembered she always smelled of lilacs.

He glanced up and saw a woman with her arm around a small boy whose blond hair reminded him of stalks of wheat before harvest. It made him think again of his mother, and he was filled with the same familiar, black regret and the fleeting wish he could go back in time. He heard it again, but it was no longer the voice of the preacher. It was coming from the preacher, but at the same time he knew it wasn't. He also knew that no matter how much he tried, he couldn't ignore it. The voice was calling him by name. It was speaking, if you could call it speaking, to *him*. Even though he didn't know what was happening, he knew he would never be able to describe it to anyone. It wasn't that they wouldn't believe him. You can always find some who will believe anything, but he knew his words would be inadequate vessels even to himself. Sometimes, words were like vapors, present but empty.

Lou felt the strong arms around him, and a dark regret rose in his throat, filling his mouth with a bitter, nauseating taste. His nostrils were filled with a putrid smell, and he felt dirty deep, deep inside. He wanted to peel his skin off in hopes he could find a clean spot. Maybe he could shed his skin like a snake and begin again with a new skin and a new life. The arms tightened, and he could hear the water cascading over the falls, a deep resounding roar. The water and the voice were one and the same. He felt his head jerk back, and he could smell the clean, crystalline water as it rushed through his nostrils. He was lost in a swirling tempest of water. Over his head there was light, and he was not in darkness.

Suddenly, the water became music all around him, and Lou could feel— not hear, but feel—the music gently pulsating through his veins. Then it passed through his heart, and he saw the black rock of regret being washed away, bobbing like a small cork until it disappeared from sight. When he realized it was gone, he began to cry. He could feel his chin on his chest, and the tears came like a flood. He reached into his pocket for his handkerchief and could tell it was not clean, but he pulled it out anyway. He wanted to stand and leave, but his feet wouldn't move; all his energy was being spent in tears while his body shuddered. These were not like the tears he had shed earlier and so often. These were tears of joy. He knew his past had been turned back and that he was a new man—maybe the man God intended him to be.

Lou wiped his face and took a deep breath. When he looked around, he thought everyone would be staring at him and the preacher would be standing there with a dim-witted look on his face, but no one was looking his way, no one except Emma Reed who had a wonderful, gentle smile on her face.

Without thinking, Lou smiled back and discovered he could smile for the first time in he couldn't remember when. As he rose to his feet, a few heads turned but showed little interest. He looked down at his hand and saw where he had punctured it with the nail. He stroked his fingers along the oak grain of the pew. "Solid," he thought to himself, "and beautiful, too."

He smiled again, this time at nothing other than the thought that the world was filled with beauty. He found himself wanting to drink of it, to be drunk with it. As he left the church, he could smell the dust of old things and furniture wax. As he stepped outside, he was sure spring was not far off, and in his mind, he saw a baby.

CHAPTER SIX

An Angel Named Hollis

Hollis wiped the black grease off his hands with the red shop rag and stared at the engine of his old pickup. He could hear his father's words: "If you can fix it, fix it. Don't be wasting your money on something new just because somebody's gonna admire it for a few minutes."

"What ya doin', Mr. Hollis?"

Hollis turned to see Kip, his seven-year-old neighbor from across the vacant lot, staring up at him. His hair was disheveled as always, and the freckles across his nose and cheeks gave him a slightly faded raccoon look. "I need to fix my ol' truck, Kip. She's got a leak. Look underneath, and tell me what you see."

"Uh, there's a black puddle. That's not good, huh?"

"Nope, it's not. Grab that bucket, and turn it over. Climb up here, and I'll show you the problem *we* gotta fix." The boy glanced up at Hollis with a surprised but eager look at the sound of *we*.

The boy carefully climbed on the bucket and peered under the hood, his eyes wide with wonder. "Now you see this? It's called a valve cover, and right here it's bolted to the engine. This here is called the block; it's the main part." Hollis slowly moved his large, dark finger along the parts and glanced at Kip to make sure he was paying attention. "Now you see all this oil here where my finger is? That's where it's leaking cuz the gasket between the two is torn or just worn out. Do you know what a gasket is, Kip?"

"Yeah, I think it's a seal thing, like between a lid and a jar to keep things from leaking. My mom uses 'em when she cans stuff."

"Right you are, boy," Hollis said with cheerful encouragement in his voice. He could see the boy's confidence increase by the look on his face.

"How, um, we gonna fix it, Mr. Hollis?"

"Well, first . . ."

"James Kiplard Mitchell, what are you doing over here? I told you not to bother Mr. Hollis."

"Uh oh, your mama's using all three of your names. You in trouble now," Hollis said with a big, wide grin.

"I'm not bothering him, Mom. We're fixing his truck. It's got a leak, and there's a puddle the size of Lake Tahoe under it. Look underneath."

"The size of Lake Tahoe, huh? It's okay, I'll take your word for it, my exaggerating son. Did you do all the things I asked you to do?"

"Yes, Ma'am, and I even put the garbage out."

"Well, then, I guess whether or not you stay is up to Mr. Hollis."

"It's okay, Maggie. He isn't bothering me. In fact, if it's okay with you, I'd like him to get on his bike and ride down to the A-Z and get me something to help fix this enough for me to drive over to Woody's to get the part I need."

"It's fine by me, but the last time I looked, this boy had a flat tire on that bike of his. Is it still flat, Kip?"

"Yeah, and Mike Sharp borrowed my pump, and he's gone to his grandma's for the weekend."

"In my shed, there's an old bicycle pump right behind a red toolbox. You run and get it, fix your flat, and then you can run my errand."

Without any hesitation, the boy hopped off the bucket and ran for the shed.

"Do you really need him to run an errand for you, Hollis, or are you just trying to get him out of your hair?" She gave him that don't-try-to-fool-me look that Hollis had seen many times before, mostly from his mama. He didn't know how women did that.

"No, Ma'am, I do need him; he doesn't bother me. He likes to learn, and he's smart. You're doing a good job raising him. I can tell."

"Thanks, Hollis, for the encouragement, but it isn't easy raising a boy on your own."

"Yeah, I know. My poor mama had to raise me, my brother, and my sissy all by herself. I'm sure some days she 'bout pulled her hair out, but the good Lord helped her get us up—and out."

"I got it, Mr. Hollis," Kip shouted. "I'll be right back with my bike."

Hollis watched the dust kick up as Kip ran home across the vacant lot, and he thought back to how it felt to be a boy who was sharing in the work of a man. How important it had made him feel, and how much he had missed his daddy when he was gone.

"I guess I'll get back to my housework," Maggie said. "You be sure to send him home when you get tired of him. I sure appreciate all the attention you give him when you can."

"Believe me, Maggie, I enjoy your son. He's a good kid. If it's all right with you, I'll take him to Woody's with me."

"Sure, he'd like that, all those men, car parts, and grease. Knowing you, you'll buy him a treat before you're done, but keep it simple, okay?"

"Yes, Ma'am," Hollis said with his usual pleasing grin.

Hollis watched the young woman as she strolled toward her house, and he wondered what could possess a man to leave a woman of such character. But he knew the answer would be both complicated and simple. Two didn't always become one, or at least not always forever, and the ugly head of sin and selfishness always reeked more than its share of chaos. He thought of Angelica and felt a weight on his heart, kicked the dust at his feet, and wondered.

While he waited for Kip to return, Hollis cleaned the area around the leaking gasket and wondered about the wisdom of his temporary repair. He sat on the running board and looked over at Peavine Peak north of Reno. It was April, and the thermostat was already pushing toward 80 degrees, a good day to work outside. But there was still snow on the peak, and it could be chilly at night, especially if you were alone.

"I'm coming, Mr. Hollis."

Hollis turned to see Kip riding as fast as he could, and when he was a few feet away, the boy stomped on his pedals to brake the bike, turned the handlebar, and leaned to the side, skidding to a sudden and impressive stop.

"Whoa, boy, you almost knocked my truck over," Hollis said, smiling. Kip looked at him from the small cloud of dust and smiled, too.

"What do you want me to get at the A-Z, Mr. Hollis?"

"I want you to take this dollar and buy all the bubblegum you can, and then chew some all the way back here."

"I thought we was gonna fix your truck," Kip said with a bewildered look on his dusty face. "Is this a trick?"

"No trick. Trust me, boy, and hurry. The days gittin' along, and we haven't gotten anything done yet. When you get back, we'll do our temporary fix and go to Woody's, okay?"

The boy stuffed the bill in his pocket and without a word turned his bike and headed for the A-Z. He had such intensity on his face that Hollis thought he looked like he was carrying a life-or-death message to some besieged army somewhere. Hollis turned toward the house and went into his small kitchen. He opened the fridge, pulled out a pitcher of lemonade, and poured himself a glass. He could feel the cool liquid drain down his throat, and it took him back to West Fork, West Virginia, sitting out back of the house under the big maple. There in the shade, it was a time of family jesting and poking. It would be hot. Daddy would be off work from the mine, and Mama might be shucking peas as they sat there. Sissy would have some kind of flower under her nose, sniffing it and pulling the petals off. He and his brother would be hitting each other until Daddy said, "Stop, you two." We would for awhile, Hollis thought, but then we would start all over again. Hollis wondered how his brother was doing in Vietnam. "Lord, be with my brother, and even if he has to walk through the valley of the shadow of death, bring him out safe on the other side. Amen." A few minutes later, he heard Kip drop his bike next to the truck, and Hollis joined him. As they drove toward Wally's, Kip was like a squirrel on a nut hunt turning this way and that, looking in every direction.

"I can't believe we just put bubblegum on your motor and it stopped the leak, Mr. Hollis."

"Engine, Kip, a motor is run by electricity, but cars and trucks are combustible engines. It's only a temporary fix, and I wouldn't do it if we had to leave town, but I'm too lazy to walk the four miles to Wally's."

The boy turned and looked out the rear window. "I don't see no grease behind us, Mr. Hollis. The bubblegum worked, but what are you gonna do with the pieces that are left over?"

"Well, it seems to me that if an assistant mechanic has to ride a bicycle on a hot day to get something for the repair, he surely deserves some gum." Hollis glanced at Kip whose raccoon mask was in competition with his own smile.

When they got back after the cover gasket was repaired, Kip's mother came to gather him up and take him to the barber for a haircut, amidst mild protest.

"You know, Kip, going to the barber shop is one of my favorite things to do," Hollis said in a serious tone. Kip shook his head, resigned to his fate, and yielded to his mother's wishes.

Tomorrow, Hollis would clean things up around the place because he didn't know if the run he was going on the following day would be short or long. It didn't really matter to him. It was a paycheck, and it was something to do with his time. There was no reason to hurry home anymore.

The following day was productive, cleaning and getting things arranged the way he wanted. After he washed his dinner dishes and the pan he had cooked in, Hollis picked up the phone and dialed a number he knew better than his own. Unexpectedly, someone answered it on the first ring. "Universal Trucking, North American Branch Office."

Hollis had to laugh every time he heard Merle's little speech. Merle liked people to think the company was all over the world and that the Nevada office represented North America. In truth, it was a small company, although a good one. "Merle, this is Hollis. Before I come in tomorrow, I want to know what you have planned so I can prepare accordingly."

"Once a Marine, always a Marine, huh?"

"Yeah, something like that."

"Okay, you're going to make a milk run from Reno to Henderson and back with no return load. You'll have stops on the way down there at Hawthorne, Coaldale, and Tonopah, an out-of-the-way offload at Warm Springs, and then on to Vegas and Henderson."

"Warm Springs? There isn't anything there but two abandoned buildings and a nice natural hot spring. What am I taking there, and for who?"

"This load is gonna be like my ol' lady's goulash, a little bit of everything," Merle explained. "Building materials, commercial air conditioners, and for Warm Springs, eight portable stand-alone buildings for a film crew out of the movie capitol of the world. There will be a crew to offload it. They went up yesterday, so you should be good."

"I'm glad I called. With the seven hours to Vegas and with Warm Springs, it looks like I may be spending the night in Henderson. If I'm on the road the next day by 5:00 a.m., I could have the rig back here early."

"Don't forget, Mr. Gung-Ho, you have to sleep, eat, and pee, not necessarily in that order. Don't bust your butt. You'll have the rest of the day off, and the rig has to be gone over before it goes out again anyway."

"Sounds good, Merle. I'll see you tomorrow morning." When Hollis hung up, he tried to envision the drive south. It wasn't vacation season yet, so the traffic would be light. Offloading sometimes took far more time than needed, depending how prepared they were on the other end and if the truck was loaded correctly. You didn't want to have to unload one thing to get to another. As he thought about the diversion east to Warm Springs and its 5,000 foot elevation, he decided he'd better take his sheep-lined jean jacket because the wind could whip up through Tonopah Basin carrying a cold cargo of its own. He wondered if the Hollywood folks were prepared for cold and wind or if they just heard Warm Springs and thought it was just another luxury spa.

"Well, ol' body, it's time to lay you down to rest again." Hollis spoke gently to the mirror image in the small bathroom and tried not to notice the wrinkle lines darting out from the corners of his eyes like tiny furrows in a miniature field and the white hairs poking their aged heads out of his dark chin. He turned from the truth-giving mirror and felt the pressure in his lower back as he sat on his bed and opened his worn, black Bible. The leather cover was torn, faded, and cracked like the dry desert under the summer sun. He knew he probably wouldn't get anything out of it tonight, but he knew the good Lord would understand. He could see the words all lined up respectfully in their places like children waiting to return from recess. The words were clear, but the ideas drifted past, wrapped in an unwanted fog.

His thoughts drifted to Angelica as they did most nights when he put himself into bed—alone. "O Lord, I messed up. It was my own fault. If I hadn't been a trucker, gone all the time, and had paid her more mind when I was home instead of working on my old pickup, she might not have run off with that fertilizer salesman from Alamogordo. I hope she is happy, I really do. It was hard at first when I got the divorce papers. Hell, who am I kidding? It is still hard, but people ought to be happy."

He remembered that he had been in Shreveport, Louisiana. He had dropped off his load but couldn't get a new one headed west, and he hated to haul an empty truck. He figured by the time he got to Texas, he could arrange a haul. It was just as well. He didn't like being in the South any longer than he had to. He knew it was the so-called New South, but you never knew when some redneck wanted to impress his buddies by humiliating the nearest black man. He wasn't easily intimidated at six feet six and 250 pounds of well-carved muscle, but he knew some people just insisted on carrying their brains in their asses, like the teenage kid who went after him in Shreveport. It could have been really bad, but fortunately for Hollis, no one was there to join in on the fun. He had finished his dinner and was sitting in the booth, nursing his coffee and trying to figure out an eight-letter word for "highly gratifying" that started with an L. That's when this kid who had been sitting at the counter called to him.

"Hey, black scum! What y'all doing in here this time o' night? Y'all can't be readin' that paper now, can ya? Cuz y'all don't have no brains. Y'all don't know how to read, or did you go to one of them A-firm-a-teeve action schools up north?" Hollis just ignored him and realized his puzzle word had to end in S because number four down was "precious," and his word shared the same last letter. It's funny the things you remember.

"Hey! Hey, Mr. Black Man! I'm talking to you. Y'all hear me?"

Hollis would have just walked away and left the kid to his own troubles, but he hadn't paid yet. He stood and tucked the newspaper under his arm and headed for the cash register, not looking at the kid.

"Son of a bitch," the kid said, as he broke a glass ketchup bottle over the edge of the counter and moved toward Hollis. An ordinary man might have been frightened, but Hollis Washington is no ordinary man. He certainly wasn't going to be afraid of some kid who was shorter, lighter, and drunk.

"Look, Son, I don't want any trouble. Why don't you put the bottle down before someone gets hurt?" It wasn't a question that awaited an answer; it was a statement that presumed reasonable compliance. But even as he said it, Hollis knew there wasn't going to be anything reasonable about this kid that night. The kid's eyes seemed to move involuntarily from side to side and then focus on Hollis. The kid took another step toward Hollis and raised his arm. The bottle dripped red streams of ketchup down his arm, which made it look like he had slashed his wrists and was bleeding.

Ordinarily, Hollis would have grabbed the kid's wrist, twisted it into a hammer lock, disarmed the kid, and left. But he had seen this kind of drunken frenzy before, and he knew he needed to end it all now without any possibility of a continued scuffle or a chance someone else might come and join in. He needed to say good night for good. Hollis reached up and grabbed the red wrist firmly in his left hand and lifted it even higher so the kid was barely on his toes, and then with one smooth, almost gliding motion, he brought his right fist up and through the kid's jaw, turning slightly and putting the force of his hips and shoulders into the punch. He heard the jawbone break and watched the kid's eyes roll back into a gray shadow. Hollis left him hanging from his left hand for a few seconds before dropping him onto the floor.

"Holy hell! That was great!" gasped a black man with a cook's hat on, while a little Hispanic man, probably the dishwasher, stared through the order-out window. The dishwasher's eyes were wide and looked like black saucers. He kept looking around like the entire INS was going to storm in any minute. Hollis checked the kid's pulse and realized he was still alive. The cook was still talking.

"Look, you better hit da road before some of his people show up. Me and Marteen will take care of him. We'll put him in the dumpster. If he's still there in the morning, we'll set him on his way, pretend we don't know nuthun," he said with a grin that betrayed his delight. "Shucks, this cowboy ain't gonna remember tonight," he said, still grinning from ear to ear.

Suddenly, the door to the women's restroom swung open, and the waitress Hollis knew only as Sharon stepped out. Her eyes were on her nails, which were redder than any shade Hollis had ever seen. She turned toward the dining area, stopped, looked at the kid on the floor, and then looked at Hollis. He was afraid she would think the ketchup was blood and faint. Instead, she took a step forward and picked Hollis' newspaper up off the floor.

"I think this is yours, and you better get outta here before somebody comes. Leonard, you and Marteen get rid of this garbage, and then mop the floor. I've gotta fill the sugar dispensers," and she handed Hollis a towel to wipe the ketchup off his wrist. "By the way," she said to Hollis as she looked down at the heap of human flesh covered in ketchup, "your dinner is on the house."

Hollis thanked them and was two hours away when it occurred to him that the word he was trying to think of was *luscious*, and it reminded him to stop and call Angelica and check in. He was surprised when she wasn't there because he knew she should be unless she was covering someone else's shift at the Broken Wheel. He waited until lunch and then called Mrs. Jackson next door. That was the agreement. Always let Mrs. Jackson know if anything out of the ordinary was happening.

Mrs. Jackson took a deep breath when she heard his voice, and Hollis knew from a lifetime of hurt that silence almost always preceded bad news. His mama called it "Da quiet before the storm."

"I'm sorry, Honey. She done left."

"What do you mean she left? Where'd she go?"

"I don't know where she go, Hollis honey, but she and dat man in the ugly polyester suit took her stuff and left, and I don't think she plans on comin' back. I'm really sorry, Hollis. Now don't you go and do nothin' stupid like gettin' all drunk and in trouble to kill your hurt. You hear me now, Hollis?"

"That man," Hollis repeated to himself. He thought the receiver was the heaviest thing he had ever held in his life as he dropped it back on the cradle. He had to turn to get his bulk out of the phone booth. The sun was shining, and there was a slight breeze—delightful weather, he thought to himself as he walked toward the truck and felt the tears drop from his chin. He bent slightly and wiped his nose and chin with his cuff.

As he pulled his rig out onto the highway, he remembered seeing a lady changing a diaper on the tailgate of a station wagon. It was the longest trip back home he had ever made. There was just no reason to hurry—no reason, no reason at all. That night, he sat on the edge of his motel bed with despair all around him, listening to the sounds of the interstate and remembering the words of the weeping prophet:

> Is it nothing to you, all you who pass by?
> Look and see
> if there is any sorrow like my sorrow,
> which was brought upon me.[4]

Exhausted, he fell asleep surrounded by strangers who did not know his sorrow.

"But life moves on," Hollis thought the next morning as he put his Bible down. "For everything there is a season,"[5] the Good Book says.

That was five years ago, and there was never a word from her except the divorce papers. He almost chuckled with the idea of running off with a fertilizer salesman as not being out of the ordinary.

Hollis had run into Shad Sparks once at a truck stop in Barstow. Shad had been running some fencing down into the Imperial Valley, and he said he had seen Angelica at a laundromat in Indio. She looked heavier, he said, but he didn't talk to her. That was the last news of her Hollis had from anywhere, and that was three years ago.

He kicked his worn, leather slippers with the matted sheepskin lining off his feet and slipped beneath the covers of his own bed. It was kind of hollow hearing only his breath instead of two, but who knows what tomorrow will bring, and hell, maybe someday he won't be alone at night. He knew that wasn't too likely, but one can always hope.

> *Thank you, Lord, for this day, and don't let my fears ride shotgun in my sleep. Be with all the orphans in the world, and let them sleep good tonight. Amen.*

Early the next morning as Hollis climbed into his truck, he could see a glow just behind the eastern horizon. He loved this time when the darkness slowly yielded to the light of the sun and the quiet darkness was gradually trespassed upon by the day's living as they awoke and started another day. But for now, at least, it was quiet. He glanced over at Maggie's house. All was dark. Mrs. Jackson's bathroom window was lit up as usual. The engine leaped to life when he turned the ignition and purred when he slipped it into gear and headed down the street. He stopped at the A-Z to get a hot cup of coffee and fill his thermos before going to the freight yard.

"You sure bought that neighbor boy a lot of bubblegum yesterday, Hollis. You got a dentist friend or something?"

"He didn't tell you he was helping fix my truck?"

"Yeah, he did, but when I asked him what all the gum was for, he just shrugged his shoulders and stuffed some into his mouth." Hollis rolled his eyes, shook his head, and laughed all the way to his truck.

His haul down to southern Nevada was uneventful and seemingly slow despite so little traffic. He was glad the movie crew at Warm Springs was so organized and the guys offloading knew what they were doing and did it faster than some Teamsters he knew. There were some wind gusts in the basin that were more of a nuisance than a problem. Watching the yellow line and scrub brush along the road and feeling the weight of the load almost gone from the trailer, Hollis thought about his future and what he might try to do. "But then again, it might just be a silly idea that would simply cost me a lot of money and confirm my foolishness," he said out loud. But Hollis could taste and smell his dream most days. When he pulled into Henderson, he caught the aroma of barbecued ribs in the air and knew he was both hungry for food and eager to try his idea of owning his own barbecue place. "Are you giving me a sign, Lord, dropping that smell on me right when I was thinking of my dream?"

Hollis wasn't just interested in the usual honey, ketchup, and Worcestershire sauce with a shot of whiskey. No, Hollis had experimented with herbs and spices from all over the world. He had one sauce that combined Worcestershire sauce, Ethiopian coffee, a very small portion of a Carolina Reaper Pepper—the hottest pepper on the Scoville Heat Scale—rum, not whiskey, and cooked bacon marinated in a solution of red wine and mango juice. It would take him more than a week to have the perfect blend, but it was always worth the wait. He modified the recipe with some additional garlic to give a boost to the Worcestershire sauce. He thought he might serve the meat with cooked mushrooms and onions occasionally. But he would have to find himself a good baker who could make great berry pies. "Not as good as Mama's," he said, "but better than most."

It all made him think about what he was doing and what he might be doing. "Lord, I'm thankful for this job and all you provide for me, but do you think just once I could carry a load that might really help someone, like medical supplies or bottled water for tornado victims or something? I'm getting a little tired of running around the country just moving stuff. I'm not complaining, but I think you know what I mean. Could I just be someone's angel, just once?"

CHAPTER SEVEN

St. Francis

"You should name it Francis."

"What are you talking about?"

"Your bug. You should name it Francis. It's like St. Francis. He was simple and unpretentious, and so is your bug."

"Maybe. I'll think about it, but no promises."

"Of course not," she said, smiling, as she went back to her reading. In the silence between them, they both knew they had shared something intimate, not in a sexual way but with a kind of touch that went far deeper than skin. After a long period of silence as they traveled, being watched by quiet trees and whispering clouds, Faith broke the silence. She spoke more softly than before.

"Thanks for that back there. We lost a little girl this week. She was four years old. It's part of the reason I left town. I just needed to get away. Her name was Hope, and we've had her since she was three. Yesterday was her funeral in Everett. She had bright red hair, and she reminded me of Little Orphan Annie. You're not supposed to have favorites, but she was mine. When the chemo took her hair, she told me, 'Mama says my beauty is inside. Can I be beautiful with cancer in me and no hair?' I told her she would be beautiful forever." Faith was tearing up again. She fiddled with her bag until she came up with a Kleenex and blew her nose and wiped her tears.

"Have you ever seen a child's casket, Pete? Death in miniature. We can't put them back together, no matter how many grants or specialists or king's horses or men or trained nurses we have." A heavy silence punctuated her words, and the only sound was the sound of the yellow bug.

Pete knew that sometimes words were like salt on a wound; they only made the pain worse regardless of the intention, so he kept quiet. He was glad the sun was coming out from behind the cluster of clouds. If it had continued to be a gray day, he would have felt like he was trapped inside a traveling tear, rolling over the mountain. All this made him think of escaping and the need to be fishing. But somehow, being with this woman was more intriguing. For a moment, he thought of Gwen, and then he didn't.

Pete began to feel the weight of his bladder and thought about the coffee from Wally's and who knows how many refills at the coffee shop in North Bend. Once they began eating, relaxing, and conversing, they hadn't been in a hurry to leave despite the continuous glares from the bottled blonde. As the bug entered the snow tunnel that covered the highway, Pete knew he would have to stop when they reached the Snoqualmie Summit.

Pulling up to the restroom, Pete glanced at Faith. "Now it's my turn," he said. She didn't move when he got out, and he was too embarrassed to look at her face.

The place looked like it had probably been part of FDR's CCC program to put America back to work in the 1930s. The construction was crude but built to last. Despite the onslaught of travelers with pocket knives, it looked like it would last forever. Pete found himself drawn to the carved graffiti on the walls. "This place could be a geography test for the Pacific Northwest," he thought to himself, reading the declarations on the walls. "Davenport Class of 41, WSU 72, Rosalia 55, Garfield 58, Sammamish 63." And there were, of course, declarations of love. "Tommy + Gwen." Gwen?

"What's going on with me and Gwen?" Pete asked himself as he washed his hands in water that he was sure hadn't seen heat in a decade. They had been seeing each other for about eight months, and he enjoyed her company, but she seemed . . . well, there was something he couldn't quite see. When he came around the corner of the old building, he looked at the bug, and Faith was gone. He had a brief moment of panic. "She must have decided to go pee after all," he thought to himself. When he reached the car, he breathed a sigh of relief. Her rug bag was still in the back seat. "Wait a minute, Pete. This is a stranger you just met. What do you care if she takes off?"

"Pete! Up here. Look! Come see." She was standing on a gentle rise under a giant Douglas fir. He walked up the rise, wondering what was so important.

"What?" he said in that familiar I-don't-understand-women tone that men use when they are bewildered and know they're missing something.

"Close your eyes, and breathe in a deep breath," Faith instructed as she did just that.

"This isn't where you knock me out, steal my keys, and run off with my car, is it?"

She opened her eyes and gave him the don't-be-ridiculous look that women often give men.

He hesitated, but he followed her orders and could feel his lungs fill with the mountain air with a scent of pine and fir mixed together and something else he couldn't identify.

"It's wonderful, isn't it? It's the smell of spring, the breath and scent of new life."

"It does feel good, but it is still a little wet around here."

"Look over here," and Faith knelt with her knees on the ground like a saint at prayer. "It's lupine. Beautiful, isn't it?"

Pete was struck by the beauty but not of the lupine alone. As she knelt there leaning over the small purple flower, a first sign of spring, the sun was shining in spots on her hair, giving it a shine of its own. He knew somehow this woman was unique in a way that tweaked his interest. She worked every day trying to save the lives of children with terminal illnesses, and here she was embracing a weed as if it were a grand miracle. He watched her fingers. They were long and thin, not cluttered with flashy polishes. There were no rings, he noted. She moved her hands around the plant, gracefully touching without imposing, with admiration and awe. He found himself smiling and feeling good.

When they were on the road again, Pete asked her, "I still don't get something. If you're a nurse with a good job, I assume, why are you hitchhiking?" Faith put her book in her lap and looked out the window at the green hills, occasional rocky cliffs, and the periodic clear cuts. She looked at black stumps standing like tombstones amid short green bushes with a few saplings standing here and there. She wondered how long it took before a forest recreated itself. *How long does it take people to put their lives back together?* she thought. *Some never seem to, and what makes the difference?*

"When I was coming back from the funeral, my car overheated. I had a busted radiator hose, and my radiator was a relic anyway, so a friend of mine is fixing the whole thing. It will only cost me for parts, and labor will cost me a good but not too expensive dinner. But I just had to get away, as you could see from my episode back there. So I did what I have always done when things get tough—I hit the road."

"Are you one of those people who run away from their problems?"

"We all run away, one way or another. That's why some people take vacations and others drink too much."

"So your boyfriend is fixing your car?"

"Actually, a girlfriend is," and she smiled.

Pete didn't want to get into self-revelation because maybe there was something to the fact he was named after a guy who talked fast and heroic but hid when things got tough. He decided to steer the conversation away from its present course because she might ask him what he is running away from. "You know, hitchhiking is really dangerous. There are too many crazies in the world."

"Yeah, you have to be careful that you don't end up riding with a serial killer," she said as she glanced his way and smiled. "Do you ever wonder who's in charge, Pete? Or is it a giant tragedy? Maybe we're all insane because we're all trying to make some sense out of it all, and maybe there isn't any sense to make, and the children suffer the most. I used to wonder and think that all the time. But despite it all, now I know there is meaning to life, but sometimes, like yesterday, I slip back and question it."

Pete drove in silence, thinking, "What makes sense? We all wonder if there is any meaning to life except the ones who claim to have it all figured out. It all comes down to two different camps—the there-is-no-meaning camp and the there-is-meaning camp. And the latter usually let God roam about their camp unless God's demands hit home and become too personal, and then they just look for another god or remake one in their own image. So if I am in the no-God camp, I must believe life is meaningless. Do I believe that? I'm not sure what I believe anymore," he told the voice in his head.

"Some people like my mom would say, 'God doesn't promise us good, only himself, and that's enough. From there we can find meaning in life.' But I don't think so, Faith. How can anyone be sure? Life is one big uncertainty; you can be sure of that," he chuckled.

Faith flipped her seat back into the reclining position and closed her eyes. "You're quite the philosopher, Mr. Reporter Guy, but I have a really deep question for you: When are we going to stop for lunch?"

"Your bladder acting up again?"

Pete glanced over to see her reaction, and Faith was smiling with her eyes still closed, but smiling. It made him feel good, and he realized maybe he had been doubting too many things lately. He realized he didn't like that about himself. Gwen came to mind again. Then she was gone. He considered himself a wordsmith. It was how he made his living—telling stories, revealing secrets. He knew how to be descriptive, but no words seemed to fit what he felt when he saw Faith smile. Somewhere in the back of his mind, he knew this smile was more than good orthodonture.

Time was losing its urgency. Pete was finding himself moving from "getting there" to "being with," and it was welcome, unexpected, and disconcerting. He was feeling an emotional weightlessness that he found unsettling, but at the same time it felt like he was moving from chaos to order. Being with Faith for only a short time was somewhat like floating down a lazy river on an inner tube in the middle of summer on a hot day. You just let the current carry you along and enjoy the warmth of the sun and the coolness of the river at the same time, the two opposites making one experience, unsure when it will end but content with just being. For now, being was all that mattered, amazingly because he had given this blonde with an oversized leather jacket and a hippy bag a ride.

They found themselves driving into a small town reminiscent of the Old West. It only had one main street, appropriately named Main Street. You could see from one end to the other. The buildings were unattractive brick blocks with facades higher than the roofs. They were probably intended to make the buildings look grander than they were, but they only made them look like a movie set. The town had been bypassed by the main highway, so it had lost or won, depending on your point of view. Pete spotted a cafe about halfway down the street and parked.

"Now remember, when you get out of this bug, no serial killer talk," Faith reminded him, "or you might get us thrown in jail, and I don't think the jail here would be too comfy."

Inside, the place looked more like some big game hunter's trophy room than a restaurant. Pete noted that it was clean and there were two families sitting at tables and a few men at the counter. He figured if they catered to such a crowd, it would be fine.

When they sat down, Faith began to think about this stranger she had grabbed a ride with. He hadn't tried to impress her. In fact, he had been a perfect gentleman. He didn't make off-color jokes or hint at anything sexual. She realized she felt perfectly comfortable with him, and he seemed like the kind of person she would like for a friend. Surprisingly, she already felt like they were friends. He didn't seem like so many guys, a square box of settled sand. Also, he was moderately handsome, and his eyes were absolutely gorgeous. She wondered what he was about. He seemed restless, searching. His cynicism bothered her because it was something she had to fight or run from most of her life.

She became excited around living things, plants, and animals. The mystery of how 37 trillion cells could organize themselves into the miraculous human body seemed to her one of life's great mysteries. It was perhaps the greatest proof of the existence of God because all the systems of the body had to start at the exact same moment, or there could be no human life. You didn't have a circulatory system without a brain or without functioning lungs. The nervous system with its variety of nerves was a mystery all its own. If the sensitive nerves in our tongue were in our feet, we wouldn't be able to walk. *The body heals itself in so many ways, but unfortunately not always,* she thought to herself. Living things always gave her a sense of hope, a feeling of a larger purpose in life. *If we could just find out the key to cancer cells, those horrid cells that mutate with each generation of new cells and resist the best treatment yet known.*

"You look lost in thought again," Pete said.

"I guess I was. So what's it like to be a reporter? What do you do? Sports?"

"No, I'm not the jock type." Pete flexed his arm, and they both laughed.

"I do investigative reporting mostly. I try to find out who's doing what they're not supposed to be doing and write it up."

"That should be easy. You can interview anybody. Most people are doing something they shouldn't."

"It's not quite like that. First, not everyone is doing something illegal, and second, nobody tells you the whole story. You have to piece it together on your own, and that's the hard part."

"Sounds like it could be a little dangerous, too."

"I suppose, depending on the story. I had a guy chase me for three days one time because I was told some county supervisors were having a private, behind-the-scenes meeting in a hotel room with some contractors who had connections with the mob in Chicago. It turned out to be one supervisor having a very personal meeting with the wife of another supervisor. It wasn't the kind of thing we print."

"Maybe not, but I'll bet a lot of people would like to hear about it. What did your boss say about it?"

"I never told him. I tell him as little as possible."

A waitress who looked like she probably had been there since the first wagon rolled into town took their lunch order and made them feel like they were at their grandma's house.

Faith picked up the conversation from before the cheery waitress interrupted them. "Is your boss Mr. Hitchcock?"

"Yeah, how did you know? Do you know him?"

"Well, I do read the paper occasionally, but before Christmas I was invited to a party in Bellevue by some of my doctor friends, and he was there. In fact, it may have been his party. It was okay, but this Idaho girl isn't much for big parties, crowds, and small talk. I think there were more people there than would have been in my high school graduating class if I had stayed in Kellogg."

"So how was he?"

"Who?"

"Winston, Mr. Hitchcock. How was he?"

"The truth?"

"Yeah, the truth."

"He was, how do I want to put this? A real jerk with roaming hands. I could say more, but I'm trying to decaffeinate my descriptive language. But I'm a miner's daughter, so I can fire it up when I need to."

"You mean he was obnoxious, arrogant, and self-centered?"

"I think that's an accurate description, but mild. Besides, he was drunk and tried to hit on me twice."

"What happened?"

"Nothing, except I suddenly became very clumsy and spilled my drink down the front of his shirt. It was a waste of a good Cabernet. When he went to clean up, I left. I had a gloating sense of victorious feminist satisfaction."

"I wish I could have seen that. So what is it you're doing that you shouldn't be?" Pete asked with a sly smile.

"What?"

"You said, and I quote, 'Everybody is doing something they shouldn't.' What's your secret no-no?"

"I said 'most people,' and you're only giving me a ride. You're not entitled to know everything about me."

Pete normally would have taken the comment as a rebuff, but Faith was staring him right in the eyes with a smile on her face—no, a smirk. There was something being said that wasn't being said. It was one of those between-the-lines comments that may be "You're invited to know, and I would like you to know" or "I'm sure you would be interested if you did know, but you will just have to wait for another time."

Pete thought for a moment and considered it more of a challenge than a rebuff and filed it away in his to-be-pursued-later file.

"Yeah, we're just strangers trucking along the great American highway," he said with a sarcastic chuckle.

After they finished their lunch, Pete leaned over the table with a conspiratorial look. "You want to share a piece of that chocolate pie?" He was staring at the bakery display in the glass cabinet. "I can't eat a whole piece, and it looks really good."

"Well, I could, but I need to watch the calories." When she said "calories," she pulled her jacket open as if to show her overweight body. Pete noticed the pink shirt slightly conforming to her figure. *There is no wasted fat there*, he thought to himself.

Pete had never thought about it before, but there is something about eating from the same plate with someone that is intimate and maybe even sensual. Or maybe it's because it's creamy, tasty chocolate smothered in whipped cream. After each bite, Faith stared into his eyes. *God, she has radiant, beautiful eyes!* Maybe it's the way she was savoring each bite, licking her lips, and moaning. The moaning added a new dimension to the experience, an unsettling one.

"Isn't this great? I really shouldn't." Faith scooped up another bite of pie and raised it between them at eye level, and Pete found himself staring across the deep-brown chocolate into her blue eyes, and without thinking, he licked his lips as she ate the bite.

"Don't you like it? You're not eating your share," she said with some mild concern.

Pete felt himself blushing. "Go ahead and finish it. I'll pay, and we can get going."

"No, here's my half of lunch and the pie," and she reached into her jeans, pulled out some wadded up bills, and threw them on the table.

Standing at the counter waiting for the waitress to ring up the check, Pete noticed that the few men at the counter were all staring at Faith. Pete wondered why he felt so—what was the word?—attracted. Yes, no, but something else, more than attraction, he felt—connected. No, it was more. Appreciative—no, closer to grateful. That's it. He felt grateful. He couldn't remember feeling this way about being with anyone else. It certainly wasn't the word he would use to describe his relationship with Gwen. *And if I'm interested in Gwen, why am I so intrigued by this woman I just met? What feelings do I have for Gwen?* Sometimes, you just get into the routine of a relationship, and I guess it's the routine you actually begin to like. The person is just there; it's convenient.

> *How can I feel grateful for someone who hasn't done anything for me? Maybe I just feel grateful because she has made the drive more interesting. She's providing me company. No, it's more than that.*

As she stepped off the curb, Faith moved toward the driver's side, "Francis says that I should drive and give you a rest."

"What?"

"This little saint of a car says he wants a woman's touch at the wheel, and you need a rest. What's the matter, Pete? You don't strike me as the male chauvinist type."

"Sure, why not?" He was still thinking about gratitude and why it seemed to be so present. His mind was derailed in a fog of male confusion.

"You seem lost in thought. You all right?"

"Yeah, I was just trying to sort some things out in my mind."

"You're getting ahead of yourself, Reporter Guy. You need to wait until you're fishing for that. It's the only reason some people fish, so they can sit by a stream or float across a lake and think or sometimes rest from too much thinking. People who don't fish think it's all about catching fish, but for the true, lifelong fisherman, it's about sorting and sifting, reaching deep within yourself and finding things there you had lost or never known before. Fishing just gives you the excuse to do what no one is allowed to do anymore—go off by yourself and think."

"Now who's the philosopher? You're beginning to sound like my mother when you talk like that."

"Is that a bad thing?"

"No, she was big on sifting and sorting, but usually over the ironing board. You sound like you're speaking from experience. Do you fish?"

"Are you kidding? Why, us Idaho gals are born with a fishing rod in one hand and a deer rifle in the other."

Pete laughed. "So you were born there, not just from there?"

"*From* is the operative word. Francis drives pretty smoothly and has punch for such a little guy, but he is definitely not a hill climber."

"I haven't named my bug, remember?"

"You can't fight destiny, Pete. You can't stifle Francis's identity anymore than you can your own."

"That's the second time today I've been told that."

CHAPTER EIGHT

Connections

W hen they began the slow climb up from the Columbia River, Faith was quiet. Pete thought she seemed to be traveling another road of feelings and memories. He wondered if she would let him on her road. He realized now that he was the hitchhiker who desperately wanted to travel with her. He wondered how many questions flooded her mind as she drove. She said she had run away from Idaho, but if Kellogg was so bad, why is she going back?

"How come you asked if I was a sports writer if you've read my stuff?"

"Because I wanted to know what you would say about yourself. You're pretty modest. I like that."

Pete didn't say anything and just watched the rolling hills of the eastern Washington plateau, sage brush and wheat, miles and miles of it, rising and falling, rising and falling. They were like a small craft on a large sea of brown, waving grain of winter wheat. Off to the northeast he could see large thunderheads clustered in the sky and wondered if it would rain on his fishing. The slow drone of the VW engine and the unchanging but rolling horizon made Pete sleepy, and he closed his eyes, hoping to find some escape.

Escape . . . esc . . . rest . . . ru . . . run . . . run. . . . run, Pete . . . D . . . the dogs, the dogs are behind you. I have to get up the hill and over the fence. Mr. Robinson's dog bit Joey Smathers and ripped his pant leg off before he made it over the fence, and Joey is faster. Run, Pete . . . run . . . he could hear his labored panting . . . feel the pain, no . . . no . . . don't look back. It will slow me down . . . keep running . . . head up, breathe deep. Oh God, my chest hurts. Past the files of words and scattered pages. Past the names . . . Oscar . . . DJ . . . Mrs. Hutchins . . . the dogs are getting closer . . . my legs . . . I can't breathe, air, I can't run from the hound . . . hound, heaven, "Hound of Heaven" . . . poetry class . . . "I fled him, down the nights and days . . . I fled him, down the arches of the years; I fled him, down the labyrinthine ways" . . . today?

Today in the Capitol, President Nixon announced that he has ordered the bombing of Haiphong in an attempt to stop the North Vietnamese march to the south. It is reported that tens of thousands of refugees are fleeing Viet Cong troops.

"I'm sorry, I didn't mean for the radio to be so loud. I was going to play a little music."

Pete shook his head, wiped his eyes, but didn't want to tell her he welcomed the interruption.

"Most of the news is bad anyway," she said as she reached over to turn the radio off. "Doesn't it amaze you that while we're eating chocolate cream pie in a cafe in the mountains of Washington, at the same time some mother might have her nursing baby in her arms and the rest of her family by her side, shepherding them like little sheep, running down some jungle path for their lives? But you're probably used to it, being a reporter and all."

"Used to what? Death or the absurdity of things? How can you get used to having war with dinner? At least in World War II, you had to go to the theater to find out the news on a cleaned up newsreel. No American dead bodies, at least not up close. Now we watch it on TV over mashed potatoes and gravy— napalm, blood, guts, and please pass the butter. But you can't stop the whole world just to take care of one person or one family. If some couple gives up their honeymoon in Hawaii, it's not going to save your refugee Mama-San or change Tricky Dicky's mind about blowing up the Viet Cong. I may be a reporter, but I'm not used to the absurd horrors that come with war or any other form of man's inhumanity to man. Besides, what does it mean to be 'used to it'? What kind of person would that make me? What kind of a world will we have if we become used to unexpected and unnecessary death? What about evil? Should we get used to it, too? Just because you report an event doesn't mean you can't feel for the people involved. You have to be careful where you let your emotions take you when you're a reporter, but without them, how would I engage life? That's one of the things that's wrong. Everyone is becoming mechanical; there's no passion left for life. I think it's one of the reasons I'm taking this vacation, because I'm beginning to feel too mechanical."

"Look, Pete, I didn't mean it that way. I just meant you're probably not as shocked by tragedies because you cover them for a newspaper."

"I understand. I'm sorry I reacted like that. I don't see as much as some, but you're right. Someone can be having a wonderful time, thinking life is grand, and somewhere else, for somebody, it's a living hell, but there isn't any connection between the two. Life is just insane that way. Educated Ivy Leaguers who studied the classics and the wisdom of Socrates and Plato are bombing the hell out of some poor peasants in the jungle who can't even read, and we're supposed to be the civilized ones?"

"I'm not sure about the no connection part, Pete. I mean, maybe there is a connection. Maybe there is something that ties us all together, and when one suffers anywhere, we all suffer in some way."

"I'm sorry, but the world just isn't that sensitive. The guys at the yacht club with their dye-headed bitches don't suffer much over their cocktails while Mama-San and her litter are being blown to bits. But I do know one thing. The more we make death a statistic, the more we diminish life as a gift. I'll tell you a connection story—true, too," Pete went on. "A couple of years ago in Chicago, a man's wife and daughter were killed in a car accident. The husband was just leaving the hospital morgue unit when he stepped into the elevator where some young kid who worked in the hospital waxing floors was whistling because he just found out he had been accepted to college. The guy almost beat the kid unconscious before the elevator reached the lobby of the hospital. The poor kid didn't know the man's wife and daughter had just died. If our joy runs into someone else's sorrow, there can be hell to pay."

"I don't mean a conscious sense of loss, Pete, but it's like the world's atmosphere. Creation is full of life, and every loss reduces all of our life's supply, and the real tension in the world is between the forces that want to preserve life and those who would destroy it. We talk about finding the meaning of life, but what if *life* is the meaning of life, and we are to embrace it, share in it, and, most of all, be grateful for it?"

"It sounds like you're saying the world is nothing but a battle between good and evil."

"Maybe. The destroyers think they are destroying only what they want to destroy, but they are destroying something bigger, something more. Cruelty is a way of pulling out all the threads of life, Pete. Cruel people reduce life, they choke on it, they make you so afraid of it that you die inside, if not really die. The ironic part is, so do they."

"This is very heavy stuff for a guy on vacation. I'm not sure I can handle all this during what I thought would be a boring ride across the state of Washington."

"Maybe you should go back to sleep."

"Maybe you should tell me more about yourself."

"Maybe you should mind your own business."

"I think my business is expanding."

Faith smiled and laughed. There was only the sound of the small engine droning on mile after mile. It seemed some of the darkness was gone, too. It was as if to speak of pain, to acknowledge cruelty, to know life is fragile in some way diminished the power of darkness. They both felt lighter. They had no answers, but the communion of questions drew them closer together. Neither of them thought or spoke or even knew the word, but it was a *shalom moment*. They both knew their experience together was a blessing, but it was also a mystery that was yet to unfold.

The radio's intermittent reports on Vietnam cast a series of dark shadows and random images on Pete's mind that he had been trying to forget ever since he left there. But they came back, especially at night. As the warmth of the bug and the lull of the engine cradled him, he fell into a deeper sleep. He was there again.

Pete could feel the sweat forming on his skin and seeping into his clothes even though it was still early. You would think the jungle canopy would keep it cool, but it seemed more like a steam bath that just kept the heat in and baked everything. He didn't have a rifle, but he did have the comfort of his Army issue 45, World War II version. While reporters were not supposed to carry firearms, he knew it would be stupid not to, and he never considered himself stupid. Besides, he doubted the VC had ever heard of the Geneva Convention, let alone read the accords. He won the gun off a pilot in a poker game in Saigon. The man said he could afford to lose it because he had a more modern, updated version. Pete had tried it out. It shot straight, and he hoped he would never have to use it, because if he did, it meant he was in a bad spot.

It always amazed him how quiet the jungle could be when you knew it was full of animals both on the ground and in the trees. When it was this quiet, you also knew something had disturbed them. The animals were like the moment of silence just before a prize fight. Everyone holds their breath for one second, the bell rings, and then the place erupts with the shouting crowd. In this case, the crowd was jungle wildlife, and the opponent wasn't standing in clear view across the ring. He was somewhere, but where? A hand went up. It was attached to the arm and broad shoulders of Sergeant Filmore Gillespi of Waco, Texas, known to all as "More." No one moved. More went to his knee, and everyone did the same. "Hanson!" More whispered. A wiry kid from Oklahoma scurried up to the Sergeant and tipped his head toward him. Pete couldn't make out what was being said, but Hanson quickly disappeared into the foliage on their right, and the Sergeant was sending someone else to the left. They all waited and listened. Pete heard the flutter of a bird toward the top of the canopy, and as he looked up, he heard rapid fire, screams, and the sound of someone running. He heard someone cock his weapon. When you're in a situation filled with uncertainty that may tip away from life and toward death, one's senses become acute. Staying alive is never a number-two priority.

Pete was aware of the smell of the earth—fresh, moist, with centuries of decomposed foliage giving way to new foliage in abundance. He wanted to lie there and smell the dirt like one would savor a fresh-baked slice of bread or the chocolate chip cookies his mother used to bake and then let him eat two before she put them away, and he had to sneak to get more. *I'll bet she knew I was sneaking them all the time,* he thought to himself. There was a sound, and Pete looked up and saw Hanson coming through the brush, bent over and carrying the other kid who looked alive but had obviously been hit. "I killed two," Hanson reported, but there were about six who ran up the trail. Barry here got winged in the leg, not bad though, just enough for R&R in Hawaii with some pretty nurse."

"The Army only recruits ugly nurses," More said, "so you guys won't shoot yourselves in the foot. You didn't shoot yourself, did you Jackson?"

The wounded man lay on the ground as a medic tended his leg. He grimaced, "No, Sarge, it's a Purple Heart getter, but I'll be back to help you fellas out."

"Don't worry about us, Jackson. We got this rabbit foot of a reporter to keep us safe." He glanced at Pete and smiled. After ordering a helicopter and making arrangements for the wounded man to be taken back to a clearing, the patrol prepared to proceed. Because he couldn't spare any more men, More asked Pete if he would help take Jackson to the pickup point, and they would meet them back at base camp later. "I'll give you a full report, just like you had been with us," the Sergeant promised.

"One more thing," Hanson said. "I saw a booby trap because I watched one gook jump it. So there are probably more, too."

"We'll have to be extra careful, then," More said, as he passed the word back down the line. "This whole encounter may simply be a trap. I'll see you tonight, Rabbit."

Pete returned with Jackson to base camp and waited for the others, but they never came. The next day, a patrol found their bodies not far from where Pete had left the patrol. They had been stripped of their weapons, and one of them had an ear cut off. No one had called in for support or aid; it all must have happened so fast. Good men, Pete thought. Men who could have become doctors, teachers, musicians, farmers, anything they wanted, but now they were gone. Their families would go through heartache, and who knows what angry young siblings would do, which wouldn't be good. A strange thought struck him. *I wonder what they were having for lunch at the Pentagon while these men died.* He knew there were those who were marching against the war at home, and some questioned their patriotism, but right now he wasn't so sure they weren't the true patriots. They were trying to stop this madness and save lives. Pete respected these soldiers, and with More, he had formed a tentative bond, but all bonds were tentative here.

These men—More, Hanson, Colbert, and the others—had given their lives for what their country had called them to do. But what was it they were called to do? Pete knew there were plans to bomb Hanoi and bring the war to an end, but the politicians, not the military, were running this war, and like most politicians, they were inept at anything but talking and taking power lunches. He could feel tears coming to his eyes, but instead, he kicked the ancient jungle soil and spit. He had had enough. When he spit, he realized how thirsty he was. He ran his tongue around the inside of his mouth and then opened his eyes. Pete knew then that he was not in Vietnam. It was only another one of his bad dreams. *It had all been a bad dream,* he thought, *for all of them.*

Pete looked out the window, listened to Francis's rhythmic whine, and tried to reel himself back into the present. Faith glanced at him and saw the perspiration on his forehead. "Are you okay, Pete? You suddenly look like you've been through hell. Are you getting sick? Maybe we should stop and get some fresh air."

"It was just a dream. No, that's not true, it was a nightmare, and every time, it gets a little worse. But I'm all right. I just need to wake up to reality, whatever that is." Pete managed to slip into a quiet slumber, void of night terrors, but when Faith flipped the turn signal, he awoke from his traveling slumber as she slowed and shifted. He glanced up and saw a rest stop in their immediate view and wondered if this gal had a bladder problem.

"I just need to stretch my legs, in case you're wondering, and you probably do, too. It's not good to sit too long without moving around. It creates problems for your circulation."

"You're the nurse," he said as he stepped out and stretched his arms above his head and closed his eyes, feeling his muscles respond to the movement. He opened his eyes, and she was gone. He heard a moan from the other side of the bug, and as he glanced around it, he realized she was touching her toes with her palms, and he couldn't help but admire the scene. Pete turned quickly as she stood up and pretended like he was watching others who had stopped.

"Want to walk down to the end and back?"

"Sure," he said with no little sarcasm, as if it were the most exciting thing on his mind. "What are your hobbies?"

Faith thought for a moment. "Hmm, I have collected baseball cards since I was about six. I guess that's my hobby."

"Really?" Pete responded with curious enthusiasm. "Do you like baseball? Did you ever play?"

"I played girls softball in high school and college. I still play in a women's league during the summers but mostly as a sub because of my schedule at the hospital. I can't commit to regular times."

"Do you have a regular position, or do you just fill in as necessary?"

"I used to play second base regularly, occasionally shortstop, but in this league, I play wherever they need me, except pitcher."

"How good a batter are you?"

"You're beginning to sound like a talent scout. I'm not a home run hitter, but I usually get on base with either a single or a double. What about you?" she asked with a smile that made him warm all over.

"I swim, water ski when I can find a boat, and I like to hike. I have thought about bicycling and taking a trip around the Olympic Peninsula, but I'm afraid I would have to work up to it. But my great love is baseball. So how many cards have you collected?"

"Well, I only have 127, but they are all pre-1955 and . . ."

"More than a hundred pre-1955? Some have to be classics worth lots of money."

"They are, but I like to think of them as keyholes to baseball history, which for me is more interesting than their monetary value."

Pete felt a little dizzy, and he couldn't believe what he was hearing. And he wasn't thinking of the value of her baseball cards. He was almost giddy with excitement, and containing it was difficult.

"So, baseball history buff, who invented baseball?"

"A former pitcher for the Chicago White Stockings, as they were called then. It was A. J. Spaulding, who batted 313 and was the first player to wear a glove on his non-throwing hand," she said with a smug smile on her face.

Pete couldn't hide his dismay, or his pleasure, but his competitive spirit also was suddenly fueled.

"Who signed the first Louisville Slugger?"

"Honus Wagner, and the year was 1900. He was a shortstop, played almost exclusively for the Pirates, and won eight batting titles, which is a record unbroken even today, despite the fact that he won his last title in 1911."

Pete was now grinning from ear to ear. It was like he had found his long-lost twin, someone who inhabited the same universe as he did.

"Okay, this is the bonus question. Baseballs had rubber centers, but during World War II, there was a shortage of rubber."

"Balata," she whispered as she stared straight into his bewildered, hazel green eyes. "It was totally predictable what a ball was going to do once it hit the ground, and it almost always did."

Pete had a hard time hiding his pleasure. He was sure he was even blushing. "So what is your most prized card?"

"There are two actually, but they're the same player. I have one from 1926 of Satchel Leroy Paige when he played for the Chattanooga Black Lookouts in the Negro League, and one from 1948 when he played for the Cleveland Indians in the Majors."

"I've never met a woman who knows so much about baseball history. You're amazing." Pete thought for a moment about how Gwen hates baseball and calls it "primitive."

"Thanks for the compliment. I'll race you back to Francis."

Before Pete could utter a sound, Faith was 20 feet ahead of him, and he knew he would have to push it to catch up, let alone win. But just as he was about to break even and pass her, two collies leaped from between two cars, and it was all he could do to keep from tripping and falling to the sidewalk.

"What took you so long?" she said with the grin he had come to appreciate as she leaned casually against the bug.

"Next time, no canine interference, okay?"

"Men always make up excuses when women beat them at something athletic, or anything, for that matter."

"I'll be back in a minute," Pete said as he walked off toward the facility, thinking what an amazing woman was riding with him and Francis. This was certainly not the boring trip he had feared.

"Okay, Pete, now that you've had time to catch your breath, it's my turn. What 20-year-old pitched three full games in a row and won all three?"

"You got me on that one. I guess I don't pay much attention to their ages."

"I'll give you a hint. He was also known later as the Big Train."

"Walter Johnson."

"You are correct, Reporter Guy. He also led the Washington Senators to their only World Series win in 1924. He had 10 shutouts, the most in baseball history, and his 3,508 strike-outs are still a record. Now I'll give you an easy one."

"Thanks a lot."

"How many children does Willie Mays have?"

"Hey, that's not a baseball question. I thought we were playing baseball quiz."

"Do you have an answer, Reporter Guy?"

"I'll say four, but I'll refer the question to the judges as to whether or not it's a baseball question."

"The correct answer is . . . ta da . . . one child. You lose. And the judges rule it's a valid question because first, Willie Mays was a baseball player, perhaps the greatest center fielder ever. And second, there is more than one kind of batting average," she laughed and showed that grin again.

Pete couldn't help but laugh and shook his head. "I have been defeated, but just for this round."

"I read that Willie's wife has Alzheimer's. Is that true?" Faith asked.

"It is, but ol' Willie is still his positive self, always grinning and encouraging kids to play well, try hard at school, and be good human beings. I was at a sports banquet last year where he was featured. He is just a great guy—kind, loving, and positive, despite the personal burden he bears."

"Like Lou Gehrig," Faith said quietly. "He was a great baseball player and a good human being, but ALS is a horrible, disabling disease for anyone. It had to have been especially hard for such a great athlete. Someday, researchers will know enough to defeat it, hopefully soon."

They were both silent, thinking of personal burdens they had witnessed and their own. *Life doesn't travel in a straight line,* Pete remembered someone saying. *It becomes weighted down in many places.* But right now it was pretty light with this beautiful, smart, and caring woman who had transformed his car from a bug into a saint. Faith began to share more of her story as they pulled back onto the highway.

"I was put in the care of an Oregon family who had experience creating a home for nonbiological children. They had adopted all their children, so taking me in wasn't anything new to them. They never legally adopted me because of my age. For the most part, all the kids handled the idea of being adopted well because they didn't care if it was something exceptional; they had each other. But there is something I learned that I didn't understand until I got into my nurse's training. It's called 'attachment disorder,' and ironically, psychologists discovered it while following the children of divorce. Then someone got the idea of investigating whether or not it occurred in adopted children."

"Never heard of it," Pete said with a question in his voice.

"Children who have been separated from their mothers, usually shortly after birth, like with an adoption, have a sense of detachment from others. It is not conscious, but they have an intuitive sense that something has been torn away. Because of this and depending on their new family environment, some have difficulty attaching to others or forming any kind of intimate relationship. It may affect all their relationships for a lifetime. They develop a protective distancing so they will not be hurt again. We all do it to some degree. When someone breaks your heart, you're hesitant to be vulnerable again. Many spend the rest of their lives distancing themselves from others because of their fear of being hurt."

"You don't seem hesitant to be vulnerable."

"I'm slow on trusting, but the children and parents in the cancer ward have taught me a lot. I haven't had any long-term guy friends, and I know part of it is my problem."

"What's the other part?"

"It seems the only ones left in the pool are pollywogs."

He gave her a quizzical look, to which she gave no response.

"Anyway, they made me part of the family and treated me like their own daughter. When I graduated, I got a scholarship to the University of Oregon. Then I moved to Seattle to get my nurse's training. I worked as a waitress at the Golden Lion and interned at the hospital. Then I got hired after graduation. Nothing unusual about all that."

"Except most runaways don't do so well."

"Well, like I said, I loved to read, thanks to Miss Mabel. And the Oregon family showed me something I had only heard about but never experienced."

"What was that?"

"Maybe later."

Pete remembered traveling across the Columbia Plateau with his parents when he was eight. He thought the trip would never end. Neither Faith nor Pete had said anything for a long time, but when Faith finally spoke, Pete knew by the tone of her voice that she would share something personal that had been locked within her.

"Pete?"

"Yeah?" he said hesitantly.

"I haven't exactly told you the whole story of why I ran away."

"Yeah, I didn't figure you had, and you don't have to." Pete could feel the doorknob turning, the tumblers retreating, drawing the latch back, and the privacy of her life about to be opened to him. Suddenly, he felt a weight upon his heart, like someone was standing on his chest. He knew he was about to hear something fragile, hidden from view, and he wondered if he really wanted to carry its weight. After all, she was just a stranger. He wondered if he could hold it without breaking it. "Yeah, you wanted to get out and see the world; not so unusual." But he knew even as he spoke that his shallow words carried only a hint of truth.

"More than that, I wanted to leave the pain, leave it behind me. I wanted to leave the cruelty because I was, like I said, dying inside. My mother was a wonderful woman, very creative. She would put notes in my lunch or my books and even in my pockets to cheer me up during the day. They would say things like "Why are you standing around with your hands in your pockets? Get to work. Have fun." I even got in trouble for reading one of her notes in class.

"Boy, sounds like you were a real delinquent. No wonder you had to run away."

"Stop teasing. I want to tell you my story."

"You don't have to tell me anything. We're strangers, remember? We just met, and you're the cute hitchhiker, and I'm the guy with the cute car."

"In one way, it's easier to tell you because you are a stranger, but on the other hand, I don't feel like you're a stranger. I mean, you seem like a friend, and I trust you. For some reason, I want you to know about me. But first, you have to promise me something."

"No, you can't have my car," he said, laughing.

"I don't want your car, although I do like Francis. You have to promise me that what I am going to tell you will not end up being printed in your paper."

"Sure, but you still don't have to tell me anything. Really, you don't." Even as Pete said it, he knew she would and that he would listen, but not just with his ears. People bear secrets, some for most or all of their lives. Most often, it is to protect themselves and occasionally to protect someone who was important to them. But Pete couldn't help thinking what a unique moment this was. He thought that this was the kind of moment most of us spend our lives trying to avoid, not wanting to be really known as we are or seeking and never finding. We don't want others to know our fears or our pain. We don't want them to know the hatred we carry in our soul because we believe we have been unjustly wronged and that others will not love us if they see our weakness and our darker side. Ironically, at the same time, we long to be known as we really are and loved anyway. I wonder how many of us really find it. I have been with Gwen for eight months, yet we know little more than biographical facts about each other. And I've been with this stranger for a few hours and know so much more about her.

"My mother died when I was 15." She said it with the same emotion one would say "I think it's going to rain." But hearing her own words seemed to relax her, like it needed to come out first to prepare for what was to follow. Pete felt sure he was being given an answer to a question he hadn't asked.

"My dad had been gone for three or four days. He did that sometimes. He would just disappear and be gone and then show up like he had been up at the mine doing his shift the entire time. You can drive for miles into the mountains on roads only a four-wheel drive or a mule can manage, and you'll come around a bend in the road, and there under the trees will be a tavern. They're in the middle of nowhere, and they always have at least one customer. Usually it was my dad. I'll bet he knows every barkeep in northern Idaho and most of Montana by their first name. They cater to hunters, miners, fishermen, loggers, and anyone who drifts into the place.

"He disappeared one night right after getting paid, but he didn't leave my mother any money, and we were getting real low on food. So my mom decided to drive down to Wallace and see if her sister could give her something to help for a few days. She couldn't call because the phone had been disconnected the month before since we didn't have enough money to pay the bill, and she was too embarrassed to use the neighbor's phone. All our money was traveling across some varnished bartop. She knew Dad would come back; he always did. Anyway, it was winter, and I was old enough to be left alone, so she went by herself. The weather was bad with fog and icy roads, and she probably couldn't see more than a few feet. There was a freight truck crossing the highway near Osburn, and she might as well have hit a brick wall. I guess she never had time to think about dying.

"So that left me alone with Daddy. I'm glad I didn't tell her before she died what he was doing, but I used to think that if I had, she never would have left me, and I would have died, too. Or the two of us wouldn't have waited for him to come back. We would have just packed up and left. Mom worked some nights at the cafe, and Daddy would stay with me if he didn't have something else to do. One night I was in bed, but I wasn't asleep, and he came into my room. I could smell his breath, whiskey and burnt, wet tobacco, before he got to the bed. He sat down on the bed and started brushing my hair with his hand. I liked that, but then he touched me in a way he shouldn't.

"After Mom died, he wanted me to sleep in his bed with him, and I did at first because I was afraid, but then something inside of me said, 'No more.' I told him I wouldn't anymore, and I didn't want him touching me. So he didn't, at least not gently. Instead, he started hitting me every chance he got. If he didn't like what I fixed for dinner, he slapped me or shoved my face in the food. I hated my own father. I used to think of ways to kill him. Do you know what that's like, Pete? To want to kill your own father? What kind of evil is that? What kind of horrible person wants to kill their own kin?"

"It's certainly understandable under the circumstances," Pete muttered without emotion as he watched the wheat do its dance across the landscape. He wondered how many acres of wheat it would take to absorb a little girl's hurt like a sponge? Was there anything in the world that would blow such a painful storm cloud away? The thunderheads in the distance no longer made him think of fishing in the rain. Instead, he thought of a young, adolescent girl without laughter and joy, trapped in a house alone with a monster.

"But that's just the point, Pete. It isn't understandable. How can a father treat a daughter who adores him and thinks he loves her like no one else in the whole world become the most hated thing in her life? He becomes what she fears the most because he makes her hate herself. He destroyed my faith in myself, in life, and in him. I used to think my father was the strongest, smartest person in the whole world. Even his leaving us was okay because he always came back.

"My hating him actually began before my mom died. It wasn't just what he was doing to me; I started to realize he was hurting my mother. She had always been happy and positive, showing me what she called 'hidden miracles' that could only be seen by eyes open to wonder—like dancing dust in the sunlight or the perfect design of a dandelion seed. But the more often my dad left, the more she became sad, especially when he came home. Some nights, I could hear him yell. At first, my mother cried, and then after awhile she stopped crying; she stopped smiling, too. In fact, she showed no emotion at all. She stopped brushing her beautiful hair and wearing her nice dresses. Some days, she would just sit by the window in her robe and stare, saying and doing nothing. It was like she was withdrawing into herself, and she would have except she had me to think about. She never drank, but she might as well have been in a drunken stupor most of the time.

"So the reason I spent so much time in the library wasn't the weather; it was my family. When the library closed, I would go to a friend's house or follow Miss Mabel home. It was the safest place, and I knew no one would hurt me there. I think now that Miss Mabel knew my situation, which is why she let me come often. That's another thing. Once my mom died and I was left alone with my dad, I started to look for the bad in others. I was no longer looking for life's hidden miracles. My eyes were no longer filled with wonder but with fear. I began to realize something inside me was stealing my life. It wasn't so much my father's abuse but how he changed who I was and how I looked at life. The real me was dying inside, and I was going to die a little every day if I didn't get away from him."

"So you ran away?"

"Well, eventually, but not as soon as I was going to. My dad got real sick, a liver dysfunction, probably alcohol-related. He had seizures without warning. He couldn't work for a long time and was confined to bed, so he couldn't hurt me. I saw it as a gift from God, even though I knew little of God at the time. He went on disability, and we were on welfare. I did ironing at night and sometimes worked at the Owl Cafe washing dishes and waiting tables, anything I could do to keep us in food. Then one day he was well enough to go back to work.

"It was a spring day in late May, and the sun was shining into the valley. I had just stepped out onto the back porch to listen to the birds and breathe the day's fresh, bright air. I was so caught up in it that I didn't hear him come up behind me. He pushed the screen door part way open and said,

'Thanks for taking care of me. I'm going on down to the union hall and give them my medical release papers from the doc so I can get back to work. You have breakfast ready when I get back, and we'll talk.'

"I stayed on the porch until I heard him start his truck. Then I packed a few clothes in one small suitcase and went to say goodbye to Miss Mabel, but she wasn't home. So I walked to the highway and hitched a ride to Spokane and then took a bus to Portland."

"How old were you when you left?"

"I was 16, going on 30," she said with a hint of humor in her voice.

"How in the world did you survive?"

"I had help from the YWCA. A family took me in, church people, and it was almost like having a normal life from then on, except for the nightmares."

Pete turned his head slightly and looked at her. Their eyes met, and he, a man of fluid words, was silent. He turned back to face the long blacktop with its dividing yellow line. Pete realized Faith had just shared with him the dividing line of her life. They were both silent for many miles.

Faith pulled to a stop and stepped out, walking around the rear of the bug without a word more. Pete stepped out and could hear the wind weaving its way through the winter wheat. It reminded him of a room full of people all whispering, each trying so hard to speak quietly, but the tributaries of their voices ran together to form a stream of sound. He felt the stream of wind brush against his face, and he could see the thunderheads clustered off to the north. But despite the breeze, the sun warmed his face. To the west he saw a semi disappear over the horizon, only to emerge again with a puff of gray smoke above it and then down again, leaving the smoke hovering above the horizon. He looked to the east and thought of Spokane—and Faith. He wished there was another mountain range to cross, one with slow, winding roads and steep hills that would make the trip longer still. A blue pickup with a horse trailer sailed by, blowing swirls of dust at Pete's feet, the rattling trailer drowning out the sound of the whispering wheat. *Maybe I should drive her to Kellogg,* he thought to himself as he slid into the driver's seat.

"It's hard to believe this wide-open Palouse country was once a bubbling, churning river of molten lava so hot it would burn anything in its path," Faith said as she looked at the panorama of gentle rolling hills, winter wheat, and gray thunderheads beyond. "My granddad once told me the earth is like a man's fist held tight without appearing to move, but inside, the fist is another world. Miners like him go into the fist to find whatever treasures might be there. When they enter the fist, their world changes from space and light, air and freedom, to darkness, confinement, and heat. The deeper they go, the hotter it gets and the more they are drenched by the sweat of the earth. But the part topsiders don't understand is that inside the fist, there is a constant pulsating of life. The miner can feel the pulse of the earth, and the sweat of its palm makes him work in rain gear unless it's a rare, dry mine. The pulse is a sound heard nowhere else. As the earth's muscles twitch, they may bring a cave-in or a rock burst and his injury or death. Despite how it may appear, the fist of the earth is always moving, pulsating, sweating, and squeezing against the intruders. The earth doesn't want to give up its treasures easily."

"Your grandfather was quite a philosopher. Is he retired now?"

"No, he was killed by a rock burst while drilling in the Bunker Hill Mine. Kellogg is a company town. Bunker Hill has been there for so long that it's like an uncle who looks out for you. The reality is, you work pretty hard to get Unc's benefits, and sometimes you die for him."

"No offense to your grandfather or anyone else, Faith, but what kind of a man goes underground day after day? I could never do it, not in a million years for a million dollars."

"You could if you just barely graduated from high school and this is where you grew up and you just came back from a war like Vietnam. You're alive, and you saw your buddies come home in body bags. You think maybe you can beat the odds. Plus, there is something in your male genes that says you have to take risks to be a real man. So boys go into the mines to prove to their fathers, uncles, and probably some doe-eyed girlfriend that they are men. The ironic thing is that they are right. It takes quite a man to bottle up his fear of the dark, trust that his partner will look out for him if things get tough, and do work that you know is slowly wearing down your body and is going to leave you bent over and maybe coughing or crippled the rest of your life.

"Sometimes they say to themselves, 'Enough, I can't do this anymore,' draw their last paycheck, and get out of the mines, but most come back. They have mortgages to pay and kids to feed, and they look around and no one is going to pay them as much with as little education. So it's back into the fist with the hope they can escape its final grasp. But it wears on them.

I don't think I understood as a kid how frightening it must be, and some people do awful things to cope with their fears. It wears on the women, too. Can you imagine sending your husband off to work every day not knowing if tonight he will come home? Of course, they usually do, and the regularity anesthetizes you to the risks and danger. But it is always pulling at you like small weights tied to your heart, and the more time goes on, the heavier they get. It's why so many of them live so hard, drink too much, and don't look to the future, because the future is as elusive as yesterday. There isn't much you can do about it but hope."

"The future is elusive for all of us," Pete remarked. "I remember the body bags, the hard drinking, and the carousing in Saigon when we had the chance. I was only a reporter and was supposedly safe, but you knew when you went in the country that you might not come back. But you went anyway because you had a job to do, either to kill the other guys if you were Army or report about how well the Army guys on each side were killing each other. And I have to admit, there was a high to the danger, a rush like nothing else, especially when a firefight started. But it was tempered by the pervasive cloud of death that hovered from the sky and seeped into the earth and into the pores of your skin after a firefight. Guys tried to shake it off with booze or weed, rough humor, sex, and prayer, but it was always there."

Faith smiled. "Which worked best, sex or prayer?"

"It seemed nothing worked at the time, but if you survived, you gave a lot of credit to prayer. The uncertainty of it all is one of the things that makes war hell. So are you going back to Kellogg to try to fix the past?"

"Are we playing Sigmund Freud now? I suppose most people would think of it that way, but I want to do something about the present, not the past. I know who holds my future. I could be fooling myself, but with God's help, I have pretty well dealt with the past being a force that was directing my life. Don't think it has been easy, because it hasn't. It still pains me at times, and this little trip is painful for a lot of reasons. But you probably guessed that part. I cried for years, but I had great help, people who listened without judgment. I was surrounded by people who believe in the power of redemptive love. They were praying people, and they prayed for me and comforted me after nightmares.

"People talk about wanting to be healed from their past, and they want one great moment to cure it all, but it doesn't usually work that way. At least it didn't in my case. Healing comes from small, daily doses of love that are given to you whether you deserve them or not. It's like the salve I put on a child's skin to help heal their lesions. The gentle touch in small doses makes things better. And some days, I took out all my anger and rage on the people who were loving me and helping me the most.

"I'm going to Kellogg because I need to see my father, and he needs to know, for his sake, that I'm okay. Maybe it will help him with the years he's got left. I'm not expecting any big Disney movie reconciliation, a father-daughter love fest. My future is not about returning to Kellogg, because I'm not going to stay there. My future is coming out of who I am now, not the little girl and angry teenager I was. It's not my earthly father who holds the key to my future, but, as the saying goes, 'I don't know what the future holds, but I know who holds the future.'"

"You're starting to sound like my mother again."

"So, tell me about her. What was she like?"

"She was a woman who loved life, didn't hold grudges, was awed by everything about life, and was as close to God as anyone on earth can get."

"I would like to have known her," Faith said, almost in a whisper.

Pete glanced at Faith as they came down the hill on I-90 toward Spokane. The sun was lighting up the buildings, but he noticed that clouds were hiding Mt. Spokane. It looked dark in the Idaho foothills. He asked if she had ever been planning to go to Spokane or if that was just a line and she had surprised him.

"Actually I plan to spend a few days with my Aunt June who lives in Browne's Addition."

"Is that some kind of retirement home add-on?"

"No," she laughed, "she lives in an apartment, and Browne's Addition was Spokane's first suburb with its first park and bandstand, which are still there. As for my aunt, she's my father's youngest sister, and I won't tell her you thought she should be in a retirement home. She's a runner and does at least two marathons a year. But before you take me there, could we get something to eat and stretch our legs, maybe walk in the park?"

At that point, Pete was glad for any excuse to spend more time with this woman who sparked something within him he had never experienced before, not even with Gwen. So he made no comment about her eating habits.

Pete took the Division Street exit and pulled into Dick's drive-in. They ordered a burger bundle and headed down Second Avenue toward Browne's Addition with Faith sneaking French fries out of the bag and pointing out significant landmarks. The park was Spokane's first, she reminded him, and some of the pine trees were more than a hundred years old. The bandstand, which stood in the center with paths emanating from it like rays from a cartoonist's depiction of the sun, looked like it had seen better days. Pete soon realized the paths were actually the points on a compass that all led to the bandstand where a small band used to play on Sunday evenings in the park's early years. The variety of trees in different areas gave the appearance of groups who could not agree, so each did their own thing. The small wading pool next to the swings was not yet turned on for the summer, but two girls were making it their own personal skating rink with bumps, falls, screams, and giggles. Faith was right. It was good to be walking and stretching his legs. Francis, as Pete was now calling his bug, was comfortable, but even a healthy man's butt can only take so much.

They heard a woman shout, "No, no, Pixie!" and they both turned to see a stoutly built woman in a multicolored moo moo chastising a white miniature poodle for doing its thing. "I think Pixie's in trouble," Faith said, her words laced with a giggle of her own. Pete smiled, but not at Pixie.

"These are some houses! They're mansions!" Pete could hardly believe the grandeur he had not expected.

"If you were anybody with money, you lived here, and then when they ran out of space because of the cliff over there, they built big houses on South Hill. You should see some of them. That one across the street is the Patsy Clark mansion."

Pete stared at the large house standing on the corner across from the park, an example of rich, Gothic architecture and an era when labor was cheap. "Who was she?" Pete asked.

"She was an Irish 'he' who struck it rich in the Coeur d'Alenes and came to live the good life in Spokane."

"It looks like it could use a little work. One of the windows on that corner turret tower is cracked, and it looks like it's competing with the park for vegetation. I hope someone buys it and restores it because it is a great house, but some of these places are just too far gone, and they won't be worth restoring."

"Everything that has ever been good is worth restoring, Pete."

"Not everything, believe me. I speak the truth," he said without smiling.

"Now, are we talking about architecture or people?" Faith asked.

Pete didn't answer. "Where does your aunt live from here?" He was not about to get into another therapy session when he would never see her again. Besides, what did it matter? But the thought of not seeing her again jiggled his mind like a minor subterranean earthquake tremor.

The outside of the apartment building was similar to many in Seattle— lots of brick with just enough variation in design to keep it from looking like an ice factory. But the inside was like Alice's rabbit hole. The wood on the entryway floor, which Pete guessed was teak and oak, was interlaced diagonally across the entrance, which had slim columns of polished granite that rose to the arch, a deep dark mahogany. The symbol of the North Wind was carved and mounted on the archway. They were standing in the middle of the living room under a chandelier that had more crystals than Pete had ever seen in one place. It looked like it should be in an opera house. The fireplace at the end of the room was formed with polished granite blocks, and the mahogany mantle matched the crown molding that circled the room. The figure on top resembled a cherub. *Not quite like my place*, Pete thought to himself.

No one had answered the door when they arrived, so Faith had let them in with her key that she had kept all these years. But as they were still admiring the apartment, the door opened, and in came a woman with a long dark ponytail and wearing jeans and a sweatshirt. After the usual greetings, hugs, and admiration for each other's looks, which Pete had concluded were lacking in no way in either of them, Faith's aunt turned and said, "And who is this?" Her smile was as contagious as she was attractive, and Pete found himself relaxing and thinking to himself, *This should be good.* "Oh, Auntie dear, this young man picked me up hitchhiking, and isn't he delightful?"

"He is my friend Pete Webb, and he's on his way to Idaho to do some fishing. He volunteered to take me to Spokane. Pete is a reporter for the *Seattle Times*, and I know his boss," Faith answered. Pete wasn't too comfortable with the examination as Faith's aunt's eyes traveled over him.

"Good to meet you. Where are you going fishing?"

"My family has a cabin up the North Fork of the Coeur d'Alene River, and I'll fish the fork."

"Sounds like fun. You two must be hungry. Do you want something to eat or drink?"

"No," Faith said, "we actually stopped at Dick's as soon as we got into town and ate in the park. Besides, Pete has to get on his way. I've held him up enough, but it was nice to have someone to talk to."

Pete suddenly realized something. Faith had not told one lie to her aunt except maybe implying that she was chummy with his boss. And he was pleased that she described him as a friend, but he also realized that he had been summarily dismissed.

"Well," her aunt said with a warm smile and a conspiratorial look in her eyes, "I'll put this stuff away while you two say your goodbyes."

Pete could swear her aunt winked at Faith, but Faith took his arm and walked him to the door, recounting the "serial killer event" in the coffee shop in North Bend and laughing. She gave him a hug and said, "Thanks for the ride, and especially for the listening ear. I appreciate it that you listened to my story."

"We all have our stories," Pete said, "but most people never know it except our closest friends, and sometimes not even them."

"When I started out this morning, I was just running from the pain, but you helped me with that, and I appreciate it more than you will ever know. And I can tell everyone I rode with a serial killer," she said with her perfect smile.

"That you can, but I'm not so sure I'm a sub for Freud. But I'm glad you're feeling better, and I hope your reunion with your father is a good one."

"Expectations can lead to disappointment, Pete, so I'm trying not to imagine anything but just let it be whatever it becomes and pray for the best. I just hope he will accept my forgiveness so his life can be free from the shadow of our past."

"Now you're sounding like my mom again."

There was the sound of cupboard doors slamming shut, some ice rattling in the refrigerator in the kitchen, and some quiet singing.

Faith opened the door and said, "I guess this is goodbye."

"Well, if I have to run to Kellogg to replenish any of my supplies, where would I find you?"

"Just go to the cafe and ask for the Markses' place, and they can give you directions. You can even walk there from downtown."

"Which cafe?"

"Pete, we're talking about Kellogg. A fast food place may have gone in along the highway since I've been there, but there's only one cafe." To Pete's surprise, she took his arm and led him down the steps to Francis. She put her hand on the roof and said, "Thanks for the ride, Francis. You are one cute bug."

Pete's grin was interrupted when Faith turned toward him, grabbed both his shoulders, stood on her tip toes, and gave him a sweet, gentle kiss on the lips. Just as suddenly, she did a quick pirouette, skipped up the stairs, and went through the apartment door without ever looking back. Pete inadvertently reached up and touched his lips and smiled.

"Francis, I think it's time for us to hit the road."

CHAPTER NINE

Cabin Life

Pete passed the Snake Pit Bar, a log cabin edifice built in 1880. It had been the primary place of refreshment for the river pigs, as they were called, who rode the logs down the river in the previous century and railroaders and Teamsters who hauled logs, minerals, and all kinds of freight. He couldn't help but think of how many stories the building could tell if only the log walls could talk. From drunken brawls, roaring laughter, quiet seductions, secret family stories, and braggadocios, they were stories meant to affirm someone's manhood.

Not long after, Pete passed a curious sign combination. The first one read, "US Government Forest Station Ahead," and about a hundred yards beyond was another sign that read, "No Shooting." While he was sure the signs were not meant to be read in connection with each other, for Pete, the combination captured much of Idaho's attitude toward government. *This may be the last place except Alaska where the rugged individual still exists,* he thought to himself.

It was good to watch the river. Pete rolled down his window so he might catch some of the smells that emanated along its banks. There was both an aged, musty smell of wet, decaying soil and the smell of fresh, new growth. The clean that hangs in the air after a good rain permeated it all. He couldn't hear the river over the bug's whine, even though the river was showing signs of the spring melt. In the high country, things were still bound by winter's frigid grip, and the thunderheads decorating the horizon only seemed to underline the fact. "This is northern Idaho," he reminded himself, "and the warmest part of spring is a long way off. There may be snow falling on this ground as late as Memorial Day. It has happened before."

Broiling mounds of water seemed to jostle one another, pushing and shoving, disappearing beneath the surface only to emerge again a few feet away, ready to thrust toward another swirl. They seemed to reach out, grasping for and slapping the riverbank. Sometimes, the water tore away small chunks of earth or freed a broken root from the earth's hold, causing the mix to turn more and more chocolate brown as the arm of gravity continued to pull at this cold, wet taffy. Pete realized he might have to limit his fishing to the smaller creeks.

As he turned a wide, slow corner, Pete saw the old bull pine that had endured lightning strikes, floods, at least one forest fire, and even some novice woodcutters. Then he saw his turnoff. It was reassuring to know the old tree was still there and hadn't been removed to widen the road or simply fallen from the fatigue of having stood there for more than a century. He pulled off the main road and followed a curving, dirt track a few hundred yards before he came to the gate hidden from the main road. It was locked, as he expected, and he was glad he got here before dark, because although he thought he could find the key in the dark, he preferred to do it in the daylight. He stood at the post, took three steps to his left, moved a thistle with the back of his hand, and spotted the rock. He lifted it, half expecting a scurry of bugs, but when he saw that the can underneath wasn't rusty, he knew Brindle had replaced the old can, and the key to the gate would be here. He lifted the coffee can out of its hiding place, took out the key, and unlocked the gate. He snapped the padlock onto the fence and left the gate unlocked. He could tell from the bent grass and the tire tracks that Brindle had driven in and not ridden one of his mules.

Pete wondered if Brindle could ride anymore. He had to be older than Methuselah. Although the grass was still high, it was clear where the road was. He saw one spot where Brindle must have cut up a fallen tree. He could see the clean cut of the trunk and the circle of sawdust on the ground. As he approached the final turn in the road, he emerged from the heavily tree-lined road and into the clearing where the cabin stood. At that moment, he found himself with a slight feeling of regret. He knew the place would not be the same. He also knew it would bring back memories of better times, of childhood times, of innocent unawareness. Though they seemed big at the time, his hurts were small, and he had not yet fully grasped the world's brokenness. His Sunday school teachers had talked about the Fall, and he always pictured broken things, torn apart, unable to be restored, like Faith's mother's vase. Childhood is a time when, for most of us, death and even cruelty are not yet known, and the knowledge of evil still remains on the other side of the garden.

Pete's mind started to go to Vietnam as it often did when it began to fraternize with the idea of evil, but the sight of the cabin jerked him back to the present moment. He had that momentary sense of satisfaction that comes from arriving at one's destination. His mother always said, "Life is a series of destinations, but it is the journey we travel and the lives we touch along the way that concern God the most." Faith, their day together, the sound of her voice, and her slight fragrance still seemed to linger in the bug. It reminded him of the joy he had felt with her. He stared at the old cabin that he knew had witnessed many arrivals before him.

When Pete stepped out of his small car, the world around him seemed to burst in size. It was far greater than the little framed front window could ever display. It momentarily took his breath away, but then he took a long, deep breath, like Faith had instructed him when they were on the pass, and thought he tasted creation itself. He stared at the cabin. The sagging, cedar shake roof had been blocked up, and the old rocker was back on the porch. A few of the shakes were askew, but all in all, the roof looked like it was still good. "Those pioneers knew what they were doing when they put up their digs," Pete thought to himself. There were streaks on the windows where someone had attempted to wipe the dust off, but you could tell they weren't real committed to getting the windows clean. Brindle was good with his hands and could fix anything if he could get his hands on some bailing wire or some rope, but cleanliness would never be something he would be remembered for. The wooden porch looked good, and Pete thought to himself, "It's like a children's choir waiting for the signal to sing; as soon as I step on the porch, the chorus of creaks and sounds of footfalls will begin, and it will be a welcoming song." It occurred to Pete, perhaps for the first time, that the cabin was more than wood and nails. It was as if someone who knew him well had waited patiently for his return and now was ready to embrace him and let its life and history settle upon him. He wondered if all prodigals feel this way when they finally return. He knew this prodigal would skip the barbecue in his honor. He grabbed his bag and moved toward the wooden edifice, feeling all the time like he was home.

The inside smelled of dust, and it had the feel of air that had been kept captive too long. But he could tell it had been aired out some, and there was a fresh pile of wood by the stove, and kindling, too. He opened the stove door and saw a teepee of wood with fine moss inside it, ready to be ignited. A new enameled coffee pot sat nearby, and he spotted a box of groceries on the small counter by the sink. He knew Brindle would provide him with enough to get by for a night and a day. That had always been the arrangement in case there was foul weather when his family first arrived and couldn't get out for supplies. Pete always thought that was strange because his mother always brought more than enough food, and there was what she made while we were here. When he turned back toward the stove, he caught a movement across the room and froze. He slowly turned and carefully peered in the direction of the movement. There, hanging on the wall, was an oak-framed mirror that had long ago lost its sheen. It was his own reflection that had startled him. "Sometimes, the scariest thing around is ourselves," he said to himself before he examined the ancient kerosene lamp on the table.

The more he moved about, the more the cabin seemed like a box of memories with a roof on it. Pete was exploring like a modern-day Gulliver. Every room contained some kind of memory, and they kept emerging with what seemed like a pulsating silence. He could see his father sitting in the old leather chair with its terrain carved out by years of use. His father would be reading as if nothing else in the world existed, with his pipe dangling from his mouth even though it may have already extinguished itself, or it might have sat in the round copper ashtray. It seemed to have never been moved, and it bore its own marks of time. It was as if the entire cabin exhaled the air of memories, from the grain of the wood in the floor and walls to the dance between the specks of dust drifting in the air to the shadows sliding along the walls.

He remembered his mother in the kitchen baking wild huckleberry pie in the old wood stove. The aroma permeated the cabin and escaped to the woods beyond. Or he could see her sitting on the front steps, her knees together, with her long, cable knit sweater pulled over her legs. She sat there, hugging herself, with her hot coffee mug steaming in the morning chill while she watched with the eyes of gratitude as the sun began to lift the night's veil from the meadow and the tips of trees while birds sang their joyful song of the day's birth. She was a woman, he realized now, who savored life rather than just lived it. She didn't dwell on her pain but found joy in small things. It occurred to him that perhaps Faith was the same about little joys like new, budding lupine.

He remembered one time his mother hurried him from the cabin and made him stand in a certain spot so he could see the sun's refraction of light on a row of dew drops on a leaf. "Look, Cub, it's a rainbow in miniature hiding here on this leaf. This entire forest and meadow are filled with tiny miniature rainbows."

Pete stood there now and stared through the dust on the window at the brush, weeds, and rich green sword ferns beyond the grove of Douglas fir. He could remember sitting on his mom's lap and asking why she sometimes called him Cub. She squeezed his shoulder, stroked his hair, separated strands with her gentle hand, and said, "Because I'm the mama bear, and you are my little cub." She squeezed him tightly and kissed his forehead.

"Where does the joy go?" Pete thought to himself and closed his eyes tightly to shut out the death of his mother. Pete thought of a journal passage he had written shortly after her death.

> *Does joy fall to the earth like rain, and then it is devoured? Or does it fly away, to land on someone else to lift their sorrow and pain and let them, at least for a moment, sing? Where it goes I do not know, but its absence leaves a dark space where one wanders, wondering if they are traveling deeper and deeper into the pit, or toward the end, or maybe a small chance at life again. At least that is the hope.*

He shook his head to cast off the thought and stepped onto the small back porch. His eyes went to the wooden plank walk laid generations before. Now encroached by a mossy carpet and growing ferns, dry rot had taken its toll in a few places. He could see the rusted heads of nails he had pounded into the plank while his father did some carpentry work on the cabin. It had been the same when his father was a child and his father before him. There were at least three generations of nails, and maybe more. "There are probably enough nails in this plank to build another cabin," he found himself saying out loud. Beyond the cluster of ferns and some small willows, he could see the original old house with its fallen-in shake roof and river rock chimney, a monument to pioneer living. Behind it was still the split rail corral for the horses. The holes in the walls were so big you could see through to the other side. He could see that the mountain peaks beyond were still snow-covered.

He thought of the trips to the high country and the dark, furry bear they saw one summer running as fast as a car up a steep incline. It hurtled itself through brush and over fallen logs as if they were not there. Pete hadn't been afraid, but he was paralyzed with a sense of awe that seemed to overpower his ability to take in what he was witnessing. There was no mechanical roar like a car or a train, but simply pure power as the animal ran from human contact. Despite how powerful anyone felt, as humans they would be impotent in the midst of such a force of nature. Pete often thought of that bear at cocktail parties when men began their subtle or not so subtle boasting. The contrast between the braggadocian men and the bear reminded him of how delusional humans can be. It also reminded him that mama bears are a force not to be reckoned with. *So let my words sink into your heart, Cub; don't forget what your mama bear taught you.* Pete closed his eyes momentarily in an attempt to bring himself back to the present.

The sound of the grinding transmission, aluminum cans rolling in the truck bed, and the distinct sound of a Jeep truck with more miles than any engineer ever believed possible broke his train of thought. It rolled along the overgrown roadway and stopped short of the cabin, bringing with it a cloud of dust. The dust came not from the wet earth but from the filthy truck, dirt and dust being its main cargo. The driver had no trouble getting out because there was no door on the driver's side. In fact, there were no doors anywhere. Anyone else would have thought this a summer vehicle, but Pete knew better.

The man came out of the dirty truck one leg at a time, and he looked like he should be getting off a horse in front of a Western saloon. He had what some teens would call a beard (most women would call it a frightening, shaggy face), and others would probably wonder if he was molting. There was no pattern, no clear lines, just patches of gray hair randomly scattered about, separated by islands of leather-like skin. His mustache was pure Western, bushy and wide, white as a snow dove. His hat looked like haberdasher roadkill, but his wide yellow, toothy smile overcame everything else, just like the aroma of a great dinner helps you ignore an unkempt house. It was obvious that he had originally been a tall man, but now he was a little bent, and his shoulders looked like they had slipped from their proper place.

"Well ain't you a sight for my bleary ol' trail-worn eyes," he said as he pushed the frame of the rearview side mirror straight up and ignored it when it immediately fell back down. He muttered something like "damn cheap thing" as he moved toward Pete. He was dressed in a gray flannel shirt cut off at the elbows, and underneath, covering the rest of his arms, was his long underwear, the white sleeves soiled and torn.

"It's good to see you, too, Brindle."

The two men shook hands like distant relatives and then hugged each other with great enthusiasm as affection, undiminished by time and circumstance, flowed through each to the other.

"It really is good to see you, Pete. I was sorry to hear about your mom. She was a great lady. She was a praying lady, that's for sure. You'll never know how much I've missed your family coming up here like when you was a kid. When I got your letter and you said you were coming, I yahooed and dosey doed all the way around my place and even got a sliver in my toe. Good thing I got no neighbors but critters."

"I'm sorry I missed seeing that, Brindle. I'll bet your hounds really appreciated it. You do still raise and train hounds?"

"Are you kidding? I got the best hounds in Idaho, Montana, and any other state, and they joined the celebration. The hounds danced with Cybal, she's my new lead mule, and Barrister my parrot couldn't keep his filthy mouth shut. I thought I was gettin' some nice bird who might hum hymns cuz she was owned by a preacher, but she's got a tongue like a sailor's whore. Embarrasses my prudences, she does."

"Your prudences?"

"Yeah, my sense of rightness, good stuff, how things ought to be. The sense of 'You better not let your daddy catch you not minding your prudences.' You know, prudences."

"Sounds like an interesting bird, Brindle. How's the rest of your life? Come on, let's light the fire, and while its warming the cabin, we can sit on the porch 'til the chill sets in out here."

"The stove's all ready. I put the tinder in and the wood next to it. The matches are where they always are by the breadbox. You notice I cleaned the place up? No point in lighting the stove if you don't put no coffee on."

"Don't worry. I stopped before I left Coeur d'Alene and got some at Gittel's store, and yeah, I noticed you cleaned. I might have to take you back to Seattle with me to be my maid."

"Not a chance! No city life for me. I went to Denver to have a tooth pulled once during the Depression years, and that was enough city life for me. I would have pulled the thing myself 'ceptin' it was all infected and more painful than a mule kick in the head." Brindle followed Pete into the cabin. "It must've been a lonely, tiring trip pedaling that kiddy car all the way from Seattle," Brindle said with a yellow-toothed grin.

"Be careful, Brindle, you might hurt Francis's feelings, and he might spit crankcase oil all over that clean outfit of yours. Have you done any laundry since Christmas?" Brindle gave a quick glance at himself and lightly brushed his arms and stomach.

"Just kidding. You look fine for an old coot. But I wasn't alone. I picked up a hitchhiker on the other side of the mountains. She was going to Kellogg, so I gave her a lift to Spokane."

"She must've been an ugly thing if you kicked her out instead of taking her all the way over the hill to Kellogg, or here," Brindle said with a grin on his face.

"She wasn't ugly by any means, but she wanted to visit her aunt in Spokane and not go to Kellogg yet. I might go look her up in a few days—well, maybe." Pete placed the coffee pot on the stove and watched as the steam soon began to rise. Brindle suppressed a smile.

"Pretty girl standing on the side of the road and riding close for half the day or more in that thing—you must have a story to tell. What did you call it? Francis?"

"That's her name for it, that's all. She said it was unpretentious like St. Francis."

"But you let it stick? I think this ride may not be over, Pete."

"Maybe not, Brindle, maybe not." Pete couldn't see Brindle's yellow-toothed grin behind his back.

With the fire lit and the coffee brewing, the stove's radiating warmth was filling the small cabin. The light and shadows played hide and seek across the walls and off the dusty glass. Pete felt a new warmth and a hopefulness as the aroma of the brewed coffee began to settle in the air. Pete was glad Brindle had the sense to buy new mugs and dishes and put them in the cupboard still wrapped in the shopping paper in case there were mice about. As they took their mugs and stepped onto the porch, Pete could see a ray of sunlight as the sun sank on the western horizon accompanied by orange and purple streams like bridesmaids at a wedding. He wondered if tomorrow would be as interesting as today, if he would be alone or with Brindle. And would he begin to miss Faith? "Hell," he thought to himself, "I already miss her, and I hardly know her. Well, actually, I know more about her than some people I have known for years." The two of them sat there for some time, silent, welcoming the coming night, drinking coffee, and knowing they did not need to speak.

There was a movement in the trees and the smell of grass and wood smoke. Darkness was slowly lowering itself upon the valley. Pete looked at Brindle sipping his coffee and playing with the heel of his boot and then looked at the earth before them. "This is holy ground," he said to himself. "Yep, it's holy ground."

Pete could remember some of Brindle's story. His mother and father had each told him bits and pieces. His people had come to the Peace River country in Canada in a covered wagon after the Civil War. His mother was the first white baby born there, so she was named Peace. When she became an adult, she married a man from Texas, and they eventually ended up back there, and Brindle was born on a ranch just outside of Brownsville, Texas.

Pete remembered when they were at the cabin after the Native American pow wow in Coeur d'Alene. Brindle had told him about watching the Fourth of July parade in Brownsville when he was a boy, with Quanah Parker the Comanche chief leading the parade in an old Ford. Brindle had helped rustle up wild mustangs, chased Mexican bandits back across the border with a posse, and labored in the fields up and down the plains. His father told him that Brindle had saved a man from drowning while pushing logs down the river, but he never spoke of it because another man did drown. Brindle blamed himself for only being able to save one.

Pete's mother told him that when Brindle and his wife, Julie, found out they couldn't have children, Brindle made sure Julie had all she needed, packed a mule, rode into the mountains, and didn't come back for two weeks. They never spoke of it again. When Pete asked, "What did she do for two weeks while he was gone?" His mother put her arms around him and said, "Well, Cub, she did what all women do. She let the tears come, felt cursed, gathered up strength deep from within, and went on giving her love to her man, knowing he would never understand her pain."

Brindle had worked briefly for the Northern Pacific Railroad as a tunnel blaster, but after a few close calls, he decided that logging was much safer. But Brindle's heart was with animals, and he had a talent for taming spirited ones. More than anything, he loved breeding animals. For some unknown reason, he had a special love of mules and had bred more than one either for himself or someone else. He was definitely a unique character, Pete thought to himself, and a man whose life could make a good movie.

Brindle sat there thinking he was glad the boy had grown into such a fine man. He had gathered bits and pieces of information over the years of separation. Whenever he was around Pete, it was both good and bad. The boy had always been curious, a quick learner, and trustworthy. Brindle could tell he had his mother's warmth and his father's strength. But it always reminded him of the child Pete's parents lost in the womb and the ones he and Julie never had. Pete's parents' marriage had been a good one, and they were both happy after that first year when the baby had died and they accepted what they could not change.

Brindle missed his Julie and helping her can the berries they picked together. You could love animals, and they could love you back, but no critter could ever give him the joy he had each time she hugged him. He glanced over at Pete and smiled, and was glad the boy had come back.

"Pete, did I ever tell you how I met my sweet Julie?"

"I don't remember hearing that story, Brindle, but I'll bet it's a good one."

"I was hauling hay down by Orofino, and the axle broke on the rig. I was stuck there until it could get fixed, which is no small thing on a flatbed. They just don't have truck axles sittin' on the back shelf. Anyway, Julie's mom had a sandwich and pie shop, and I wandered in there waitin' to hear how long it was gonna take to get a new axle. The place smelt like fresh apple pie, fresh brewed coffee, and grilled pastrami. My nose could have stayed there forever in sniffing heaven. But the highlight of the place was my Julie. Every man in the place thought she was the most beautiful girl they had ever seen, and their eyes popped out like bacon grease on a hot skillet every time she walked by.

"I always sat in a small booth in a corner, and she knew right off I was a stranger in town. When she discovered my plight, she always asked how I was and how the repair progress was goin', like it was her rig. I got so I went early to lunch when it wasn't busy so I might get a chance to talk with her. I was pretty shy, and she did most of the talking, but she was not all gabby-like, just friendly. In fact, one day she sat down and visited until her mother scowled at her and called her away. Her mother made great pies, but that woman would make a grizzly run in fear. Before I left, Julie told me of a dance at the grange hall the next night, which was a Saturday. Well, it turns out my rig was all ready to go Saturday morning, but all I could think about was Julie. So I told myself, what's one more day now?

"I went to the dance, and guys were pushin' and shovin' to see who got to dance with Julie next. I'm no boot stompin' or soft shoe guy, so I just stood in a corner sipping what I think was lemonade, with a little Jim Beam one of the fellas probably poured in. Then they announced it was going to be the last dance, a slow one. Before anyone knew what she was doing, Julie marched over to me and said, 'Brindle the dance is about to end, and you haven't danced with me once. This is your last chance.' I was so surprised I almost choked on my lemonade, but she took my hand and led me to the center of the dance floor. The next thing I know, I got my arm on her back and her hand in my hand, and then she looks up at me with those beautiful, brown eyes. She whispers real soft in my ear, 'Hold me closer, Brindle.' By now, my heart's palpitatin' so hard I think my ears will burst, and then I knew I wanted to spend the rest of my life with this gal. So as the music was stopping, I looked into her eyes and said, 'Miss Julie, I got somethin' to say to you. I would consider myself the most blessed man on this earth if you could find it in yourself to accept me as yours. I'm not the smartest man alive, but I will always provide for you, and I will never, ever harm you. Will you marry me?'"

"You proposed after one dance? You had never dated her or even kissed her? My gosh! What did she do?"

"She said, 'Do you have an engagement ring?' That took me back for a second cuz I didn't think she was that kind of girl. But I knew by the look in her eyes that she loved me more than I could imagine. So I reached in my pocket, pulled out a piece of leather twine, and said, 'Will this do?' She laughed and nodded yes, so I took out my pocket knife, cut a short piece, and tied it around her finger. She looked at that piece of leather, smiled, and said, 'It's the most beautiful engagement ring I ever saw.' Then she gave me the heart warmin' smile, threw her arms around my neck, and gave me one of those tongue-swallowing kisses that almost sent me into the rafters. When I opened my eyes, I realized we were standin' in the middle of the place, and everyone was watchin' us. Then she shouted, 'I'm getting married!' All the women smiled and applauded, but a lot of the guys gave me hard stares. Cuz that was Saturday, we had to wait for the courthouse to open on Monday morning before gettin' hitched. Then we packed her old truck and left. That's our story."

"That's amazing, Brindle. After only one dance, you proposed. What on earth led you to do that?"

"Well, Pete, it doesn't take a lot of courtin' to know someone is right for you. That week in the sandwich shop we had talked about a lot of things, and apart from her obvious beauty, I knew she was a young woman with depth of character, and she had an anchor in her soul. And as it turned out, she needed it."

"I still think it's amazing."

"When you find the right one, you don't wait for somethin' to mess it up. There was a lot of competition for her affections, and I knew if I waited, things might not turn out well, and I might lose her. If you find your mystery girl, don't wait, or you may be sorry."

Pete's mind went to Faith and Gwen. He imagined them on opposite ends of a teeter totter, with Gwen up in the air and Faith sitting on the ground with him standing next to her. *More depth,* she whispered and stood up while Gwen unhappily crashed to the ground.

Brindle and Pete sat on the porch until the night's chill drove them inside. Although Pete had invited Brindle to stay, Brindle said he had brought a session of mules up from New Mexico the week before and was trying to breed his own to expand his high country pack train business.

"This stallion is a strong horse, but so is the donkey. She is one stubborn cookie. I hope their mule isn't as stubborn," Brindle told Pete as he left.

Pete was glad to finally be alone. He wanted to bundle up and sit on the porch and listen to the night sounds, but when he opened the door, he realized the temperature had dropped quickly. He reminded himself that he was in the mountains, even though it would soon be May. He tempered the fire in the stove and slipped into his sleeping bag. He didn't really want to sleep. Most of all, he wanted to relive the day, beginning with leaving the gas station in Issaquah. He recalled his disparaging opinion of Faith as she stood on the side of the road. Then there was the unexplainable compulsion to stop for her. He recalled her walking casually to Francis, who was not yet Francis. That was another thing. He let her name his car, and he liked it. There was her interview of him and his serial killer response. Then there was the lupine and her story of running away from an abusive father. Even more surprising was her willingness to forgive him. Where did that come from? Her laughter and tears. It all began to be twisted in his mind with diversions to Brindle, DJ, Winston, and something about Gwen. Oh Gwen, what are we about? But his last vision was of Faith smiling over chocolate cream pie as he sank into a deep, tranquil sleep.

Before he opened his eyes, Pete heard a scuffling sound and then a twig breaking right outside the window. The smell of the cabin gave him a nesting feeling and a lingering sense of peace, despite the intruder outside. He listened for a moment, and the sound stopped. Just as he was about to move, he heard it again, only this time he sensed it was closer to the back door. "It could be a bear," he thought to himself. "It's too big to be a skunk, or it could be a man. Brindle wouldn't sneak around. Besides, he has a key." He opened his eyes and glanced at the dust-wiped window and saw only gray sky and a light, feathery mist rising upward above the dark green curtain of trees and the tops of the silver spruce. He quietly placed his feet on the floor and was immediately struck by how cold it was. His first thought was, "Oh the hell with it, get back in bed." But then he heard a sound again and the sound of movement on the back porch. Something seemed to bump the door. He grabbed his jeans and guided himself into them as quietly and quickly as possible. Now, whatever or whoever it was sounded like they had turned the corner. Pete knew if he crawled into the kitchen, he could probably rise up to the window and get a good peek. He crawled across the aged planks and had a quick flashback of his mother wiping up spilled spaghetti sauce on this same floor. Just before he reached the kitchen wall, he turned, reached toward the stove, and grabbed the black iron poker. He took some minor comfort in having a weapon. He balanced himself on the balls of his feet and slowly raised his eyes to the window's ledge. Suddenly, a face was staring at him on the other side of the pane, only inches away—eyes large and a hairy face. He fell backward and felt a pain in his wrist as the poker went crashing to the floor like an iron bird. Pete took a deep breath and laughed at himself as he stood and watched the white tail of the startled deer bounce up and down as it headed for the trees. "I guess we both got a start. I hope the rest of your day goes better, and mine, too."

Pete went for his socks and finished getting dressed, putting on a sweatshirt that any self-respecting mother would either trash or give to Goodwill. There were still hot coals from last night, so starting the fire was easy. The coffee's aroma quickly filled the cabin, and as soon as it was ready, Pete went to the front porch and was mildly shocked by how much cooler it was outside. He sat in the rocker and noticed how the wooden arms had been polished by time and wear. He wondered if he should buy a pipe. He had seen the round, copper ash tray in a corner of the kitchen, but he knew he hated even the idea of smoking. Besides, he was not his father, and times had changed.

He remembered the story he had done on cancer research for the *Times* and the first time a link was found between smoking and cancer. Without any laboratory verification, a researcher, on a hunch, had taken a registry of doctors and found out what the doctors died from. It turned out all the doctors who died of cancer had been smokers, and none of the nonsmoking doctors had died of cancer. Pete always thought it ironic that dead doctors who smoked gave the first hint of a connection between smoking and cancer. He smiled but immediately felt a pang of guilt. Cancer is no laughing matter, he thought to himself, and thought about yesterday and Faith's struggle with the death of a little girl. He wondered how it would be when Faith met her father and how he would react to her return. The thought of yesterday was pleasant, and he didn't know what to do with it. "I'll probably never see her again," he said aloud, but just as quickly as the sound of his own voice ceased, he knew it was not true.

He breathed in the morning air and the aroma of the coffee, the foliage, and the earth, and allowed himself a smile. Beyond a grove of sword ferns, he caught sight of a woodpecker on a dead Tamarack about a hundred yards away and listened to the rhythmic hammering of the bird. He watched as it traversed the tree, reaching, pecking, diligent, and deliberate. It reminded him of the Apostle Paul's words, something like "If you don't work, you don't eat." He knew that from the frequent repetition of his father, not from diligent reading of the Bible. The sound of the bird's tapping expanded beyond the tree, carried down the valley, and evaporated into a distant silence. The night's moisture seemed to gently rise from the valley as it slowly awoke to a new day. It was like heat itself was awakening from its night of sleep.

Sitting there on the porch looking at the cabin brought a faded memory of his mother bending over and reaching into the cupboard next to the sink and removing a box. He didn't remember anything about the box except that it was important to her. He finished his coffee and wondered if the box was still there. He decided to find out. "This is silly. I'm sure it's not here, and besides, there probably is nothing in it." Pete went inside and knelt before the cupboard. He felt as if he had been tricked into a position of prayer. He remembered visiting the beautiful cathedral in Seattle with a Catholic friend and how awkward he felt kneeling in the pew. He opened the cupboard and only saw a cookie sheet and two old bread pans. He rattled them around but saw nothing. "It must have been something I dreamed as a child or thought I saw. I think I'll go for a good walk."

It didn't take long before the morning's wet grass had dampened Pete's boots. Crossing the creek that flowed toward the North Fork didn't help, either, but he didn't care. The boots were good, and his feet were not wet. He had bought them at REI in Seattle the month before and worn them every weekend around the apartment and to the market to break them in. As he came to the edge of the meadow, he could see the birch trees standing like sentinel guards in front of the forest at the far side of the meadow. The morning mist was all but gone now, and though the sky was gray, he could feel the increasing warmth as the valley heated up.

Pete remembered how he had pestered his dad to make a birch bark canoe so they could go down the river in it. He was disappointed when his dad came up with a Coleman aluminum canoe; that is, until they put it in the river, and then the adventure was on. The trees looked almost majestic with their paper-thin, white bark against the dark wall of the forest. A shadow crossed his path, and looking up, Pete saw an osprey with wings spread wide, gliding in a curved pattern across the meadow. Quickly, it seemed to fall from the sky, and just as it looked as if it were crashing, it splashed upstream in the creek and arose into the air with a fish clenched in its mouth. It was thrilling to see the magnificent bird flying so effortlessly. Ironically, Pete's mind went to the fish. Only moments before, those fish had probably been gliding in their own world, unaware of the threat from above. "Death doesn't always fire a warning shot," he had heard a beat cop say once. He knew it was true. By the time cancer fires the warning shot, much of the race is already lost.

His thoughts went back to his mother and her lying there in University Hospital, pale, jaundiced, her skin a yellow, tallow color and the veins in her hands and arms coursing her limbs like red and blue highways on a road map. She had, of course, lost her hair long before the end came near, but it was her eyes that he could not forget. They had always been bright and full of life and delight, but in the end, they had become dull and cloudy. But her mind never became cloudy; she was clear right to the end. Pete remembered her eyes because so many times as he was growing up, they had been a comfort to him. He didn't even have to be in her arms as a hurt little boy; he could look across a room and see her watching him, and it was as if she were pouring confidence into him through her dark, brown eyes. Her last words still echoed in the back of his mind. *I love you, Peter. Nothing can separate us from the love of God. I'm going now. I will be at peace. Trust your heart, Son.* Pete stopped to catch his breath. The memory caught him by surprise and had taken him to grief's door. It was a place he tried not to visit, but he kept showing up there despite himself. He stood and looked to the sky. There was no sign of the osprey, but the valley pulsated with life. He took a deep breath, felt gratitude, and wondered about Faith.

CHAPTER TEN

The Sleuth

A fter the movie with Betsy, DJ had spent some time with his friend Kurt, a mechanic for the Washington State ferry system who lived in a convenience apartment just below Queen Ann Hill. It was convenient, DJ thought to himself, because everything is in one room— kitchen, bed, living area, all in one, and the head was the original closet. He wondered how people slept in those places. You never knew when some Seattle rain might be overly aggressive and the hill might come sliding down, sending you into the city toward Puget Sound. But Kurt had the finest collection of Louis Armstrong records in all of Seattle and probably the whole West Coast. So to DJ, it was worth the risk to camp on the hill one night and listen to the genius on the horn making sweet music that others could only dream about. He rubbed his arms at the thought of it. He was glad the rain had stopped, although it had seemed to beat a rhythm with Louis as he played.

Now he was going to investigate, just like Pete had asked him to. He liked doing it. There was a sense of adventure, plus you were out in the world instead of being in a cramped sound booth. He had once considered applying for the FBI, but those haircuts were just too much. Besides, he figured they hated rock and roll because they use it as an interrogation technique. He knew his destiny was to be the country's best disc jockey, and he couldn't fight destiny. Right now, he was hoping destiny was on his side because he was going to meet a guy at Oscar's newsstand who wasn't known for his gentle disposition. DJ only knew the guy as Little Fritz, but there was nothing little about him. DJ had once seen Fritz airlift a guy off the sidewalk and throw him over a parked car into traffic. DJ winced, thinking of the pain. He had put some feelers out before going to the movie last night, and there was a message for him when he got home to meet Fritz at Oscar's this morning.

Oscar's newsstand was a pick-up and drop-off point for almost anything—messages to friends or mistresses, hidden cash payoffs, or just meeting up for a date. Oscar never dwelt in anyone else's business, and most of what went on was legal, except for the betting. Oscar kept his racing sheet posted on the stand, and bets were always welcome. But he only carried bets on horses, never football or the fights or anything else. He considered his newsstand an off-track convenience window for the serious racing fan. He probably had as many customers as any window at Long Acres. Street kids, business execs, secretaries running bets for their bosses, and even cops stopped by, sometimes to bet, sometimes to get helpful information to keep the city clean.

Oscar sat on his wooden box, his bald head covered with a watch cap. He wore short, baggy pants, a leather jacket, and Redwing work boots. Oscar had rings on three out of five fingers on each hand, but they looked like tourniquets on his chubby little fingers. No one would ever think to make fun of his dwarfism and his smallish stature because he looked like a cross between a cheerful clown and a mob boss. DJ considered Oscar one of the best people on the planet, and he knew if he took a poll, so did a lot of other people.

"Hey, Oscar, who's the lady who just left? The one in the green coat? She looks familiar."

"You ever had an appointment with the mayor?" Oscar asked, glancing at the woman moving gracefully down the block.

"Are you kidding, Oscar? He hates my Meet the Mayor shtick. So who is she?"

"She's his secretary. If the truth be known, and it never is in politics, she probably runs the city when he doesn't get in the way."

"Well, is she betting for him or for herself?"

"Mr. big shot disc jockey and amateur private detective, I have to keep my confidences, ya know."

"Oscar, you little . . ."

"Don't state the obvious. They're both betting, but she's smarter than her boss; wins more money, more often. But don't you go making that a part of your mayor thing on the radio, or I'll be busted for sure."

"Don't worry, I won't blow your cover, as if it were a secret."

"Isn't this an odd time for you to be here, or are you just dying for one of Wally's hot dogs? *Dying* being the operative word."

"That's not a bad idea—not dying but eating. No, I have an appointment with Little Fritz."

"DJ, you got a death wish or sumpin'? He's probably the number one provider of fish food in all of Puget Sound. You're street smart enough to know that. Never mind, it looks like your date's here." Oscar nodded toward the street. DJ turned to see a shiny, black Lincoln with dark tinted windows pull up to the curb. The driver got out and walked over to Wally's. He was over six feet, at least 275 pounds, and had a scar that went from his lips to just beneath his right ear. He looked mean, but he wasn't Little Fritz. "Too small," DJ thought to himself. As "Scarface" walked back toward the Lincoln, the rear window lowered slowly, and one hot dog went into the massive hands of Little Fritz. Scarface stood on the curb eating his hot dog, all the while watching DJ and Oscar and occasionally surveying the intersection. DJ started to move toward the Lincoln, but Oscar whispered, "Wait!" A moment later, although to DJ it seemed like an hour, the hand emerged again from the back of the Lincoln and motioned DJ forward. DJ wondered what kind of noise his body would make when it hit the ground and if he would be able to hear his own bones break.

Fritz's face was pudgy and somewhat bloated, but his shoulders were broad and seemed to crown a massive chest with little or no stomach. He appeared to take up most of the rear seat. DJ stood at the window and was glad he was outside the car.

"You a snitch for the cops?"

"No, no, nothing like that. A friend of mine is a reporter, and I dig up stuff for him. No cops, no way, man!"

"So what does your friend want to know, and why is he looking for me?"

"He isn't looking for you; he isn't even in town. I thought you might be able to help me; that is, if you want to," DJ said with a little hesitation in his voice. "All he knows is that someone is running up bills on credit cards of folks who aren't with us anymore." DJ hesitated to say "dead" to Fritz. "He's trying to find out how whoever it is got the cards in the first place."

"Your friend ain't very smart for a reporter." Little Fritz reached behind his ear, and a cigarette appeared in his hand like some party trick. DJ wasn't sure how to take the comment. Was it a warning? But before he could give it much thought, Fritz lit the cigarette, blew smoke in his face, and DJ started coughing. "What's your friend's name?"

"His name's Pete Webb. He writes for the *Times*."

"Yeah, I know him. He does his homework. He wrote about that Addison kid. Stupid kid shoulda stayed in Canada. And that lawyer, he sure got his. But I'll bet that crybaby of an editor doesn't like your reporter friend much."

"Why do you say that?"

"I say lots of things, and most people are smart enough not to question them."

DJ quickly scolded himself. *I should have kept my mouth shut. Now I won't find out anything.*

"Didn't hear you on the radio last night. I was busy—business, but you're funny. I love it when you pretend you're the mayor. He's such an ass."

DJ was amazed at how soft—not quiet, but soft—Fritz's voice was. He realized that when Fritz picked the guy up and threw him over the car, he hadn't spoken a word. It seemed out of place. He wondered if it was some trick of nature.

"Everybody knows where dead people go, well, before they go under, I mean. Somebody has to bury them." The window went up, and Scarface slid into the driver's seat after giving DJ a look that made his heart skip a beat. Before DJ could move, the window slid down halfway, and he heard Fritz say, "Thanks for the hot dogs." The window closed, and the car merged into traffic like a shark leaving on a hunt.

"Hey, Oscar. Guess who likes my mayor act?"

"Be glad he likes something 'bout you, but next time, don't meet him at my place."

"Oscar, this is a public street, a public sidewalk. Besides, I met him in front of Wally's, and he's not complaining."

"That's because Wally don't understand the complexities of evolution because he sells hot dogs."

"The complexities of evolution?"

"Yeah, it's so simple, it's complex. The big fish eat the little fish, and soon there are no little fish, so the bigger fish eat the big fish, and Little Fritz is about the biggest fish I know, and I'm about the smallest fish I know except for Stella."

"Who's Stella?"

"None of your beeswax. You never heard the name. Got it?"

"Sure, no problem. Fritz is pretty big, but I'll bet you five bucks he can't swim, so that leaves him out of your evolutionary complexity. Say, what do you know about funeral homes?"

"Excuse me, can I get a *Post Intelligencer* please?" asked a man in a red beret.

"Sure, here you are." Oscar passed off the paper and turned to DJ with a frown on his face.

"Come on, Oscar, when was the last time you went to a funeral?"

"Ouch! I don't like those things. They make me feel like my number's up next. I went to my brother-in-law's funeral. Ah, that was the last one. It was in a little Catholic church up on Capitol Hill. He converted during Korea, a foxhole thing and all that. He figured if the Virgin Mary could save his ass when he needed it the most, then he should be loyal to her."

"Thanks, Maxy," Oscar said as a man in a blue windbreaker walked away waving the paper over his head that he had just purchased. He didn't look back.

"So, one day he's up on a ladder," Oscar continued, "painting the house, and my sister's screaming for him to come in for lunch. She had fixed him a meatball sandwich, his favorite. She was about to kill him she was so mad. The meatballs were getting cold, but the guy's already dead. They said he had a heart attack and was dead before he hit the ground. What can she do? Man, she was a mess. She drove me crazy, at least until she met Jack."

"Excuse me, Sir, do you have any Spokane papers?" She was a matronly woman who spoke with an accent, either Canadian or British, DJ couldn't tell, but you could tell by the tone of her voice and the way she said "sir" that she was speaking respectfully, not sarcastically. Oscar glanced over his shoulder and looked down at a small pile of papers.

"Spokane? I only have *The Spokesman-Review,* not the *Chronicle,* but it's a day old, and you can have it for nothing if you want it."

"Thank you very much, but here is your money, and I prefer the *Review* anyway, so this will be good. I have to keep up on things over there. I have family there. You gentlemen have a good day."

"Nice lady," DJ said.

"Yeah, but Jack, her new hubby, he's a real piece. I don't get to see her no more, my sister, I mean. Always driving down to Vegas or some other warm place where people get crazy in the sun."

"Probably beats rain, Oscar. Back to my question. What do you know about funeral places? Anything?"

"Yeah, they charge you for breathing in those places. It's like they got something against the living. Why? Somebody you know kick off?"

"That will be two bits."

"I'm sorry, I don't have any change. I only have a five dollar bill."

"Well, this is your lucky day, cuz I got lots of change," Oscar said sarcastically as he reached into his apron and pulled out a fold of bills and change from his apron pocket.

While this exchange took place, DJ glanced at the pile of papers and wondered how many trees it took to supply all the dailies in all the cities of the world for one day. "It's probably a good thing most of the world is illiterate," he thought to himself.

Oscar poked DJ and whispered. "He does this once a week, says he has no change, like I'm here to give papers away."

"But have you heard anything about any of them, anything questionable?"

"What are we talking about? You lost me."

"Funeral homes, Oscar. Have you heard anything? Something weird you might remember?"

"Nah, there is one thing, though."

"What?"

"They burn ya."

"You mean they cremate the stiffs?"

"I mean they're as crooked as a mountain road. Their whole place is probably a front for something phony. You shoulda seen what my sister had to shell out. Hell, I could dig a hole for a lot less and say some good words, and it would have saved her plenty. I never met two guys so weird."

"Let's face it, Oscar, we'd be weird, too, if we were sitting around with dead folks all day. What two guys? What's the name of the place? Let me see your phone book."

"MacDonald Funeral Home & Crematorium, Northwest Funeral Home, The Hyde Brothers Complete . . ."

"That's their name, crooked as Tricky Dicky, just not so successful."

"Here it is, Hyde Brothers Complete Funeral Services. I wonder how complete is complete? Good, they're all out past Green Lake. I can take the bus. I'd better check them all. You may not be right about the Hyde Brothers."

"Mark my word, your friend Oscar called this one, just like the filly in the second race last Saturday."

"See ya. I gotta go make arrangements for my favorite uncle's demise."

"I didn't know you got a sick uncle."

"I don't. I don't even have an uncle. Well, that's not quite true, but that's another story, later." DJ crossed the street just as the northbound bus arrived. It felt good to sit down. He closed his eyes and immediately wished he hadn't.

DJ had read somewhere that fathers and sons were always in competition of some sort. He was wise enough to know his situation was unique. Few fathers lose their profession, health, and future in the prime of their lives. They don't slip into alcoholism and a life of resentment and bitterness that becomes toxic to everyone around them. He remembered when he was little and they went to the coast, camped on the beach, and dug for razor clams. His father would fry them in a batter of some kind, and they were so good. "The secret is two minutes on each side," he remembered his father telling him. DJ had thought his father was the wisest man in the world for knowing the "secret" of frying clams. The thought of his father at a better time brought him around to consciousness as the bus braked to a sudden stop.

DJ had only been to a funeral home once in his life, and that was when his grandmother died. He was sure most funerals weren't like hers. The ad had said, "Hyde Brothers, Complete Funeral Service," and DJ wondered how complete and what incomplete might mean. What would you leave out? He had checked the other funeral homes first, and they seemed fine. As he entered the lobby, he heard a muted chime ring somewhere beyond. He could hear music in the background, which he was sure was supposed to comfort the grieving. But he couldn't help but think, "Is this what happens to worn-out elevator music?" The place was amazingly quiet, and there was no sound coming from the street. As soon as the door closed behind him, the world outside ceased to exist. DJ wondered if he was about to live out an episode of *The Twilight Zone.*

"May I help you, Sir? My name is Franklin Hyde."

DJ hadn't even heard the man approach, which was kind of creepy. The man stood ram-rod-toy-soldier straight before him in a brown polyester suit, white shirt, and K-Mart tie. He looked about 50 with varying shades of dyed black hair. His skin was a pasty white, and for a second, DJ wondered if one of the cadavers had actually come to meet him.

"Yes, I think you can, Mr. Hyde. I uh, um," DJ did his best to look sorrowful and tentative. "I need to make plans for my uncle's . . ." He choked on his last words and thought, "Mr. Jalesco, my drama teacher, would be so proud if he saw me now."

"Let's step into my office, Mr. . . . ?"

"Robinson, Dustin Robinson."

"Just follow me, if you would, please." As DJ followed Franklin Hyde down the hall, he noticed some gray strands of hair on the back of the man's head. "You should be more careful, Franky," DJ thought to himself. "People will know you're not a young stud."

The hallway was carpeted in a chocolate brown, the same as Mr. Hyde's suit, and the walls were covered with cheap prints of mountain scenes and Grecian porticos leading to unseen gardens. It was obvious to DJ that these were message pictures. Franklin Hyde's office looked more like a small living room than an office. Behind the desk was a large picture of the ocean with a glowing sun dipping behind the horizon. The meaning was clear: "Time runs out for us all. Your loved ones are on a wonderful journey. Do not be sad." For a brief moment, DJ forgot about his role as a grieving nephew and thought about his own mortality, the life he is living and the years ahead. He wondered about his father and whether bitterness shortens your life or prolongs it. As he looked at the other furnishings, he figured the Hyde brothers must be preferred K-Mart shoppers.

"Now what is your uncle's name?" Hyde said as he pulled a manila folder from his desk. He daintily lifted a fountain pen from an etched glass container.

"His name is Uncle Burl, I mean Matthew Burl Scott, but he goes by Burl. He doesn't have long—a few days, no more. They say the muscle is dying and soon the valves will cease to function." To his own surprise, DJ shed a tear.

"I know this is difficult, Mr. Robinson, but there is some information we need to know. What hospital is your uncle in?"

"Oh, he's not in a hospital. He's at home. Mary Ann and Jewel take care of him, but Jewel is actually the maid. Mary Ann takes care of him during the day and Jewel at night. But there is also Millbrook. He's the butler. He helps, too. I'm his only relative."

"Butler? Well, can you give me your uncle's address?"

"Gee, I don't remember. I just know how to get there. He's on Westlake Drive. It's the house with the golden eagle on the gate. It's not really gold, though. It's just brass, but it's golden in color. I can get the address for you and call."

"Why don't we just look it up in the phone book?" Hyde suggested.

"Oh, it's unlisted. I'll call you," DJ said tentatively.

DJ had driven by this house many times, admiring it, but he had no idea who lived there. It never occurred to him that he would have to provide a home address for his "uncle" to die in. He just hoped the house didn't belong to the Hydes. "Can you tell me what happens? I mean when he goes . . ."

"When your uncle expires, someone . . ."

"What do you mean 'expires'?"

"Well, you know, when he is no longer with us."

"You mean when he *dies*?" DJ said the last word like he was trying to get the attention of a friend in a crowd. He wasn't sure if he managed it, but Mr. Hyde appeared to duck and looked like he might hide under his desk.

"Why, yes, that's what I mean," he said as he straightened his tie. "When your dear uncle expires, someone from his premises will call us, and we will come and pick up your uncle and transport him back here and prepare him for inurnment or internment."

"What's inurnment?"

"Well, yes," clearing his throat. "When someone is cremated, their remains are placed in an urn, so it's called *inurnment*. Do you know whether or not your uncle wishes to be cremated?"

"No, I guess I'll have to ask."

"Do you know if your uncle has funeral insurance?"

"Is that in case you drop him or something?"

"Absolutely not! They are insurance policies that pay for all the expenses incurred by the funeral home."

"Boy, I didn't know this would be so hard. I know he doesn't have life insurance because he doesn't believe in it. He says, 'Why should I pay them? They aren't doing anything to keep me alive. I'll leave more than enough behind without any insurance company's help.'"

"I assume, therefore, that our services will be paid for by Mr. Scott's estate."

"Yes, his attorney will take care of all of that."

Franklin wanted to ask the name of the attorney, but he thought that might be pushing the boy, and he probably wouldn't remember the name anyway. Anyone with enough money to have a nurse, a maid, and a butler in this day and age certainly would have enough in their estate. In fact, Franklin thought to himself, there may be more opportunity here yet.

"I assume there is no Mrs. Scott?"

"No, my aunt died several years ago, and Uncle Burl took care of all the funeral stuff."

"Uh huh. Could you tell me who your uncle used, perhaps?"

"No, it was in France. I said goodbye at the airport and never saw her again." DJ managed to bring up another tear and moisture to his eyes.

"I'm sure," Hyde said, "that a man of your uncle's stature wants the best of the services we provide?"

He's moving up for the sales pitch, DJ thought. "Sure, nothing but the best for Uncle Burl. Money is no object, but the Fortune 500 will have to replace him. Fortune 499 just doesn't have the same ring to it." DJ looked at the floor as if he were lost in sorrow, wiping his nose with his sleeve, purposefully ignoring the box of tissues sitting prominently on Hyde's desk and on every table in the room. Looking up, DJ said, "I'd better go find out about the internment stuff. I'll get back to you."

"Of course, Mr. Robinson. Here, why don't you take one of our pens? Our number is on it. And here is my card."

DJ took the cheap pen with satisfaction. Franklin Hyde walked him to the front door, and when he opened it, DJ heard the chimes. He looked around, "Where is your brother?"

"I beg your pardon?"

"It says Hyde Brothers. Where is the other Mr. Hyde?"

"Oh, Henry is out on a call."

DJ noticed the change of air immediately as he left the building. He found himself taking large gulps of it. The term *dead air* just took on a new meaning, and it was totally unrelated to his radio broadcasting. DJ thought about the golden eagle house. He may have painted himself into a corner, or as his grandpa used to say, "Wasn't there another way to make it more difficult? No point in putting a mountain in your way." *What's the secret to moving mountains?* he thought as he stepped onto the bus.

"DJ, I used to think you were a smart guy," Betsy scolded, "but now I know that you are a complete, totally qualified, certifiable idiot. What are you going to do, just walk up to some stranger's house and ring the bell and say, 'Excuse me, I was wondering if I could bring a dead body into your house to try to catch a crook'? It all sounds perfectly reasonable to me. How about all you other people out there in radioland? Does your favorite late night disc jockey sound sane to you?"

"Betsy, keep your voice down! Look, I was just trying to get a feel for the guy, and my gut tells me he's a sleazeball."

"Well, that may be true, but there are a lot of sleazeballs out there who never commit a crime. They're just sleazeballs, and that's all. Just because he's in the funeral business and is a sleazeball doesn't mean he's stealing credit cards from the dead. Besides, how are you going to find out? Do you really think you can provide him with a dead 'Uncle Matthew' who doesn't exist and a wallet full of credit cards assigned to a man who isn't real?"

They were sitting in Skippers by the window near the ferry dock. DJ watched the seagulls as they sat on the pilings and hustled an occasional French fry from those eating outside. He watched the ferry as it approached across the green-gray water, its wake cresting in white foam. He figured by its size that it must be the Bainbridge Island Ferry, but he wasn't sure. He looked over at Betsy who was looking at the menu like it was an ancient document just discovered and never read by anyone before her.

"I don't know what I'm going to do, Betsy, and you're right. I'm an idiot."

Betsy reached across the table, almost spilling the salt, and put her hand on his. "No, you're not, and I'm sorry I said it. You're just trying to help Pete and stop some crook. Both of those are admirable ambitions, but you are not Captain Midnight, superhero. You're a sweet guy who loves music and likes to play detective. You're hopeless, but I care about you anyway."

She really does care about me, he thought to himself, *like no one else in my life, except for Mom.* Betsy had big, brown eyes that either looked like she knew everything or was taking it all in. Her hair was dark but not black, and her lips were thin and always ready to smile. Most people would call her cute, others pretty. "Maybe I should just wait," DJ lamented.

"Now that sounds reasonable, rational, and, I must say, totally out of character. I think there's another possibility."

"What's that?"

"If your funeral director has used those credit cards to buy things, it may not be possible to prove anything unless there are large, conspicuous purchases. They would need to be obvious so it would be worth taking it to the police."

"The only thing conspicuous about this guy is that he buys cheap clothes and has no taste. He . . ."

"But," Betsy interrupted, "we know some of the cards were used for trips. If we could find out if the Hyde Brothers, or one of them, had gone to any of those destinations at the same time, you would have a pretty good idea if they're involved. But I don't know how you could find that out. I can get you a record of the trips, where and when, but I don't know how you can find out if either went on a trip. They would have had to travel under the name on the card."

"Betsy, you are not only sweet and beautiful but a genius. You get me the credit card records, and I'll do the rest."

"You'd better be careful."

"Don't worry. I used a fake name. They won't figure it out."

"I hate to ask, but who are you this time?"

"I'm Mr. Robinson. Very common, Mr. Dustin Robinson." DJ smiled as he said it.

"I get it. *Mr.* Robinson instead of *Mrs.*, and *Dustin* for *Dustin Hoffman*! At least you didn't tell them you're Captain Midnight."

Franklin Hyde was sitting in the bar area of the Olympic Hotel contemplating the next phase of his life. The booth was large, and even with

Franklin's ample frame, he looked like a man in a dinghy waiting for the other passengers to arrive. Dave Brubeck's "Take Five" seeped seductively from the hidden speakers. It was a sassy number that couldn't help but lift one's mood, although at this point, Franklin's mood was above normal. Three guys at one end of the bar were arguing whether or not the Pirates would take the World Series again this year. The first thought they would. The bald one thought the Dodgers might come through. The third lamented Seattle's lack of a baseball franchise. Franklin noticed two women at the other end of the bar. They were busy tearing some other woman apart piece by piece like jackals in the desert. Franklin would have put money on the fact that the victim was better looking or at least made more money.

Franklin had gone into the funeral home business because his ex-father-in-law had made it sound so pleasant, and he didn't have to put out any money. But unlike his father-in-law, Franklin didn't like people. His father-in-law and many others he had met in the profession called it a "ministry" and saw themselves helping others in a great time of need. And sometimes, God forbid, they even swallowed part or all of the costs themselves. It was something Franklin could not comprehend. Life was about getting what you wanted, and you couldn't get anything without money. "So, why give it away?" he pondered as he swirled the ice in his drink. He momentarily thought of Shelley, his ex-wife, but it was a very brief moment as their marriage had been.

Six months to the day, she had left him for an alcoholic dock worker in Bremerton. Just two weeks later, the two of them ended up on the wrong end of a fatal traffic accident. Shelley's grieving father gave Franklin the business and left town. Franklin recruited his younger brother, Henry, and they became the Hyde Brothers.

"Henry thinks of himself as a partner and equal to me, but that's just not the case, neither legally nor practically," Franklin thought to himself as he emptied the glass and raised his hand to catch the bartender's attention for another. While Franklin watched the ice in his revived drink, he thought about Dustin Robinson. He was an odd young fellow, but evidently he had a very wealthy uncle who would soon pass. He decided that if the old man died before he and Fan Kim left, he and Henry would take the call and maybe pick up a few things of interest if they could. He wondered if the old fellow would have any credit cards. He was beginning to think the credit card scam had run its course. If it's too frequent, the authorities are going to begin figuring out how it can be done, and there would be inquiries. Franklin looked at his watch and wondered if Fan Kim was going to make it or not. She sometimes got tied up and couldn't get away. After all, she was a very important business lady in Chinatown. He decided he would give her another half an hour. Besides, it was pleasant here, and it would give him time for another drink. What were three drinks in the afternoon, anyway? Maybe a kick-start for the evening, depending on Fan Kim's plans. "I may not go back to work today," he said to himself as he watched the ice float in a circle around his glass. He took a deep breath and sat back, relaxed. The music was soothing and the lights were muted, and he tuned out those at the bar. It all put him in a relaxed mood, and of course, the vodka helped. He thought everything was going as planned.

"Soon Fan Kim and I will be starting new lives in Barquisimeto," he thought. Neither of them wanted the Far East, and Barquisimeto has a large enough Chinese community to make her feel comfortable. Hell, he thought to himself, there are Chinese everywhere, which was fine because he liked their food. As long as he had Fan Kim, her exotic beauty, and their combined accumulated wealth, he didn't care where they lived, as long as it was beyond the reach of the American legal system. They would have new identities. He wondered what name she had chosen for him on his new passport. She said she would take care of that part because she had some "connections." Franklin suspected that Fan Kim had been dealing in false passports, among other things, for years, but it mattered little to him. He knew he would spend the rest of his life with her, without his bungling brother, grieving spouses, and Seattle's dismal rain. "Boy, how I hate the rain," he muttered to himself.

DJ couldn't stand to go to the funeral home again, so he decided it would be more prudent to call. He listened as the coins descended down the track inside the pay phone and a moment later heard it ring.

"Hyde Brothers Complete Funeral Services, Henry Hyde speaking. How may I help you?"

"I'm Dustin Robinson, and I already talked with the other Mr. Hyde about my Uncle Burl, and . . ."

"Yes, and my brother mentioned you. Has your dear uncle expired?" he asked with sweetness dripping from each syllable.

"Expired? Oh, you mean died? No, but I got to thinking, and I thought I would call and ask you something if it's okay."

"Of course. We are here to help any way we can. What is your question, Mr. Robinson?"

If it were true what DJ had read, that 70 percent of communication is carried by the tone of your voice, then DJ was sure Henry could care less what he wanted.

"Well, your brother, the other Mr. Hyde, said to call when Uncle Burl died, and I got to thinking. What if he dies in the middle of the night or when you're on vacation or something?"

"Well, Mr. Robinson, there is always someone on call, day or night. People don't always expire eight to five," he chuckled.

DJ could tell the second Mr. Hyde thought himself quite humorous. "But don't you ever take vacations? Go to Disneyland or something?"

"Disneyland? I can't even imagine it with all those germ-ridden crowds and snot-nosed children. Oh, oh, I'm terribly sorry. I got carried away for a second."

DJ could tell number-two brother was getting impatient and was also embarrassed he had revealed his mysophobia. The idea that he and his brother would ever think of going to Disneyland was obviously an insult.

"As I said before, we have someone on call day or night."

"What's his name, in case Uncle Burl dies at a bad time?"

"His name is Prescott, not that it matters, but while he is not as experienced as my brother or me, he will be able to assist you in those first moments."

How experienced do you have to be to load a dead body into a car? DJ thought. "Is that his first or last name?" DJ asked somewhat timidly. I wouldn't want to insult him by using the wrong name."

"His name is Percy Prescott, and you should, of course, call him Mr. Prescott. Now, is there anything else I can help you with? I happen to be quite busy at the moment."

"Thank you, Mr. Hyde number two. I'll be going now." Number two didn't bother to say goodbye.

Betsy had provided DJ with a complete record of the fraudulent credit card purchases. In the process, she realized there was an easier way to figure this out and shared the idea with DJ.

When DJ arrived at Oscar's newsstand, Oscar had on his blue Dodgers baseball cap, the one from the 1930s when they were still in Brooklyn. He was handing out a paper and giving change. DJ looked at the headlines related to Vietnam and wondered for a moment if the children of the students of the '70s would have their own war in some jungle somewhere, or would this one still be going on? But he decided not to think about it today.

"Hey, Mr. Rock and Roll, Disc Jockey of the Night. Whatcha up to today?"

"I'm off to the Seattle Public Library, Oscar. I'm going to eat the fruit of knowledge and drink the nectar of wisdom."

"Sounds to me like you've already been drinking something, and it's too early for that stuff. You want a paper to wrap your fruit of whatever in or sop up the nectar of whatchamacallit?"

"No thanks, they've got free papers at the library."

"I know, I know. Damn socialists don't know how to support capitalism and a free country. Don't let any of those bookworms bite you," Oscar yelled as DJ ran across the street against the light to catch the bus.

After Betsy had called and shared her idea, DJ knew the library was the place to be. It was a large building, a monument to the architectural movement begun in Scotland in the 1700s called Vitruvius Britacannicus. The building had smooth stone walls and large classical pillars and, of course, marble steps. The steps didn't exactly lend themselves to the quiet, which seemed more important to some librarians than the books. DJ knew from many a librarian that libraries were first for quiet and second for reading.

Betsy had realized that DJ could match stolen credit card owners and their obituaries and see if the Hyde brothers were involved. The library would have past editions of obituaries. DJ went through 30 obituary notices before he began to see a pattern. He only found three obituaries tied to the Hydes where no cards were involved. DJ bounced down the library steps and was now on his way to Lake Union to find one Percy Prescott.

The boathouses that decorated the southern portion of Lake Union in the shadow of the Space Needle had not yet become the trendy yuppie location they would achieve a decade later. They were a cheap housing alternative for those who couldn't afford Seattle's escalating rents and mortgages. Despite the view of the Space Needle and the tranquility of being on the water, this housing secret had not yet been discovered. DJ noticed that some of the houseboats had potted plants marking the deck corners and colorful banners hanging in the windows or from poles. He noticed one with a pirate flag on a pole and a Confederate flag in the window of another. He noticed motorcycle parts on the deck and was hoping this was not Prescott's or he might be in for some trouble. But thankfully, it wasn't the right number.

Prescott's houseboat was white, or once was, and was mostly faded, peeled wood with an aqua trim that was not in much better condition. The paint was peeling just above the water line, and DJ, not being a great swimmer, wondered if it would hold two people. He couldn't remember any credit card purchases for paint. "What is the way you're supposed to enter a houseboat?" he thought to himself. "Do you yell and ask permission to come aboard like a sailor on a ship in the movies, or do you just get on board and knock on the door?" Before he had resolved this dilemma, the door opened, and a chubby, cherub-like fellow in a Rolling Stones T-shirt stepped out.

"You'd better come inside. It looks like it's going to rain any second. You'd better get in here before you get drenched," he said invitingly. "You must be Mr. Jansen."

"Yes, but please call me DJ."

The inside was larger than DJ expected and immaculately clean, which came as a surprise by the appearance of the outside. The heater in the corner made the place warm and cozy.

"Now let me get this straight. You're thinking about doing a comedy sketch about funeral homes on the radio, like you do the mayor thing. You're looking for material?"

"Yep, that's right, Mr. Prescott, I'm . . ."

"Call me Percy. Don't worry, I've gotten used to it. It was my mother's maiden name, and they say if you want to teach a boy the art of self defense, name him Percy. So I boxed in college until I dropped out."

DJ liked Percy immediately and felt bad for lying to him, but for now it had to be.

"Why did you come to me? Why not go to my bosses?"

"Do you really think the Hyde Brothers are into comedy?"

"You've met them?"

"Not exactly. Let's just say my alias has, and he's a good judge of personalities. Besides, you're not a real funeral home guy, and you might have a more objective perspective. I don't think funeral home guys are going to help me make fun of them. I see by that poster hanging there that you're a Stones fan, Percy. So you must have good judgment. Do you like 'Jumpin' Jack Flash'?" DJ had heard Pete say one time that if you compliment someone and share a similar interest, it breaks down any defenses they may have and makes them more comfortable about sharing information.

"Man, yeah, but my favorite song is actually "Joy to the World," Three Dog Night. It just does something for me. It's got the right vibe."

"How 'bout a few questions? Why don't you tell me how you got into this business, how long you've been doing it, and what has surprised you the most."

"Well, I got into it because I needed a job and want to save up for my dream. I'm trying to get my pilot's license so I can do that for a living. And I've been with the Hydes for three years now."

"So how long will it be before you can fly?"

"No, no. I don't mean an airplane pilot, I mean a tug boat pilot so I can work on the Sound. I love being on the water, as you can see."

"You must like boats a lot, Percy."

"Yeah, I was born in the wrong century. I would have been a tall mast guy climbing the ropes and sailing the seas."

He had a far-off look and a grin as wide as the ocean. DJ had difficulty imagining this round cherub going up the mast of a ship without causing some tipping, but Percy was an affable kind of guy, and the inside of his houseboat was amazingly clean. *Shipshape*, DJ thought to himself.

"The Hydes aren't exactly funny guys," Percy noted. "Neither one is married, and they don't have hobbies or anything. Franklin is the boss, and he watches everything. I take calls at night when someone dies, and Harold and I go pick them up and bring them back to the funeral home."

"Who's Harold?"

"He's the caretaker guy. I answer the phones at night and cover things when the Hydes are gone."

DJ saw his opening and plunged in. "Are they gone much?"

"They didn't used to be, but this past year, they took several trips to San Francisco and one to Las Vegas."

"Funeral home business stuff?" DJ asked.

"Nah, I don't think so. I'm having a hard time thinking of funny things. I can only think of one. The deceased was a vet and was getting a 21-gun salute from an honor guard from the VFW. Evidently, the old soldiers spent the morning at the VFW bar getting warm for the cemetery. It was January. When it came time to fire their rifles, they not only didn't fire in unison, but at least two had live ammo, and one grazed the officiating pastor's ear. The other one killed a neighbor's dog. I think it cost the brothers a bundle before it was all settled."

"I might have trouble making that sound funny. It sounds more tragic. Maybe this wasn't such a good idea," DJ said. "Hey, it's almost lunchtime. You want to go find some pizza? I'll buy."

"Hey, man, I'm always up for pizza. I know just the spot, not far either."

DJ enjoyed his time with Pizza Percy and was convinced that Percy hadn't taken any credit cards. It was doubtful that Harold had either. But narrowing things down to the Hydes now meant he had something he could work with. "I wonder how Pete is getting along," he thought, "and if he can handle all that quiet and solitude."

CHAPTER ELEVEN

The Diary

Pete was waking up from his nap, slowly realizing where he was. He had snoozed after lunch. He looked at his watch, surprised that he had slept more than an hour. His mind played with the realization that he didn't have to do anything. He had no deadline, no meetings, no dates, nothing that he had to rush out and buy. He just let his father's old armchair continue to embrace him, and he let his mind wander. He was looking into the kitchen and could see the sink and the window above it. He had always thought windows above sinks were there so mothers could keep an eye on their kids, but Brindle told him that before indoor plumbing, it was the practice to throw dirty dishwater out the window.

As Pete thought about it, his eyes cast down to the drawers, to the bottom drawer. He realized as he stared at the face of the drawer that it was about 12 inches deep, but when he had opened it earlier, it was only about six inches deep inside. Maybe it was deeper than he thought. Could there be a false bottom to the drawer? He slowly pushed himself up and shook the last of the fuzziness of his nap from his head. He opened the drawer and removed its contents. It was then that he noticed a hole about the size of an index finger near the back of the drawer. He put his finger in and pulled. The "bottom" of the drawer came away easily, and underneath was a cedar box. Pete knew immediately what it was. It was a manuscript box for holding journals, book drafts, and legal documents so they could be transported undamaged. He gently removed the box from the drawer and returned to the chair in the other room. He sat with it on his lap. He wondered if it would just be paper, maybe blank paper. But he doubted it. Why would you hide plain paper? He figured it was just something his mother didn't want anyone, including his father, to see. He lifted the lid and stared at a blank piece of old cardboard. Printed on it were these words: *The Cabin.* When he removed it, he saw something from his childhood. First was the compass from old Murph with "Find your way" still clearly inscribed on the back. Second was his mother's diary in her wonderful script handwriting—a window to her heart.

He looked around like he wanted to share this discovery with everyone there, but then he remembered that he was alone. Pete looked at the writing, and a warm tear formed in his eye. He began to read.

July 2, 1941

Dear Diary,

We are at the cabin again. It is always such a delight despite the lack of conveniences. The weather is perfect; there is no smell of pulp mills, like Bellingham. Just fresh trees, wild flowers, and damp grass morning and evening. Charles has relaxed a bit already. It is such a peaceful place; the peacefulness is even more telling because of what is going on in the world. It seems everything is changing. The war in Europe keeps getting worse. Charles says it is only the English Channel and Winston Churchill that is keeping England from defeat. Charles says it is only a matter of time before we will be at war, too. It is hard to believe I may be bringing a baby into a world at war. I pray it will all be over and there will be no wars when my child is grown. Maybe it will be a girl.

I haven't told Charles yet, it is early, but there is no doubt in my mind he will want a boy. Men always do. It is a woman's curse to bear a child in pain and then have them die in a war in a foreign place, a victim of other men's evil nature. Even if only half of what they say is true, "the little German" could not be more evil. Charles says he believes the rumors are true about what he is doing to the Jews.

Charles went to the river to fish. I read my Bible and prayed for the world and my baby whose life I am beginning to feel within me. I even prayed for Roosevelt, but I would never tell Charles. I hope having a child will make him a gentler man. He is good to me in his own way, but it is hard for him to let others know he has hurts, too. Men are such fools in that way! The oven is about right for baking the biscuits now, so I will be going. I'm glad Grandma Graham taught me how to cook on a wood stove all those times when we rode the ferry and visited her farm on Orcas Island when I was a young girl, or else we would be eating a lot of burnt things. Until next time.

July 3, 1941

Charles and I were intimate last night. He was more patient and less hurried; it was better for both of us. Afterward we just lay there. He stroked my hair and cheek, staring into my eyes until he tired and drifted into a peaceful sleep. This morning he got up before daylight and stoked the fire in the stove and came back to bed, and he whispered love to me. I decided it was a good time to tell him I was pregnant. His first thought, bless his heart, was if our baby could be hurt by our activity the night before. I assured him he needn't worry, but we would probably not be having many nights like that again until after the baby comes. I began kissing him gently, then more passionately, and he simply followed me into another moment of marital bliss. The baby will be fine. Until later.

July 4, 1941

We thought about making the trip to Prichard or Kellogg for the 4th of July celebrations, but we will have such a long drive back to Bellingham that we decided to enjoy ourselves here. Charles had brought a box of sparklers, and we stood on the porch and waved them around and yelled. We probably scared the animals in the woods half to death. It was a warm night, and we sat on the porch and cuddled. Charles kept touching my stomach, but I assured him there was nothing to feel. Silly man started talking to our baby. Later, we came inside and sat by the fire and drank tea.

Charles told me of his grandfather coming by himself from Scotland when he was 12 and traveling by train to Bellingham. He said when our son (notice he has decided it's a boy) is older, he would take him back to Scotland to see his ancestral home. (Maybe she won't want to go!) Until later.

July 5, 1941

This is our last full day here, and the weather is beautiful. I packed a picnic basket, and we had a picnic just below Steamboat Rock. The rock does look like the back of a boat. Charles stopped and fished at a few places on the way back but didn't catch anything. But he was not upset. In fact, he thought it was kind of funny. "A big, smart man, not able to trick a few dumb fish," he said. Ever since I told him of the baby, he has been in the lightest mood I've seen him in since we became engaged. I hope it continues in him. We leave early tomorrow, so I probably won't write again this trip. It has been a wonderful time. Charles says we will have to return with our "son" in the future. Until I return, blessed cabin sanctuary.

Peter folded the crisp paper, gently laid it beside the box, and carefully lifted out the next one. He thought about what it must have been like for her, bringing a baby into the world during the war. The country was in the war by the time of his birth. Pearl Harbor was in December 1941, and he was born in February 1942. He wondered if his mother was disappointed that he was not a girl. She never showed it or mentioned it. He had never felt second place with her. Those must have been scary times. He was embarrassed reading of his parents' sex life. It was strange to see his parents as lovers, not just parents, and his father's joy and anticipation of having a son surprised him.

His father had been exempt from the draft because the government wanted newspapers to publish the news of their victories and propaganda to push support for the war. The newsreels were really popular, but in truth, people devoured every bit of news they could, trying to figure out how it applied to their sons or husbands. Pete knew his mother had been a Red Cross volunteer and also helped train nurses who volunteered as Army nurses. World War II was a global effort to stop an evil tide, but Vietnam was about misunderstanding history, the fear of communism's spread, and misplaced power. There would be no good end to this war. He decided to wait on the second sheet and not try to absorb it all at once. Besides, he didn't know what kind of thing would be there.

Pete stepped out onto the porch with his coffee mug in one hand and the box in the other. "What is it about nature that sooths your soul?" he asked himself. "It's more than the lack of human hustle and busyness. Everywhere you look there is something simply living—trees, leaves, berries, bugs, and, of course, the animals of the forest and the great birds of the air, simply being, living. People have plans and schedules; nature has itself, seasons, and life."

For some reason, he thought of the story of Jacob in the Bible, a man who was a great schemer until he wrestled with God who blessed him and gave him a new name, Israel. It means one who wrestled with God.[6] He remembered how Jacob had limped away from the encounter. "Is that what I'm doing, wrestling with God by turning cynical and mouthing denials every chance I get?" His last sip of coffee was cold. He glanced at the sky with its threatening, dark clouds and went back inside.

The second sheet of paper in the box was a different color, not from aging but from the tint of color in the paper. Pete guessed it was originally beige, and it was heavier and a better quality. He opened it gently and was careful not to tear the folds. The handwriting was his mother's same beautiful script. He held it in his hand, not yet focusing on what it said. "It has to be at least nine years after she wrote the other ones," he realized. "With gas rationing, they would not have been able to come to the cabin during the war. Once they came back, I was eight years old," he thought to himself.

July 21, 1950

We are finally back at our cabin sanctuary, and the world has been turned inside out since our last visit. We now have what they call "atomic bombs," and they are the most hideous weapon ever devised. One bomb can destroy an entire city. Wars now are not just fought between soldiers alone. They now kill thousands of women and children also. I fear for Peter's future, everyone's future. But we will continue to have babies as an act of faith. He is the best thing to come from these war years.

I'm pregnant again! Peter is eight. We wanted a child earlier and almost did, but I had a miscarriage. They tell me it was a girl. Margaret would have been her name. I feel stronger this time, but I haven't told Charles yet. He was so devastated when we lost Margaret that he went into a deep, dark fog and wasn't himself for months. If I hadn't had Peter to keep my attention, I don't know what I would have done.

Spring rains turned everything green this year, and I understand it was a difficult winter out here. The animals seem to be rejoicing. We saw several doe and fawn on our way up by the river. We even saw two otters playing in the water from the bridge at Enaville. They are such clowns! Peter is like the animals, running and prancing, chattering about fish and deer, birds, and trees. He saw an osprey in flight yesterday, and I never thought we would hear the end of it. I get exhausted just watching him run about. He is always exploring or whittling with the pocket knife Charles gave him for his birthday. He thinks of it as a "rite of passage" into manhood. It is such a joy to be here. The "men" are fishing and should be back soon, so I'd better prepare their lunch. Charles wanted to bring electricity to the cabin to make it easier on me, but I told him no. Sometimes, simpler is better. Until later.

July 22, 1950

Charles talked last night about Senator Margaret Chase Smith, a freshman senator who attacked Senator McCarthy without mentioning his name. Charles says she is being attacked by McCarthy's people, but in the end he thinks she will win if she can endure. She and some other senators made a Declaration of Conscience, and she even made an allusion to the Bible by saying her party should not ride the Four Horsemen of Calumny—Fear, Ignorance, Bigotry, and Smear. She must be a very courageous woman, and I intend to pray regularly for her and her protection from the likes of Joe McCarthy. I knew bullies like him when I was a girl, and they destroy everything around them.

Charles and Pete came home with five nice brook trout yesterday, and we fried them up for dinner. I boiled some carrots and potatoes, and with the homemade bread, it was a feast! I make a loaf every other day. After we cleaned things up, we sat on the porch; Peter whittled, I knitted what will be the baby's blanket but told Charles it's going to be a scarf. He's reading a biography of Woodrow Wilson and keeps muttering how you can never trust the government and how important a free press is to the country. It's close to work, but he's still spending a lot of time with Peter, and the two of them are a joy to watch. Until later.

July 24, 1950

I didn't write yesterday because we left early and went to Coeur d'Alene and got back late. It was the annual powwow of all the Indians in the region. The Spokane, Kootenai, Nez Pierce, and others I can't remember. There was traditional dancing, games, and exhibits. I didn't think Peter would ever be able to put his eyes back in his head! The costumes were beautiful, and there was an actual wedding in the afternoon, and the bride was absolutely gorgeous in her traditional garb. It was as fine as any wedding dress I have ever seen. I bought some beads for a bracelet or something, and Peter got a small drum made of deer hide, which we forbid him to play in the car. He is out prancing around in the woods beating on it now. Charles is getting some peaceful fishing without a little boy's tangled line.

Me, I'm writing my silly thoughts, and then I'm going to chop some chicken and get it ready to fry for dinner. Charles bought two chickens from a farmer near Prichard; he already plucked and cleaned them, so all I have to do is chop, scrub, and bread them. Until later.

July 25, 1950

Charles picked up a newspaper when we were in Coeur d'Alene, and he read the most amazing thing. There's going to be an award for any singer who sells a million records, and it will be a "golden record." Why, if it was me, I would never want to play my golden record because it might scrape some of the gold off! It's the strangest thing. Charles wants to know why I'm making such a large scarf. "Is it for Johnny Weissmuller?" he asked me. It isn't for Esther Williams, I told him. We both laughed at ourselves. I can't believe it! Charles said General MacArthur has asked permission to use atomic weapons in Korea. I pray it will not happen. It will only mean death to a lot of innocent women and children who have nothing to do with this war. Why do we women always pay for the arrogance of men? Why can't we follow the Lord's teaching, "Blessed are the peacemakers, for they will be called 'Children of God.'" Until later.

July 26, 1950

This is our last full day here. Charles says we have to leave tomorrow. At least we don't have to prepare the cabin for winter. Brindle will do that for us. He is such a good man. It is too bad his wife died so young. Peter and Charles are making the most of this last day. They got up early and headed up the North Fork. Charles said they would try two or three spots, depending on the fish, and not to expect them until after lunch. I sent them with snacks but have prepared a good lunch with cantaloupe we picked up in Coeur d'Alene and some wild blackberries I found by the creek. It's funny, I don't remember any blackberries being at this spot before. Nature has its own way with things, I guess. Until the next visit.

Peter folded up the last paper, gently placed it back in the box, and went inside. He put the box back in the drawer and walked back outside. He looked toward the large cluster of blackberry vines. The sky was even darker now, and he smelled rain. He started to cry.

CHAPTER TWELVE

Dreams

"Right here is where we'll put our house, Em, with the kitchen and living room downstairs, our bedroom upstairs, and all of them looking over the river. We'll live out our last days here watching the sun rise up canyon and set down canyon. The seasons will change before us. On snowy days, we'll curl up in front of the wood stove and watch the flakes come down. I'm gonna put a salt lick on that grassy knoll, just below the willows, right over there, and we can watch the deer when they come out to the lick."

Charlie Reed looked at his wife of 35 years, and the many lines on his face signaled nothing but joy. They were in love the moment they first saw one another on the first day of high school in Wallace, Idaho. Charlie's family was new to town. His dad had just been hired as a pipeman for one of the mines. They went up the front steps of the school near one another as complete strangers and came down the same steps at the end of the school day destined to be partners for life. Other people thought it was such a strange thing, but to Charlie and Emma, they couldn't imagine it any other way. The last day of their senior year, they walked to the courthouse as soon as school was out and nervously stood before the justice of the peace, ready for marital bliss. They celebrated their high school graduation and honeymoon with a weekend in Coeur d'Alene at a cheap motel on Sherman Avenue. They took walks through the park by the lake and ate dinners at the Topper Drive-In. Their union was sealed by indulging in deep-fried onion rings and the gentle innocence of first discoveries.

Emma stood with her arm around Charlie's waist. "He's a solid man in more ways than one, and I love him more than ever." She could feel the tall grass, wet against her jeans as she watched the rapids of the Clark Fork River dance before their future home site. Across the way, an osprey circled its nest, which crested a snag where the river began its turn to the west. Emma breathed deeply and took in the terraced forest of rich, deep green beyond, stretching upward until it met the sky. "I want to keep this moment forever. I wouldn't care if there never was a house if I could stand here with you and look at all this beauty, listen to the river, and watch it change in the spring and be framed in snow in the winter. Charlie, this is as close to heaven as we'll ever get."

"Well, it might be a bit cold standing here in the middle of winter with no house. Besides, my long johns are still hanging on the back porch."

He made her smile as he always did. Suddenly, she slapped him on the butt and ran toward the river. Charlie followed, but he could no longer run. He was a strong man, although he looked older than his 53 years. Too many years in the mines holding a drilling rig hour after hour had taken their toll on his back and legs. As much as he would like to build this house himself, he knew it was unlikely he would do more than the small stuff. Some days after Charlie's shift, Emma would rub liniment oil on him for as much as an hour. Charlie Reed's body told him every day that it was running out of patience, but he kept pushing it, hoping for a few more dollars, just enough to build this house and settle in before he was another mine cripple, broken and bent, or a walking corpse with silicosis from too many years breathing quartz dust.

Emma was trying to skip rocks but wasn't having much luck. The river was turbulent with spring runoff. She thought it looked like dark chocolate churning its way down the canyon, and it seemed to eat the rocks before they had a chance to skip the surface. "I never was any good at this," she said in frustration.

"You'd better find yourself some flat water if you wanna take up this sport, and we'd better be heading back. There's a union meeting tonight, and I don't want to miss it."

"What's so special about this one? Tag Reynolds going to tell about his latest visit to the cathouse?"

"Em, how you talk," Charlie said with a smile. "No, it's about some safety report and violations that the company has ignored, even recommendations from their own safety guy. He's a good man, but he can only do so much. We'll see whether they're bad enough to have a protest strike over it."

"The last thing any of us needs is a strike. The last one put some folks under. And if you strike, we'll never catch up and build this house. We can count on spending our days looking at the big K on the brown hills of Kellogg."

"We're not gonna strike. It's just the union scratchin' and hollerin' like dogs who want to look mean but don't have no fight in 'em. Nobody's got any heart for a strike after the last one. And Tag Reynolds probably couldn't find his way to the cathouse in the middle of the day, let alone stone drunk in the black of night."

"Charlie Reed, I do believe you're all fired up. Then how did he become union steward?"

"Politics, Honey. Dirty money, union politics, out-of-state money."

Emma stood next to the old red pickup that she knew had too many miles. Charlie started it up and took a last long look at the brown river. Emma was one of those people who tried to plant moments in her mind so the pictures could be reviewed when needed. She knew life could hit you like a freight train while you were bent over to smell the daisies, so you'd better hold the good moments tightly. As a child, she had often found herself seeking the spots where the sun would touch the notch in the valley where the town of Wallace had sprung up. She wanted to hold the sun's warmth for those frigid, dark, winter days and months when the sun was only a memory because the hills were too high and the sun too low, only a hope for the future. You just hoped the shadows didn't remain long. There was another kind of shadow, she knew, in the valley. If your man was a logger or a miner, he might go off to work just like any other day and come back a cripple or not at all. The longer he kept at it, the more likely the outcome would not be good. She looked at Charlie and closed her eyes.

Emma got into the cab and slid over until her leg touched Charlie's. She thought about a strike. "I hope you're right, Charlie. No strike. I sure hope you're right." She could see the osprey taking flight toward the horizon and disappearing behind a stand of tamarack not yet green after their dormant winter brown. She closed her eyes and rested her cheek on Charlie's shoulder. She could see the river churning in her mind's eye, the osprey seeming motionless, and her baby lying face down in the crib, no sound, no color, no life. She ground her teeth and breathed deeply as if she were trying to breathe for little Jacob. But Jacob would never breathe again, and she felt the weight of the scars on her heart as the old truck skidded on the shoulder and went up onto the highway.

CHAPTER THIRTEEN

By the Numbers

Greg heard the buzzer on his desk at the Sunshine Mine office and knew his boss wanted him again. He grimaced as he lifted the papers off his desk, stood up, and moved toward the door. For a second, his mind went to the memory of training his dog, Agustin (Gus for short), and he thought he now knew how Gus must have felt every time he blew his training whistle.

"Yes sir, Mr. Nims," the young intern from the University of Montana said respectfully, although he wanted with all his being to scream at the balding man behind the desk. Greg Powell wondered why he had ever left the family ranch outside of Missoula. He thought industrial management would be an exciting field, but now he found himself working for a man who would have been more comfortable with slaves than employees of the free enterprise system. Nims never looked up or spoke as Greg placed the report on the top right-hand corner of the desk with the pages facing Nims. He was careful not to let either the top of the page or the right edge extend over the desk's edge. He had made that mistake once, and he seriously wondered at the time whether he would live to tell about the absurdity of it. He would have left that day, but he needed this internship so he could graduate and move on to a real job with a normal boss. As he closed the door behind him, he wondered, not for the first time, if his internship was just a bad dream.

Nims never heard the young intern leave, nor did he care if he came or went. He had assigned Greg Powell the number −10. He assigned everyone and everything a number. The range was −10 to 10. There was no one involved in the mining operation that he gave more than a 7. His eyes were dry from not blinking, and he felt a slight cramp in his left leg, the one he broke trying to please his wife by taking ski lessons. He knew he couldn't move, yet things appeared to sway before his eyes like a seductive dancer, slowly, without sound, while rhythmic vibrations seemed to reach for him. The light from the western window made it shine on the left side of the curve and at the same time caused a shadow inside the circle. How can it appear to be light and dark at the same time? To Nims, the ordinary play of light and shadow made it all the more mysterious. "There are ancient mysteries waiting to be mined by the inquiring mind," he thought to himself and chuckled.

A cloud must have moved across the sky because the light changed in Orville Nims's office, and the solid silver number six paperweight sitting on his desk ceased to shine as brightly as it had a moment before, and he felt like a child whose toy had suddenly been taken away. But six was his favorite number, and the solid numeral on his desk was one of his most cherished possessions. If there ever was a fire in the building, Nims knew what he would grab first, not because it was solid silver and weighed one pound exactly but because Orville Nims was in love. He knew a psychiatrist would wonder if he was obsessed or addicted. But such evaluations were too simplistic and failed to understand the importance of numbers to Orville Nims. Each night he would gently say good night to the paperweight before locking it in his safe.

His father had recognized his son's intelligence at an early age and determined that his son would follow in the family tradition of mining. He would make sure he became a mining engineer and eventually operated or, better yet, owned a productive mine. Nims's grandfather had come out of the coal mines of West Virginia and taught himself through a correspondence course. But no one in the Nims family would ever do the underground work again. They would supervise others who did. So it was no surprise when young Orville Nims entered Georgia Tech, graduated with honors in civil engineering, and then went on to the Colorado School of Mines. He cared little for engineering and even less for mining. Orville had only one love— numbers. He saw the world only in terms of numbers. They were important because you could calibrate, divide, and measure anything with numbers. Money, men, time, energy, space—everything was discussed, evaluated, and measured in the language of numbers. But unlike those who love mathematics and play with theoretical equations, Nims was obsessed with the numbers themselves.

Behind his desk was an ancient Aramaic scroll with numbers carved into a goatskin. Each numeral was repeated 10 times. Nims would occasionally rise from his desk, lock the door to his office, and let his fingers trace the delicate cuttings in the animal hide. He would talk to his "spunky 3s" and whisper to his "plump 8s." But with 6s and 9s, he was silent and allowed his fingers to very gently caress their gentle curves. He sometimes laughed at himself when he thought about it all. Here was the supervisor of the richest silver mine in America producing tons of precious ore daily. Men bent their backs, breathed dirt, and lost an eye from a flying quartz chip or a hand in an errant pulley wheel, all for silver. They brought him production reports, and he gave speeches at the Chamber of Commerce and wrote in the company newsletter about how well they were all doing. But in reality, he cared little for any of it. He didn't care if it was men, payroll, production, or profit, he only wanted to see the numbers. The mine's owners in New York cared about production numbers, labor costs, the price of silver, and profit, so at their meeting in Coeur d'Alene this week, he would show it all to them, but they wouldn't appreciate the beauty of the numbers alone. He would endure their meeting, and then he would return here, lock his door, and admire his paperweight.

CHAPTER FOURTEEN

Body Snatchers

DJ had arranged with his friend at the morgue to call as soon as a homeless "John Doe" arrived and to not let anyone freeze him or touch him. He needed a recently deceased body that he could turn over to the Hyde Brothers without any suspicion. Cecil had just called, and even though DJ was just settling in with pizza, beer, and Betsy, he knew he needed to go now. Another opportunity could be a long time away.

"I'm sorry, I have to go," he said tentatively as he hung up the phone.

"But DJ, we just got the pizza, and the movie comes on in five minutes. Did something happen to your folks, your dad?"

"No, it's nothing like that. You know how I told you I had a plan to catch the people who were stealing credit cards from dead people and then alert the police? Well, that call starts the whole plan, and I have to go now or it won't work." DJ looked both saddened and excited, and Betsy understood the saddened part. She knew he hated to disappoint anyone, especially her, and she loved him for it. But the excited part awoke something in her she was not expecting; she was not going to miss out.

"I'll go with you and help," she blurted out.

"No, it might be dangerous. No, it won't be dangerous; it just might be stupid." He looked at Betsy and then at his shoes. "Let's go! Grab the pizza!"

"Is this your stupid body-snatch idea?" Betsy asked as they ran down the stairs, their shoes echoing on the metal steps.

"Yep," DJ said as he turned on the ignition in the small Datsun. They both kept saying "I can't believe we're doing this" all the way to the loading dock of the Seattle morgue. DJ thought "dock" was a strange name when the cargo was always a stiff. It wasn't like they were delivering apples or salmon or some other important item. The building was two stories with windows that had wire running through them. It made the place look like a prison. It was gray and brick with some moss-covered parts of the north wall where water seeped from leaky gutters, not the kind of place one usually takes his girlfriend for a date. *Hey, you want to go out for pizza and a trip to the morgue?* he tried out in his mind. "You okay?" he said out loud as he turned off the lights.

"You asking me or you?" Betsy said with a smile.

They tiptoed up the concrete steps and knocked twice on the back door, but no one came. DJ began to wonder why. Had something gone wrong? Where was Cecil? Suddenly, the door opened. DJ was so startled that he jumped back from the door.

"Who's she?" came a voice from inside as Betsy grabbed DJ's hand and pulled him through the door. She said, "I'm the Chief of Undercover Operations. Now where's our body?"

"Shh! Not so loud. He's over here. When you get to wherever you're going, and I don't want to know where that is, get rid of the sheet. It has the morgue's stamp on it, and it can be traced back to here and to me."

"All right, we got it. Let's get him in the car."

Just as the three of them stepped onto the dock, headlights from a car swung into the loading area but just as quickly turned away. They stood in the darkness holding their breath with the heavy body sagging between them.

"Cecil, you could have gotten us a shorter guy. He won't fit in my trunk."

"You think the morgue is a pick-out-your-body buffet? You're lucky I got one at all and that everyone else is out of town at a coroners' convention. Otherwise, I couldn't have helped you at all."

"Coroners' convention. Now that sounds like a lively get-together," Betsy said, smiling.

They decided the least obtrusive way to haul their "client" was to sit him up in the back seat and make it look like he was a passenger. After lifting, pushing, and pulling the uncooperative subject, they finally got him into the car.

"Thanks, Cecil. You're doing a good thing here."

"Just don't breathe a word of this to anyone, ever, even if it all works out, which I'm sure it won't. No late-night storytelling."

"Now I know what they mean by dead weight," Betsy said. "He weighs more than my Aunt Clarice does alive, and she's twice his size."

"I'm not sure I ever want to meet your aunt," DJ said as they buckled up.

As they pulled away, DJ looked in the rearview mirror and saw Cecil sitting on the steps shaking his head in the universal pose of, "I can't believe I did what I just did."

"I'm going to have to stop somewhere and call Mrs. Crownherst so she can be ready," DJ informed Betsy. He pulled up to a 7-11 a few minutes later. "Do you want anything while we're here?"

"Yeah, get me a Coke so I can wash down some of this cold pizza. You know it's weird. I've never eaten with a dead man before."

"Don't worry. I don't think he'll snatch any of it. Do you want anything, 'Uncle Matthew'?" DJ said with a grin and got out of the car.

Mrs. Crownherst was brushing her hair as she did every night with her pearl, inlaid brush. She gently stroked her thick, lavish hair that young men used to want to touch and other women envied. It was white now, but she liked to think of it as silver. She couldn't believe her own excitement. She was going to help capture some thieves, squash a scam, fight evil, and uphold the good, and all in her own house. She would be like Miss Marple and solve a crime, catch the bad guys. She had read all the Miss Marple books and even watched a few of the movies based on them, and she knew she was up to the task. She took her opal brooch that Phillip, her late husband, had given her for their 50th wedding anniversary. She held it in her bony fingers, her knuckles smooth and swollen from arthritis, and gently opened the locket and looked at his picture. She looked admiringly at the photo. "You were a good man overall, Phillip, but you had some very bad habits."

Just as she was slipping off her gold-colored slippers, the phone on the bureau rang. She picked it up and heard the nice young man's voice. If she had ever had a son, she would have wanted him to be like, what was his name? David, no Darcy—DJ for short. He was so enthusiastic and knowledgeable about music and had spent an hour listening to her music and about her time in New Orleans with the great Louis Armstrong. "That young man knows his jazz," she thought to herself.

"This is it," the voice on the other end said, and she smiled.

"Roger that," she said, as she admired herself in the mirror and placed the phone back on its carriage. She went to the oak dresser, pulled out the beige pajamas she had bought for the occasion, and retrieved Phillip's robe from his closet. She thought about taking them downstairs to his lounge chair but decided to wait until DJ arrived with "Matthew." "It was a good thing you died in New Zealand on one of your archaeological digs and not here so there was no chance of accidentally using the same funeral home," she mentioned to her dead husband's picture. She had left him in New Zealand. She knew Phillip liked it there, or at least he said he did. He died there while "coddling" a young archaeology intern. Coddling is what he liked to call it. The intern said Phillip loved New Zealand. Mrs. Crownherst wished her better luck in the future and withheld the urge to tell her to keep to men her own age. She figured her husband may have died happy. She hoped so.

When DJ appeared at her door the first time, she thought he was lost. He looked lost. She was on alert. He didn't know it, but she had her hand on a no. 9 golf club behind the door. She was flexing her fingers and tightening her grip as he spoke. But when he asked her if it was Beethoven's "Hallelujah Chorus" he was hearing from within and then agreed with her assessment of Beethoven's version over Handel's, she just knew she should let him in although she had no intention of letting him use her house for an "event." But she knew such a cultured man would be safe.

However, when he told her why he had come to her house, she was absolutely delighted. "Oh my, won't the girls at the country club be surprised at what I am about to do." She stared at her image in the mirror, and the years raced through her mind as she looked at her face—the lines and wrinkles. Some years had been hard, but if you're open to it, life can always bring joyful surprises. "As Phillip used to say, 'This one is a humdinger,'" she said to herself.

And now, DJ finally had a dead body, and the plan was in motion. Betsy sat in the car waiting for DJ to return with her Coke. The smell of pepperoni pizza permeated the small space, and she wondered if anyone would ever believe her if she told them she helped steal a dead body. It just didn't fit her character. Betsy was noticing the graphics on a red neon beer sign in the 7-11 window, tracing them in her mind as a car pulled alongside and parked. Betsy glanced over and froze, holding her piece of pizza midair. It was a police car. Her heart began to race. She didn't dare look back at "Matthew" for fear it would draw the policeman's attention. The policeman who was driving got out with his back to "Matthew" and Betsy. He yanked up his utility belt, stepped up onto the sidewalk, stretched his arms, and headed for the front door of the 7-11. Betsy didn't want to look, but she had to know if there was another policeman and if he was watching her. She glanced over, and there was another policeman, but he had a clipboard in front of him. He was paying no attention to them at all. She sighed and directed her stare to the front door of the store.

"Come on, DJ, hurry up!" The minutes passed as Betsy watched the doors. Suddenly, they swung open, and out stepped the first cop with two steaming cups of coffee and a bag of something, probably donuts. He went to the passenger side of his patrol car and passed both coffees through the window. When he stepped around the car, he looked over at Betsy, and their eyes met. She smiled. He smiled, too, but he tilted his head so he could see the person in the back seat. He signaled her to put down the window, and as she did, her heart traveled quickly to her esophagus. Thousands of scenarios raced through her mind, but they all ended at the King County Jail.

"Excuse me, Miss, but your passenger seems to be wasted. Is he okay?"

Betsy gulped and thought, *Oh good, I'm still breathing.* "Yes. Dad has a real problem. He's signed up to enter a treatment facility next week. I think he thought this was his last hurrah, but we'll soon have him in bed and under careful watch until he's committed."

"You sure he doesn't need medical attention right now? He looks pretty bad. He looks like he needs a medical detox."

"No!" Betsy said, a little too emphatically. We've been through this before, Officer, and as unpleasant as it is, he will be fine by noon tomorrow."

"Well, if you say so, but I would keep an eye on him tonight if I were you. He doesn't look like he has much life in him. Good night, Miss."

Betsy forced a weak smile as the officer got into his patrol car. Just as the police officers pulled out, DJ emerged from the store with her drink and what looked like a coffee. She wasn't sure if her blood was circulating, but she was sure that "Dad" looked better right now than she did. "What took you so long? I just held off the entire Seattle police force."

"I had to use the restroom, and I had to wait. Did they say anything?"

"He said that 'Dad' looked like he needed medical attention since he was so wasted, but I assured him that we knew what we were doing, which is a big enough lie to bolt the Pearly Gates against me forever."

"Well, if he had suspected anything, he would have checked 'Matthew' out, and he didn't."

While DJ was assuring her, Betsy turned around to see how "Dad" was doing and noticed that the seal from the morgue was partially exposed to full view. Evidently, the policeman couldn't see it through the glare on the glass, and she wished her Coke was a beer or maybe even a whiskey. "You talked to Mrs. Crownherst?"

DJ nodded as he passed through an intersection, carefully watching the traffic.

"What did she say when you told her we were coming, DJ?"

"Roger that."

After they reached Mrs. Crownherst's, they managed to half-carry, half-drag "Matthew" inside with the help of the butler. They needed to put him in the pajamas and robe. When DJ started to remove the sheet, Betsy realized for the first time that "Matthew" was naked. "Oh my gosh! I can't look." She turned away and stepped into the adjoining parlor.

"Don't worry, Betsy, I'll do it."

"No, let me," Mrs. Crownherst said as she stepped in front of DJ with the packaged pajamas. "I haven't been this close to a naked man in years." She deftly pulled the rest of the sheet off and pushed it into DJ's arms.

"My, my, he certainly is a fully equipped gentleman." She put the pajamas on him, and DJ held him as she put on the robe. "There. He looks splendid, but there is one more thing needed," and Mrs. Crownherst disappeared into the next room. She returned soon with a glass of bourbon and a cigar. She took a sip and set it on the table. "Who wants to do the honors on the cigar? It's one of the illegals from Cuba. My Phillip loved them."

168

"I'm game," DJ said as he reached for the cigar, wondering if it would be better than a cigarette. Mrs. Crownherst reached into her robe, pulled out a gold Zippo lighter, and lit the cigar. She had already clipped the tip. DJ took a couple of drags and immediately started to feel lightheaded. "No more for me or I'll be too sick to go through with this."

Betsy came back into the den and reached for the cigar, but Mrs. Crownherst reached out and grabbed hold of her wrist.

"You're not pregnant, are you, Dear?"

"No, not at all."

"Well, then help yourself." Betsy discovered she liked the mellow taste of the cigar. It had a richness that cigarettes didn't have, which was only one of the reasons she didn't smoke. But this was more like drinking wine instead of lemonade. She sat down and took a few more puffs.

"That should be good enough, Dear. Put it in the tray here, and here's Phillip's wallet with all the credit cards you gave me. How did you get cards in the name of a dead man? I mean, a fake dead man?"

"Betsy arranged that. It wasn't easy, but because the card company and banks want to stop these thefts, and we assured them we could, well, they gave us the cards. I guess it's time to phone the Hyde Brothers."

"There is one little thing you have forgotten, but I took care of it," Mrs. Crownherst informed them. "When a person dies at home, the police are summoned to make sure there has been no foul play. Well, my nephew is a policeman, and he said he would take care of it. I'm just to call him when I'm ready so he can convince the funeral home that all is legitimate."

"You told a policeman what we're doing?"

"Trust me, it's all right." Mrs. Crownherst turned, picked up the phone, and dialed. "Hello. Yes, Michael, it's me, and now is the time. All right, Dear, see you soon."

"He said he would be here in 10 minutes, so I guess you can call the Hyde Brothers."

Ten long minutes later, a police car pulled up in front of the Crownherst home and parked at 2 o'clock in the circular driveway. Mrs. Crownherst opened the door, and in stepped the policeman from the 7-11. Betsy and DJ froze. He hugged his aunt and turned to the two of them. "I thought I might see you two again when I saw you at the 7-11."

"You knew then what we were up to?"

"Well, I figured not too many people would be transporting stiffs, and besides, I could see the morgue's sheet under the blanket you had over him. I saw the stamp. Have you called the funeral home yet?"

"Yes, Michael. I called them right after I called you."

"When they get here, I will tell them they are free to remove the body, and I will leave. This is going to make some story someday." Betsy and DJ were just beginning to recover from their shock.

The Hyde Brothers were used to late-night calls, even though Prescott handled most of them. It seemed to them that most people preferred to die at night. They weren't sure it was actually true, but between the two of them, they were convinced it was true. Franklin thought it was because people knew they were dying and didn't want to face another day. Henry thought it was because they were full of food they couldn't digest. Of course, this only applied to people who knew they were dying, and it didn't count heart attacks, strokes, car crashes, and the like. The Hyde Brothers really didn't like to do accident victims since it could get messy. They liked calls like tonight's where an elderly man died peacefully at home. What could be better than that, especially a rich one? Normally, Percy Prescott and Harold would answer the call, but Henry Hyde had read an article about giving your employees unexpected perks and benefits, how it boosted morale and job performance. He had nagged Franklin to do something, and he finally agreed to give them one night off a month. Besides, it would reduce their payroll costs.

Tonight, Prescott and Harold were both off, and Henry had answered the call. On their way to the house, Henry said, "Do you think this old guy had any credit cards, Franklin?"

"It's hard to say. Being an old guy, he may not have been too receptive to this new credit card idea, although it's been around a while, almost 10 years since it started with gas companies. But now they can be used for anything. We'll have to wait and see, but this guy would have a big line of credit if he does have any cards. We'll just have to wait and find whatever we can."

"This must be it. Wow! Look at the size of this place. Look at that gazebo, Franklin. It's bigger than my house!"

Franklin saw a small, Japanese-made car in an off-driveway parking space as he drove the hearse up to the front door past the police car, which was no surprise to him. He went around to the rear of the hearse and laid a folded, extra-large sheet on the gurney. They rolled the gurney and pushed it to one side of the front door.

"The name's Scott, right?"

"Yep."

"Then I wonder why they have this big C on their front door."

"Maybe they never changed it when they bought the place."

"I tell you, something's fishy, Franklin. Rich people always want people to know who they are. I don't know, but I don't like it. Maybe we should just pass on this one and take the body and nothing else."

"Don't be so paranoid," Franklin said as he pushed the brass door button and smiled.

"You hear those chimes, Franklin? They sound like bells from a cathedral." The door opened, and a butler stood in the doorway.

"Yes? You must be the gentlemen from the funeral home. Please come in, and I will escort you to Mr. Scott, Mr. Robinson, and Ms. Jewel, who will give you any assistance you may need." In the power recliner, dressed in a black silk robe and beige silk pajamas, was "Matthew Burl Scott." His head was turned to one side, his jaw was slack, and his color was an ashen gray. A cigar sat in an ashtray next to a drink Franklin thought was bourbon. As they entered the room behind the butler, Franklin could see a woman he presumed was the housekeeper, Mr. Robinson, and a police officer who was just setting down a cup of coffee. The maid grabbed it before it could even settle on the table. When Henry saw the policeman, he reflectively stepped behind Franklin.

"Gentlemen," the officer said, "as you know, this is Mr. Scott. He was under doctor's care, heavily medicated, and just died normally. There is no foul play here, and you are free to take the body. I'll be leaving now, Mr. Robinson. Thanks for the coffee, and I am sorry for your loss."

Ignoring the policeman's words, Franklin walked toward "Dustin Robinson," took both his hands in his, and told him how sorry they were for his loss and that they would do all they could to see that his uncle was treated with respect and dignity. "Do you want to have more time with the deceased?" Franklin asked in a voice that could just as easily have said, "Would you like to drink your poison now or later?" with the same expression. The empathy was so artificial that DJ thought it might crack and fall on the floor.

DJ put on his most sorrowful face. "I've had my good times with Uncle Burl. You can take him now." With that, Henry turned and headed toward the front door to retrieve the gurney.

"You can come to our office tomorrow when we can finish making all the arrangements." When Henry returned with the gurney, Franklin said, "Maybe you all would like to step into the other room. This can sometimes be a little awkward, and it is best if your memories don't include these mundane moments. Nodding in agreement, DJ suggested to Ms. Jewel that she might want to return to the kitchen and see if there was any coffee left. DJ looked at "Mr. Scott," wiped one eye, and told Millbrook he wanted him to join him in the kitchen. As soon as they were out of sight, Henry started scanning the room for valuables, and Franklin began checking the pockets in the black robe.

"Psst, his wallet's here, and there's a bunch of cards. Let's get him out of here." With that, they carefully wrapped up their victim, placed him on the gurney, and rolled him to the front door. Franklin slipped the wallet into a compartment under the gurney that was supposed to carry the gurney's adjustment tools. As they reached the front door, Millbrook and DJ appeared, and Millbrook stood ready to open the door when all was ready.

"I'll come to your office tomorrow," DJ said, trying to sound sorrowful.

"Again, we are here to serve you, and please, if you can, call ahead. We are very busy, you know." Franklin turned toward Millbrook who was moving only his hand while standing at perfect attention. He pulled the door open and gave a slight bow and mournful look at "Mr. Scott" as they rolled him away. Unknown to the Hyde brothers, Mrs. Crownherst and Betsy had been peeking through a pass-through window the servants used and had seen Franklin take and hide the wallet.

After the Hydes were gone, they all gathered in the library. Just as they were about to confer with each other, the chimes rang out, and Millbrook sprinted to the door. He looked through the peephole. "It's the police," he said, smiling, as Mrs. Crownherst's nephew walked back into the house. Before anyone could say anything, Mrs. Crownherst turned to Jewel. "Do you think you could go to the kitchen and get the refreshments I have prepared for our little party, as long as you're the maid for the evening?"

"I'll help you," Millbrook said as he smiled at Jewel. She took his arm, and they skipped to the kitchen.

When they returned, including the police officer, DJ said, "I want to thank all of you for your part. Millbrook, I mean Mr. Arturo, this is Mrs. Crownherst's nephew, Michael, our diligent policeman, and this is Mrs. Arturo, our maid, Jewel. The Arturos are in charge of costuming for the drama department at Seattle University, and they graciously not only volunteered to supply us with costumes but to play the characters as well, and they did great."

After the light applause, Mrs. Crownherst turned to them all and said, "I want to thank you all for bringing some excitement into an old lady's boring life, and you all may come back anytime. In fact, I want to invite you all to my birthday party on June 30th, and DJ, bring your friend from the morgue who helped us all."

"I don't think we will be seeing my friend anywhere that this incident might be spoken of or even hinted at. By the way, I know I shouldn't ask this, but how old will you be on your birthday?"

"DJ, you never ask a woman her age," Betsy scolded him, and Jewel nodded in agreement.

They all looked at Mrs. Crownherst with a certain anticipation. She had an annoyed look that he would ask such a thing, but then she smiled. "Well, in 1910, I went down the Grand Canyon on the back of a smelly mule. That was before they built that big dam for all those people in Los Angeles to have electricity. It was a different river in those days, wild and free, but then so was I," she chuckled. "The mule didn't smell all that good, but he was sure-footed and got me down and back up alive or I wouldn't be here now. As to my age, I was an adult." She smiled broadly, unconsciously brushing her hand through her thick, white hair.

PART II

Fire!

For everything there is a season, and a time for every
matter under heaven:
a time to be born, and a time to die; . . .
a time to weep, and a time to laugh;
a time to mourn.

—Eccles. 3:1–2, 4

CHAPTER FIFTEEN

Sisterhood

The music was almost cloud-like, it blended so well with the rhythm of the room. It felt more like it was part of the air than something being introduced into the space. The lights were low, but the sky was getting brighter every day, and it was still light out even after 7:00 p.m. The sun sneaking through the New York skyscraper windows put a glaze on the entire room. Agnes had gathered with her colleagues, members of a secret sorority, listed nowhere with no office or letterhead. They had all fought in a field dominated by men and done well. They had endured insults, long hours, sacrifice of personal time, racial and sexual slurs, and even sexual assaults, but all of it was what bound them together. They were sisters. These women were more than survivors; they were victors, and they knew it. They came together each week to celebrate and encourage each other.

As Julio, their bartender friend, filled the last glass, they looked at one another, smiled, and gave their usual opening toast from Hemingway's *The Old Man and the Sea* with a slight modification. They shouted, "Man was not made for defeat. And neither were women!" Julio smiled like always and returned to the bar with his white towel over his arm and a slight dance in his step. While the women had no way of knowing, they sensed there were other women like them all across the country who held it together because they drew strength from each other. Some, like Beth, were committed feminists, but mostly they were just strong-willed and determined women, despite the odds.

There were seven of them. Agnes McDonnel was the acclaimed leader because of her demeanor and common sense but also because everyone just knew from the beginning that she was their leader. Crystal Long worked in the same building as Agnes. One day three years ago, Agnes had rescued Crystal from an emotional breakdown in the elevator and invited her for a drink after work. Kate was from a small town in Iowa and had gone to Vassar on a scholarship. She thought she wanted to be a teacher, but business became her passion, so she headed for New York City. Beth Wizard was born and raised in New York, in Harlem, and knew more places to eat than the Dining Club. Beth was a very attractive African American woman whose father was killed in a construction accident, and her mother raised her and her two brothers while working two jobs until the kids were old enough to help. She called herself the Black Wizard, and no one disagreed. Rosalyn, Donna, and Ruth finished out the group. They were all native to the East Coast. Rosalyn and Ruth were both divorcees. Donna and Crystal were the only married ones in the group. After they had been meeting for a month, Julio began reserving them a table. They treated him with respect, and he returned the favor. The group had been together six years.

"Have any of you seen *The Godfather*? It's great, and the men are so sexy."

"Rosalyn, they're all gangsters."

"I don't care; they're still hunks. Marlin Brando is the Godfather, and his mumbling voice is so sexy. I just want to hear him whisper in my ear."

"It's just a movie, and they are hunk actors or they couldn't play gangsters," Ruth inserted before taking another sip of wine.

"Did I tell you what Guy, the mail guy, did last week? Well, he brings in the mail . . ."

"Wait, Beth, you talking about the mailman or the courier?"

"Okay, sassy ladies, let me finish. It was the courier guy. You know, the Italian one with the gold chain and the Frankie Avalon haircut."

"Yeah, the one with the sticky eyes that make the typical leer look like a blessing from the Pope."

"That's him. Like I was saying . . ."

"Frankie Avalon? You're dating yourself, girl. Besides, Frankie just copied Elvis."

"No, Frankie had that dangling curl in front, and Elvis had his hair combed back more."

"No, it's the other way around. Elvis's curl is in front, and Frankie combs it all to the back."

"Will y'all shut up and let me tell my story?"

Agnes was the unofficial arbitrator of all disputes within the group, and all eyes turned to her. She took a sip from her wine glass, glanced at the ceiling as if she were weighing some great matter in the tradition of Solomon. Then she nodded for Beth to continue. Crystal began staring at a nail on her left hand.

"So, Guy comes in and drops off . . ."

"His name is Guy?" the sextet queried in perfect unison.

"Damn it! You are the most impolite bunch of women I've ever seen! How did you get to where you are being like that?"

"We're talented, hardworking, beautiful, and smarter than men," they whispered and clicked their glasses together. Julio just smiled from behind the bar.

"Granted, but when he's done delivering to the building, he comes back to my office. 'You forget something?' I ask. He says to me, 'I just stopped by to say how beautiful you are, and I thought we should spend some time together, say, this weekend. My brother's got a place on the Jersey Shore, and he lets me use it anytime I want. Bet you and I could have some real fun together.'"

"What did you say?" Donna, Kate, and Rosalyn all asked together. "Oh, this should be good," and the glasses clinked again. Julio could not help but show his interest.

"That's a bet you'll lose," I say to him. "But you are right about one thing. I am beautiful. This brought a round of laughs, giggles, and the quiet pause of expectation. "But I've got no interest in going to some beach shack full of sand and fleas with some man I don't know, don't want to know, and don't care if I ever see again."

"Beth, you shouldn't have been so subtle." By now they were trying not to spill drinks as they were laughing so hard.

"What'd he say?"

"All I can say is that some men are missing large sections of their brains, if they have one at all. Guy is the number one specimen for the species, for sure. If he were to think out loud, there would be nothing but silence. He says to me, 'I thought you might be hesitant at first, but I know you want to go with me.' I think to myself, 'Is this a white man's disease, or are all men this dumb?'"

"All men!" the sextet in practiced unison responded and then bathed themselves in laughter, clicking their glasses of wine sloppily.

"Look, jerk," I say to him. "I got two brothers, each weighing more than 300 pounds, and one has liked to beat on things since he could move his arms. The other one likes to cut things up into tiny little pieces. If I pick up this phone and call 'em, you won't ever be delivering anything to anyone again. Now, do I make myself clear, or do you want me to escort you to the elevator so you can go down the elevator shaft without the elevator?"

Over the uproar of laughter, someone managed, "And he said?"

"No, what did he do?"

"He didn't say nuthin'! He just looked around like my brothers were standing in the corner and hustled himself right out of my office, gold chain and all. I think he took the stairs down cuz he was afraid to get too close to the elevator. I need another drink. Thanks, Julio."

"That man had bueno taste but nada sense," Julio said, and they all laughed.

"Crystal, you going to stare through that nail, or do you have a plan?"

"I think I'll have it gold-plated. No, I'm kidding. I was just thinking how much time and money we spend to look attractive and wonder if I should be doing more."

While the girls couldn't see him, this brought a big smile from Julio.

"Crystal, honey, with that long blonde hair of yours and those blue eyes and that figure that I would die for, you couldn't be more beautiful if you gold-plated your whole body."

"No, I mean more with my life."

"You are doing more, girl. You're making big bucks so your man can go to law school and make a future for the two of you. That's important. Besides you don't want to look shoddy; you like to have men look at you even if you are married."

"I suppose, but think about it. We work hard in school, we work at getting our parents' approval, we go to college or secretarial school, and we either get a man or a job or both, and then we work our butts off, but what for?"

"Come on, Crystal, you know what for. We work for money. We are among the highest paid women in this city. We can go anywhere and do whatever we want," Beth said with a conspiratorial smile.

Crystal looked at the tabletop and ran her finger along a spot where someone had left a cigarette way too long. "It's just that I was thinking about a gal I know who makes far less than I do, is single, and takes care of an ailing mother. At the same time, she volunteers at a free food kitchen, and she is one of the happiest people I know. I'm not sure work can fill a person's heart, that's all."

There was a long pause, and the sorority girls all seemed to be lost in their own thoughts. No one looked at anyone else.

"Well, we can do whatever we want if you get time off and your boss lets you go, but when you come back, there is hell to pay in catch-up work," Ruth interjected.

"Amen, Sister!" The glasses clinked together. "Julio, there's a dry spot on the bottom of my glass," Rosalyn commented.

"What Ruth says is true, and Crystal raises a good point."

"Is your glass empty, too, Agnes?"

Agnes looked into her empty glass like it was going to tell her the answers she was seeking.

"No, girls, maybe there is more to life than just getting to the top," Agnes said. I wonder sometimes if the gals in the secretarial pool on the fourth floor are happier than I am. I have a bank account larger than I ever dreamed of having, a beautiful condo overlooking the city, no husband, and I'm married to a corporation that doesn't keep my feet warm at night."

"I'll bet it would if you let it," Rosalyn said.

"Well, I'm not letting it."

"Agnes, don't you go getting philosophical on us. We all worked our butts off to get where we are and put up with a lot of stupid men along the way. We've got nothing to be ashamed of, and besides, if you're talking about L-O-V-E, I'd rather be wealthy without it than poor with it, 'cause, Sister, I been poor!"

"I'm not ashamed, Beth. I'm just thinking, that's all. I will admit that love looks good if you can find it."

"And that, my girl, is the universal problem. Do I hear an amen?"

"Amen, Amen!"

"I'll drink to that."

"And a lot of other things, too."

"You shut up, girl."

"Well, here's a question for you, Agnes. What does a high-powered executive assistant like you do when all the men in the office are out of town?"

"The mice play!" the others shouted.

"Not this mouse. In fact, I have a lot of catching up to do, and besides, they call if there is something they need, like making appointments with their golf buddies for when they return. That reminds me, I still have a few things to do tonight, so this mouse is leaving." She gave the expected pecks on the cheek and hugs and slipped Julio a $20 bill as she left.

Agnes McDonnel came from a long line of Scot-Irish known for their loyalty, reliability, and dogged perseverance. She was a descendant of the clan of McDonnel of Antrim. Her ancestors had come to America during the great potato famine of 1845 rather than be among the millions who starved to death. Her grandparents did survive and came later. She had spent 25 years working her way up the secretarial ladder in lesser firms, but now she was at the top. Her boss had a history of seizing opportunities. A decade before, Mr. Bartlett had put together an investment group and purchased the Sunshine Mine in Idaho from a group in Washington State. Then the price of silver began to rise, and even Mr. Bartlett's expectations were exceeded. It was one of the richest mineral sites in the entire world. Agnes had been impressed by all the wealth this one mine had created. In the office, Agnes reviewed the financial sheets again and then called security to escort her to her car.

In her apartment, Agnes poured herself a glass of Cabernet from Frog Leap Winery in the Napa Valley. She was there last summer with some West Coast friends. The congenial owner told her, "People forget we're just farmers. You can have all the viticulture degrees in the world, but when it comes down to it, it's about hard work, sweat, and good luck. The wrong bug or weather at the wrong time for too long can wipe out an entire harvest, maybe even an entire vineyard, permanently."

"I wonder," she thought, "how many other human endeavors are really so fragile and think they are indestructible? Is it the human flaw that we think the familiar is permanent?"

As she sipped her wine, Agnes couldn't get Crystal's question out of her mind. *Couldn't we be doing more? Isn't there more?* The bells of St. Patrick's Cathedral began ringing the hour, echoing all over the city, and even though she was Protestant to the core, Agnes always listened. There was something about the tonal pulse that resonated deep within her. It spoke of hope. Maybe it was what the early Christians felt when they thought they were listening to God. She remembered her grandmother's meal bell in Vermont and how every time she heard it, she knew she was wanted. "Is that why churches have bells, to remind us we are wanted?" She sighed, rinsed out her glass, and made her way to the bedroom. As she entered, the phone rang by her bed.

"Agnes, it's Conrad. I hope you weren't in bed yet."

"No, it's just fine. What do you need?"

"Mr. Bartlett just wanted to be sure you had the copies of the financials and profit analysis available in case there is any confusion on this end. We will be taking a close look at the production reports."

"I went over it all again tonight, and I will be in the office before you are up in the morning and have it all ready. There wasn't much information on safety concerns. Is that a problem? How is it going out there?"

"It's okay. The weather has been a pain, but we will be in and out and back East before you know it. Safety is all under control. We have all the up-to-date devices, and procedures are clearly outlined. Everything is fine. I think the safety guy may press us on some things, but I think we're good."

"That's it, then?"

"Yeah, I guess. Good night."

"Good night, Conrad."

CHAPTER SIXTEEN

Higher, Higher

L ou Marks stared into the ebony-glazed coffee as if it held the key to his future, but he thought little of the future these days. He knew he had spent his future, and it was gone like last summer. But summer would come again soon, if only to be overcome by the chilling winds of fall as they blew into the valley from the peaks above. But he also knew the future doesn't come twice. It's put in your lap like a great big present on Christmas morning, but as soon as you touch the red and gold ribbon, it is no longer the future but the present. More importantly, it is not some abstract concept; it is your life.

"Your life," Lou thought. "Not some getting ready for life. It doesn't matter whether you spit or shit, from then on, it will be your past. You can't set it all aside and save it; you can't keep it for later because there is no later. There is only the moment of the gift, and when it comes, you should smile and laugh and love; you should do the work of your hands well because this bright and beautiful present will never sit on your lap again," he said to himself.

Lou felt like he was being given a second chance, and he hoped it included Faith. It must. Despite everything, for some reason, this morning—this normal Tuesday morning—he felt like a new man; something was different. But then again, he had felt the same way yesterday, like someone had taken a huge weight off him. He knew it was about what happened in church that one Sunday, but he had no language or vocabulary to describe it. He didn't feel holy, however that felt. But he also no longer felt like his soul was filled with tailings from his evil past anymore. Something or someone had cleaned him out, and it felt real good, even better than good, and maybe that's what God does to folk when there is no hope because they have allowed themselves to become rotten to the core. He remembered a scene from *Pilgrim's Progress*, which his mother read to him over and over when he was a kid.

> *I saw in my dream, that just as Christian came up upon the cross, his burden loosed from off his shoulders, and fell from off his back, and began to tumble, and so continued to do till it came to the mouth of the sepulcher, where it fell in, and I saw it no more.*[7]

He could remember sitting in the pew that Sunday, hearing the water and the music and the voice calling him by name, and watching his regret and darkness being washed away, out of sight, gone.

"Regardless of how I feel, I still have to go do Jason's shift. I think it's time for him either to stop patching up that chameleon of a truck or admit he's not the mechanic he thinks he is." Jason had called last night from Harrison and said his truck broke down again, and he was having it towed back to St. Maries where a friend of his brother-in-law could fix it. He wouldn't make it back for his shift on Tuesday and asked if Lou could take it for him. Lou always felt that being busy was preferable to sitting around where you might think too much, as was his habit. He realized a long time ago that people who do things they regret spend a lot of time trying to unthink those things, but you only wear down the gears in your brain, and you can't heal your own heart.

At the mine and after they cleared the hoist, Lou and the others rode the train, which was more like a kiddy train, the mile from A shaft to No. 10. When they reached their drift, Hoyt began setting up his drill, and Lou scanned the area like he had done each time he came into a mine, even though he may have been there the day before. Although the inside of a drift was familiar to him, he knew things had changed. If you weren't aware of the changes, you might miss a rift or a shifted timber, or not notice a wire with the insulation off, and a thousand other things that could cause an accident.

He wasn't a fearful man, but he had always been a cautious one, at least when he was underground. But topside it was another story. He took in the darkness and the dim light cast by the miners' lights on their hard hats. He set up the large floods to illuminate the space, and the brief section lit up like daylight. This world was familiar to him, and he was comfortable here. He didn't understand, like, or care about everything on the surface of the earth, but down here there was a certain comfort. Unlike above, this world was more consistent. It changed, but at least here he understood the changes.

After some time, Lou could feel the muscles in his back and legs ache, and he wanted to take a break, but he never did before his partner did. It was a way of making sure his age wasn't getting in the way. Hoyt was younger, a hard worker, so when Hoyt wanted to take a break, Lou knew it was time. He watched as Hoyt stretched his aching muscles, and he could see how Hoyt and Jason would make a good team. He didn't know how long they had been working that morning, but he knew they had done good work. Lou glanced at the jack leg drill, then the lights, and then Hoyt.

"Hoyt, you smell smoke?"

Hoyt was wiping his face with a blue bandana and hadn't heard what Lou said. "What did you say, Pard?"

"I think I smell smoke. Is it the drill?" Hoyt stepped back to the drill and gave it a quick look.

"The drill's fine, Lou, but maybe it's one of them fan motors. You know how they get."

Lou was now like a hunter in the woods, a man so familiar with all that was always there that the slightest change was like the crash of a falling tree. It screamed out for attention.

"You smell that? It's got a putrid tinge to it, but it's smoke."

"Shit, Lou, there ain't nothin' to burn in this place except a few timbers. Even if it is a fire, it sure as hell ain't gonna be big enough to hurt anything, and if there is, they'll sound the alarm to tell us to get the hell out."

The sweaty wet hair just below the back rim of Lou's hard hat was beginning to tell him there was danger. He turned and saw the black smoke coming along the drift. "Holy shit! What is that? That's smoke! Hoyt, we gotta get outta here—now!" They turned and ran from the smoke. They were staying ahead of it when Lou heard someone shout behind him. He saw three men running toward them, followed by the smoke creeping along the drift, and now the putrid smell was overwhelming. He recognized two of them but not the third. "Where's your fourth man?" he shouted as they all continued to run along the drift.

"He fell," one of them shouted. "He's probably dead by now," the man yelled as he continued to run.

"How far back is he?" Lou shouted.

"About a hundred feet, but you'll never make it. The smoke will eat you alive. Never seen anything like it."

Lou turned and headed back up the drift. He remembered seeing the small box on the wall, and when he reached it, he pulled out the breathing device and stuck it in his mouth, ducked into the darkness of the smoke, and, bending, moved forward. He didn't know how far he had come when he stumbled into a body and fell at its side. He turned the man over and heard a moan, so he lifted him up and began his return trip. He felt like he was moving in slow motion like they sometimes do on TV. The breathing device was burning his lips, but he kept moving. He was pushing his muscles as hard as he could, but they weren't working right. He stumbled twice, and the other man moaned. "At least I'm not carrying a dead man," he said to himself, "at least not yet."

The dark smoke was all around him like the tentacles of some subterranean monster. He could taste a putrid taste in his nostrils and mouth, and he felt himself getting dizzy. Suddenly, it cleared slightly, and he heard voices in front of him. He recognized Hoyt's voice and saw the huddle of men in a smokeless space by an air vent. He dropped his load at their feet, slid down the wall, and sat like a pile of dirty laundry. He spit out the breathing tube. His lips were burning like hot coals; they were blistered and cracked, and he could barely see. He heard Hoyt's voice, "Lou, get up! We have to keep moving. We'll carry him from here, but you have to get up."

It seemed like Hoyt's voice was from a faraway place. Lou tried to stand, but he couldn't. But he was no quitter. Somehow, he found the strength within himself to stand, and he began to follow the sound of the others. Someone dropped in front of him and rolled to the side, and Lou bent to lift him to his feet, but as he bent over, his head seemed to leave his shoulders and look back at him. He saw himself fall to his knees and roll on his side.

He saw Claire and Faith in the park in Coeur d'Alene. He was pushing Faith on the swing set, and she was yelling, "Higher, Daddy, higher." Claire was laughing. The wind off the lake was blowing her hair back across her face . . . the sun was shining . . . he could feel his fingers touch the edge of the swing . . . his legs were in the grass . . . he was kneeling beside Claire's casket . . . the swing was empty . . . going back and forth . . . back and forth . . . Faith wasn't there . . . he could still hear her calling to him . . . "Higher, Daddy, higher."

CHAPTER SEVENTEEN
The Executive Meeting

B ob Templin was a short man of medium build with dark hair and a
sense of "let's get this done," which had made him a leader in business,
his church, and the community. His staff knew he worked harder
than anyone there. He expected them to work hard as well, but he was always
fair and generous. The staff at Templin's North Shore Resort on Lake Coeur
d'Alene had been preparing for this meeting for weeks. Some had worked the
weekend just to be sure everything was ready for Tuesday morning. This was
to be a major meeting of the owners, operators, and stockholders of the most
productive silver mine in North America. Their job was to impress and serve
these folks and do it well. Bob Templin knew good things didn't just happen;
you had to work hard and make them happen.

The World's Fair would be in Spokane in just two years, and he wanted
these people to become unofficial delegates, encouraging others to come this
way. He knew most families would drive, and after a long drive across the
Dakotas and Montana, a stop at Coeur d'Alene would look like paradise—
because it was. His place was the premier place to stay on the lake before
going on to Spokane.

They arrived carrying their briefcases like agents on a mission, all in suits
and Florsheim shoes except for the one woman in a conservative, navy blue,
working woman's suit. The 40 minutes in the shuttle had made them talkative.

Not one of them looked like they had ever been outdoors longer than getting from a hotel to a cab, let alone down a mine shaft. They carried *The New York Times*, *The Wall Street Journal*, and *The Spokesman-Review*. Templin could tell these folks were used to being up early and going at it hard. They joined the part of their team who spent the night at the North Shore. Listening, he picked up the news that was supposed to be important. It was a presidential election year, and Senator George McGovern was challenging Vice President Hubert Humphrey for the Democratic nomination. Humphrey was saddled with Johnson's fumbling of Vietnam, and McGovern was determined to be the peace candidate riding the anti-war sentiment into the White House. But he would first have to take that hat off of Ed Muskie whose popularity seemed to increase daily. Overhearing them, Templin, although no academician, knew it was easier for a general to ride into the White House than a peacenik. Humphrey was no general, but he had supported the war. It would be an interesting election either way—a feisty Humphrey or an anti-war candidate against Richard Nixon.

A balding man with a comb-over hairdo and a dark blue tie with gold florae was telling a fellow with a red bow tie how the world was really changing, because two days ago, on April 30th, Arthur Godfrey's broadcast contract ended, and he was no longer on the air. "Can you imagine?" he said. Here it is 1972, and Godfrey has been on the air, radio or television, since 1929. The man has no talent, except he can get people to talk and do what he wants. He should have been a CEO."

"I saw the replay last night in the hotel lounge," the bow tie commented through his tears as he headed toward the meeting room. A few of the women in the lounge were crying a little.

When they entered the room, the mine operators who had arrived a half hour earlier were standing at the window, obviously not wanting to sit in the wrong place until they were told where; that is, except Nims. He had placed himself and his reports at the middle with his back to the lake. Nims knew he shouldn't sit at either end. Bartlett, the chairman, would sit at one end, and whoever wanted to challenge his authority would sit at the other. By sitting in the middle, Nims knew it would appear that he was trying to be where all could hear, but he also knew it meant he would command the meeting and the chairman, and his rival would, in reality, be sidelined. It was all a matter of perspective, and most of the others were irrelevant.

With the exception of Nims, whose suit was special order from Hong Kong, the mine operators all looked like they had dressed in the dark or they couldn't make up their minds what to wear. Their ties were at least a decade out of fashion, and at least for one, it didn't quite make it over his stomach. Their shoes weren't Florsheim, but they were all polished. They looked like they had never been worn other than on a Sunday or at a wedding or funeral. This wasn't so much a meeting of East meets West but rather a meeting of office-bound venture capitalists whose work was in their heads and files meet men who had worked with their hands and sweated underground in the dark depths of the earth all their lives. The miners had become so good at what they did and had acquired enough experience at mining operations that they were now in charge of others, a position with which they were not at all comfortable. They were like their counterparts in the Forest Service who began because they loved the out of doors and being in the woods, and then, as they gained experience, they were promoted to an office and a desk and were lucky if they had a window to see a tree or two.

The men from Kellogg who were standing at the window were talking about fishing. Nims ignored their banter. He never fished. He didn't talk with the men except when he was giving orders. When they looked at the lake, they could talk about nothing else. Sure, this meeting was important and their work would be discussed, but their real joy wasn't in the mine. It was beyond that window, around Tubbs Hill toward Arrow Point, or into Mica Bay, or down near the mouth of the St. Joe River, or the North Fork of the Coeur d'Alene River. The places were endless, and they had spent every opportunity they could on the lake, by the streams, or by the rivers. It was one of the things that made mining tolerable, the life you could have above ground and the world you could enjoy. When it wasn't fishing season, there was hunting season. If anyone asked them, they might even say, "It made the hard work worth it," but no one asked. As they moved toward the vacant places at the table, one operator whispered to the man nearest him, "Richard Petty won at Martonsville this weekend. I hope this meeting will go as fast." The other man nodded with a slight smile.

"Well, we've come a long way," Bartlett announced, signaling to a young man with a plastic file box labeled "Sunshine" to sit on his left. The young man nervously took his seat. "Let's not waste any time. Mr. Nims, would you please share the production reports for the last six months?" The meeting was thus convened.

The first call came sometime just before noon. The operator had specific instructions not to interrupt the meeting under any circumstances, so she offered to take a message. The caller hung up. When the second call came, what she heard would wake her up at night for the rest of her life because her brother worked at the Sunshine Mine.

"There's a fire at the Sunshine mine . . . men are trapped . . . some are already dead . . . and we . . ." She didn't listen for the rest of the message. She hung up the phone. She stood and left her post, and as she was about to enter the meeting room, she saw Bob Templin emerge from his office. She beckoned him toward her but didn't wait for him. She marched into the meeting room and repeated the message word for word to the startled faces. She turned and walked past Templin who was waiting for an explanation. Her eyes never met his; she simply hurried into the ladies room and, as the door closed behind her, vomited all over the clean tile floor.

CHAPTER EIGHTEEN

Breathless News

Emma Reed was at the Methodist Church sorting clothing for the annual rummage sale on Saturday. Everyone in town always came, even if they didn't buy anything. It didn't hurt that they had all-you-can-eat chili for lunch and free donuts and coffee all day. In fact, it had become so popular that they no longer used recorded music. Seth Miller, the custodian at the high school, came and played his accordion. Emma smiled as she thought how Seth had everyone tapping their feet and swaying to his music. Folks came from Wallace, Osburn, Pinehurst, and other parts. She couldn't believe it when she heard that the new preacher, Pastor Mason Chalice, wanted to cancel it this year.

"Emma," Gertrude Rubbins whispered, "did you know Pastor Chalice wanted to charge for the donuts and coffee? Can you imagine?"

"It was a good thing the Mary Martha Circle marched into his office," Sally Cunningham added. "It was quite crowded with all eight of us. We told him the world was changing fast enough and that certain traditions are worth preserving."

"I told him other preachers had come before him, and others would come after," Gertrude added.

"We told him we enjoy his preaching, although sometimes we don't always understand what he's trying to say, but we're sure it's good," Alice Underwood said.

"When Clara told him we were sure the Bishop would agree with us about the rummage sale, Pastor Chalice paled at the mention of the Bishop."

The thought made Emma giggle to herself as she folded a pair of faded jeans and added them to the pile. She looked around the room, looking for Pastor Chalice, although she didn't expect to see him. She heard that some of the men had bets on how long he would last. She didn't think it was very Christian of them, but she did understand.

Wham! The fellowship hall doors crashed open, slamming against the wall and sending a small amount of dust airborne as the doors vibrated on their hinges. More than one woman jumped and squealed. They stood motionless, staring at Georgia Redstock's son, Case, who was half bent over, panting, red in the face, with his hands on his knees. He was trying to catch his breath and talk at the same time. As he wiped his nose with his arm, he raised his head, and Emma could see a dark fear on the boy's face. She realized the only sound in the room was Case's labored breathing.

"There's a fire at the Sunshine!" He paused for more air. "Most of 'em got out, some dead, some still down there."

The peaceful busyness of the room was instantly transformed into communal fear. As Case tried to catch his breath, his mother's face froze in a blank stare. Then she moved toward her son, put her arms around him, and lifted his head to her chest, cradling him as he continued to gasp for air. Emma knew Case was Georgia's son from her first marriage. Georgia's husband had been killed in a logging accident near Lake Pend Orielle when Case was only two. She and Joe, her second husband, had met through some cousins. Now, 17 years later, Georgia might be losing another husband.

Emma looked away from the boy to the other side of the room where she saw Bill St. George, a retired miner, sitting below the picture of Jesus praying in Gethsemane. Bill had been eating donuts and drinking coffee while he teased the women sorting clothes. He lowered his head and crossed himself. He sat with his head hung between his shoulders. Emma saw him turn his head back and forth, shudder, and then lift his head up. He was crying. The room was in mild chaos. Women were grabbing their purses and coats and moving through the doorway into the unknown, powered by fear.

"I have to get to the mine. Charlie's there," Emma said, louder than she intended as she grabbed her purse and pushed two women aside. She gathered up her coat and left quickly. Emma was glad Charlie had left her the truck in case she needed to pick up things for the sale. *Oh Lord, please let my Charlie be safe. He is a good man, and he deserves to have some years of rest. Oh please, Lord, and all the others still down there, please let them out alive. Please, dear Jesus, please.*

As Emma passed through town, she saw others hurrying to cars and trucks. She could hear sirens. She wasn't sure which direction they were coming from, and she didn't care. "You'll have to push me off the road, but first you have to catch me," she said to her empty truck cab. Emma could hear the familiar rattle of the old truck, and she knew it wouldn't let her down. Staring down the highway, she realized she had been hearing the bells from St. Rita's Catholic Church ringing continuously in what she knew now was an alarm for the entire town. Racing up Big Creek Road with the truck sometimes grabbing for traction like a man desperate to hang on at all cost, she saw a woman with no shoes running up the road. Emma pulled alongside her and came to an abrupt stop.

"Get in, Honey. My guess is we're both going to the same place." The young woman climbed into the cab of the pickup, and Emma noticed her enlarged belly. The woman was pregnant. She had dark, curly hair that seemed like it was a world of its own and wore a cardigan sweater and simple dress.

"Thank you, Ma'am. My name's Brenda, and my Georgie's in the mine. There's something gone wrong. There are all kinds of trucks racing there, ambulances, and that awful siren."

"There's a fire, but a lot of them got out safely, Honey," Emma said with as much reassurance as she could muster in the midst of her own fear.

"We've only been married a year, and Georgie was so excited to get on at the Sunshine." They turned a corner too fast, and Brenda gasped as the rear of the truck slid off the road. Brenda clung to the door as gravel spit out the back of the truck.

"Sorry," Emma mumbled, and Brenda forced a smile, all the time clinging to the door. Emma could see the fright in the young girl's eyes, but she didn't let up on the gas pedal. They passed the company office and the superintendent's house, and there was no one to be seen at either place. "They must already be at the mine. Good. The sooner the rescue operation starts, the sooner they can all get out," Emma muttered. She pulled to a stop about a hundred yards before the parking area. She didn't want to be in the way of anyone who came to help. She could see a large, black cloud coming out of the mine vent like a serpent emerging from the bowels of the earth and then drifting off into the wind. She knew it was bad, but how could you have that much smoke in a hard rock mine? What was burning?

There was already a cluster of pickups and odd cars that probably had more miles than any should have, just like Charlie's truck. Emma jumped from the truck and started to run, and then she turned around to help Brenda.

"Thanks."

Then Emma thought of something. "Wait, Brenda." She went back to the truck, reached behind the seat, and pulled out what looked like old slippers. "Here, put these on. Charlie keeps them in case he has to go in someplace and his boots are too muddy. They'll keep your feet from getting cut up." They hurried toward the mine with Brenda scuffling along. There was a cluster of people, miners who had come to help and others who Emma knew had come out of the mine. Some were talking quietly, and others farther away were raising their arms and yelling. She heard, "We can't!" and "We have to!" and "We sent some in already, and they're all dead!" Her heart skipped a beat.

"Georgie!" Brenda yelled, and broke into a run. Emma saw a young man who looked like he had aged 20 years in the last few hours. He was standing there with his arms out as Brenda raced into them. The tears rolling down his face made white streaks through the dirt on his cheeks. Brenda sobbed, kissed his dirty face, and sobbed some more. Then she took his hands in hers and pulled him to the ground where they knelt and embraced. Emma could hear her whispered prayer. As they rose to their feet, she heard Brenda say, "Now go. See what you can do to help."

Emma thought to herself, *She already has a miner's wife's heart. Her man is safe, so how can we help the others?* It's a mentality that people whose loved ones don't work at risky jobs don't understand. You walk a tightrope every day, and when someone falls or is dangling, you do what you can to help.

"Harvey!" Emma yelled, and a weary-looking, stoop-shouldered miner turned and walked toward her, his eyes on the ground. He wiped his mouth with the back of his hand before he spoke. His voice was almost a whisper.

"Charlie was in the Jewell Shaft, Emma, but he was supposed to move near No. 10, and I don't know what level. The guys on the upper levels got out, some in the middle died, almost instantly, but we don't know about the guys below the 3,700 foot level. Because smoke and fire rise, we think they might be okay. I'm sorry, Emma, but I just don't know anything yet."

"Thanks, Harvey. You all right?"

"Yeah, but we are in for a world of hurt. Do me a favor, and keep your eyes out for Pearl. Let her know I'm okay as soon as she gets here. I have to help set up whatever rescue we can put together."

"She'll be at the Red Cross station as soon as they get it set up. I haven't seen her yet, Harvey, but I'll let her know you're fine." Emma forced a smile, but Harvey didn't respond.

"Is it true, Harvey, that you sent some in and they didn't come back?" He looked at his boots and whispered, "Shit to hell. Sorry for swearing in front of you," and he wiped a tear from his eye. He turned away. "Gotta go."

Emma knew it was no good asking about Charlie. The news wouldn't change until they got some communication with the ones below, so she turned to a gathering of women who were trying to bring comfort and press down their fears with hugs. It was a ritual she had participated in before but not with Charlie missing.

CHAPTER NINETEEN

Change of Plans

Penny and Sybil were in Wilson's Pharmacy in Coeur d'Alene looking for some clever gift items and picking up some needed things because two of Penny's boys were having birthdays soon. Sybil was munching on popcorn and giving sisterly advice to Penny, not paying much attention to the rest of the store. Penny heard a phone ring, and a moment later she saw the store's owner, Chuck Sears, with his face all flushed coming down the aisle. "Excuse me, please," he said to the woman at the counter as he pushed open the front door and turned toward the bakery next door. A minute later, two men came running past the pharmacy, jumped into a truck, made a U-turn against the light, and headed east up Sherman Avenue. Penny thought she recognized one of the men, but she wasn't sure.

Chuck Sears's face was still flushed when he came back into the store. Penny noticed that his eyes flicked around like he had done something wrong. He went straight into the back and picked up the phone. "I found them. They're on their way. How bad is it?" By the look on his face and the sudden slouch of his shoulders, everyone knew there was bad news. By now, the few customers in the store were giving all their attention to Mr. Sears. People knew innately that something terrible had happened. Mrs. Sears, Lorna to everyone, put down the paper in her hand. "What is it, Chuck? What's happened?"

"There's a fire at the Sunshine Mine, and some men are dead and many more are trapped inside. Looks really bad."

Sybil dropped her popcorn and grabbed her sister's arm. Penny just stared at Chuck Sears. His eyes met hers. They both knew they were in the midst of something horrendous and life-changing. Sybil reached down to pick up the popcorn. Penny and Chuck held each other's gaze for a moment, and then he dropped his eyes and whispered, "Go!"

"Forget the popcorn," Lorna said. "Go look after your family and your men. We'll keep you all in our prayers. Now go!" Penny turned slowly as if she were trying to figure out which direction to go, but then she grabbed Sybil's hand and ran for the door.

As they left, others in the pharmacy scattered, spreading the word like gossip locusts. Some were excited because they knew something important that few knew yet and others because they had already traveled the road of pain and loss. At the same time, announcements were made at the high schools in Kellogg, Wallace, Osburn, and Pritchard. Signs were going up all over the Silver Valley—"Fire at Sunshine—Pray." "Closed Cuz of Fire."

That evening, every newspaper in the country would have the Sunshine Mine fire with almost a hundred men inside as their lead story. Regional papers and television would carry the disaster to its final conclusion, and in Idaho there was a feeling of "this is happening to all of us."

Cable was supposed to be at school, but school was boring, and Mr. Postalink made it even more boring. Besides, Cable was in the seventh grade and figured he knew everything he needed to know by now. His dad was at work in the mine, and his mom said she was going to Coeur d'Alene with Aunt Sybil as soon as he left for school. He waited until lunch and then skipped out during the chaos of everyone running to the cafeteria. He would be back in time for the end of school, and his mom wouldn't even know he ditched. He walked two blocks and then jumped into a small ravine shrouded by maple trees. The trees sheltered him from the light spring rain that made everything smell fresh. He knew no one driving by could see him because the tree branches formed an umbrella over the ravine. Maybe he'd go home and have some more cereal. He could feel the Hershey bar in his pocket and knew he needed to wait until later to eat it, but he didn't want it to get too warm and melt. "I hate it when that happens," he thought. When he got to the small creek, he sat on "his rock" and threw pebbles at the water. Cable often came here when he needed to think without anyone around. He wished his friend Eugene was here, but he had the mumps and was at home with his ma and grandma. He lifted himself up off the rock and brushed the dirt off his butt. He wondered if Linda Gregory was in class today. He liked seeing her, and for some reason, he was noticing more things about girls this year. Linda was special, and if Cable believed in girlfriends, which he didn't and knew he never would, she would be his. "I wonder who gets to decide if you are girlfriend and boyfriend, her or me?" He had to admit that there was a lot about girls he didn't understand. He decided that eating the Hershey bar might give him more energy to think, so he unwrapped it as he climbed up the side of the ravine.

Cable was headed for the gas station when he saw a blue pickup race past with four men in the back. They were too far away to see their faces, but he could tell something was up somewhere. As he turned to march away, he saw old Amos Hamilton getting into his truck.

"Amos, what's going on? Somethun's wrong, ain't it?" Amos had on his bib overalls and his Texaco cap and was struggling with the ignition in his 1947 pickup. The old truck made a heavy grinding sound and backfired twice before it started.

"There's a fire, Boy!" he shouted. "Hop in!" Just as Cable put his foot on the running board, the engine died. It took three more cranks and some colorful words from Amos before the old engine kicked over. Cable saw blue smoke reflected in the cracked outside rearview mirror. It took a few jerks and jolts, but they were soon on their way.

"Amos, you said there was a fire. Where? In the woods somewhere?"

"No, Son. It's the Sunshine. There's a fire in the mine. Say, aren't you Butch and Penny's boy?"

"Yeah," Cable said with a lump in his throat. Faster trucks raced past them, and Amos cursed his old truck under his breath. "My daddy's in the mine today." Cable looked at Amos, and Amos looked out the corner of his eye.

"Don't fret, Boy. People are always gettun ahead of things. We'll find your pa sure enough."

"My dad always says, 'Miners are people of hope.' He's always quoting some guy named Frodo Baggins: 'Where there's life there's hope.'[8]"

Amos shook his head. "Who's this Frodo guy? I never heard of him. He work around here?"

"No, he's a character in a book. He's a Hobbit."

"What's a . . . a . . . hobbit?"

"They're short people who live in houses that are partly underground."

"Sounds like they're miners to me," Amos said, gripping the steering wheel like he was wrestling it to the ground.

"I'm not sure. I haven't read the book yet. But I will cuz Pa likes it." Cable didn't say any more. He just thought about his dad and wondered if he was fighting the fire in the mine.

"We're here, Boy. Looky, looky. It looks like the whole valley's already here. You stay out of the way, Boy, and let's pray your friend Frito is right."

"Frodo!" Cable yelled as he bolted from the truck and started running up Big Creek Road toward the mine. The ground was wet, and he could smell the mud mixed with the odor of diesel oil and car fumes. Ordinarily, he would wander to the creek and throw rocks or find a good stick. Now wasn't about exploring; it was about finding out if his dad was all right.

"Damned kids these days don't listen to nobody," Amos muttered to himself as he tramped up the road.

When Cable turned the last corner, he was breathing heavily, and he bent over his knees to rest and catch his breath. The rain had stopped, but there was still mud everywhere. As he stood up, he could see a cloud of black smoke spiraling up from the mine and rising into the air. Men were lying on the ground coughing, and some weren't moving. He glanced quickly over at the men, looking at their left arms, looking for an orange band, but he didn't see it. It was an old headband his mother sometimes wore to keep her hair back. One day, his dad took it off her head, kissed her on the forehead, and said, "This is my good luck band, and I'll wear it on my left arm just like I wear my wedding ring on my left hand."

"You sure you know which arm is your left one?" his mom had said. It was a family joke because both of them were so nervous on their wedding day that they almost put the rings on the wrong hands. Cable couldn't see any orange bands, and he didn't know whether that was good or bad, but he sure wanted to see his dad.

Breathless and hacking from his hike up the road, Amos said, "You stand here, Boy, and I'll see what I can find out. I don't suppose your mom knows you're here, does she?"

"Nah, she's in Coeur d'Alene shopping. She doesn't know anything yet. She thinks I'm at school."

"Yeah, I figured you weren't where you were supposed to be, but none of that matters much now. I'll see what I can find out."

"I'm coming, too."

"Umm, of course you are," Amos said as they moved toward a group standing near the mine office.

More and more cars and trucks were arriving, and Cable could hear sirens coming toward the mine. Men were yelling around the mine entrance. Some were going in and coming right out again, and some were watching. It reminded him of the change on the field during the offense and defense at the high school football games. Suddenly, two more fire trucks pulled up to the mine. One was so close that Cable could reach out and touch it. The lettering on the side said Wallace Fire Department. There were more sirens, and three Idaho State Police cars arrived. Two of them started pulling yellow tape that said "Caution" off a large roll, which Cable thought was kind of funny in a way because the fire had already started and was in the mine, not in the parking lot. There wasn't anything to do but stay out of the way, so he talked to some of his neighbors. Mrs. Maryott was crying and looking for her husband and her brother, all the time wiping her face with a red bandana. After a while, they started bringing men out of the mine in black bags. "It's just like the ones on the news when they report on Vietnam," Cable thought to himself.

Several big, black cars drove right up to the yellow tape. One of the police officers started toward the men as they were getting out of the cars, but one of the men held out his arm, and the officer stopped while the men went on. They were all in shirts and ties, although one man, who looked familiar, had taken his tie off.

Someone shouted Cable's name, and he knew who it was before he turned and saw his mother running toward him. She threw her arms around him and seemed to hug him tighter than she ever had before. "Mom, I can't find Dad!"

"You stay here. I'll find out what's happening."

"No, I'm coming with you. We're together, Mom. That's what you always say." Penny looked at her son and saw a resolve she hadn't seen before. She took Cable's hand and moved toward the yellow tape, and two state troopers stepped in front of her.

"Sorry, Ma'am, you can't go any closer."

"I just want to find my husband." Glancing down at her son, she said, "We need to know he's okay."

"I understand, and as soon as they can, they'll give a report on the men. But right now, there are still men in the mine, and you don't want to hamper any rescue effort, do you?" The officer cleared his throat and stared into Penny's eyes. "Look, Ma'am, I'm a miner's son. As soon as I know anything, I'll come and find you, okay?"

"Yes, but . . ."

"Ma'am, I promise. It will be better if everyone cooperates."

"Okay, we'll be over there by that power pole, out of the way." Penny turned to Cable as if she needed a distraction from the reality she was experiencing. "How come you are not in school, young man? Did they let everyone out?"

"I was skipping, Mom. Please don't be mad. We have to find Dad."

"You're right, we do. We can deal with you later."

As Penny retreated and moved toward a group of women in search of news, the younger trooper said to his partner, "How come you didn't tell her you understand because your dad died in a cave-in?"

"Because that's the last thing she needs to hear right now. All these families are standing on an emotional ledge looking into a pit called the Sunshine Mine. When they find out their man or son or brother isn't coming out alive, some will go over the edge, and some won't ever be the same again. I know. I saw it with my mom. She was never the same after she lost my dad and brothers in that cave-in. Brokenness takes many forms, and maybe the worst are the ones we can't see."

"Sorry. I guess I wasn't thinking."

"It's okay. You haven't been there. We're here to keep order, but we'd also better be a comfort to these folks. We're all in this together."

CHAPTER TWENTY

The Return

"You sure you're gonna be okay, Missy? It's still a little dark."

"I'll be fine, thanks, and thanks for the ride."

Faith had gotten a ride to Kellogg after sneaking out of her aunt's apartment. She knew her aunt would have wanted to take her to Kellogg herself in order to protect her, but Faith wanted to do this alone. She had left Kellogg on her own; now she was returning on her own.

"I'm glad you aren't traveling far because it's too dangerous. I got two granddaughters almost your age, and the idea of them being out on the road scares me to death."

"I'm home now, and things will be fine," Faith said. The word *home* seemed foreign under the circumstances, but she thanked him for his generosity and realized the reality of her return was about to unfold and would no longer be formed by her imagination.

"Anybody who takes care of sick kids can ride in my rig anytime. You take care of yourself. Those kiddos back in Seattle need you, you know."

She turned away from the diesel exhaust and looked up the hill toward town. She noticed there were a few more lights than when she left, but not many. The good thing about darkness is that it hides the blackened stumps, the old rusted mine equipment that sits by the highway, but she knew it was there. She could smell the mix of minerals, fir, and cedar, and she knew exactly where the house stood from here.

Faith could see herself 13 years ago, just a young teen, standing on the other side of the highway with the wind coming through the valley beating against her cheeks to provide a rhythm for her fear. It had been daylight then when she had grabbed her ride to a new life. She had been picked up by a couple hauling freight, and they alternated between trying to make sure she wasn't running away and trying to help her out. She told them her mom was in Deaconess Hospital in Spokane recovering from an appendectomy and she had no dad. She told them the hospital said she could stay in her mom's room. Faith knew they weren't fully convinced, but they dropped her off somewhere downtown below the hospital, and then she found the bus station and headed for Portland.

A lot had happened to her since she ran from the evil that invaded her life, destroying her body and soul and tearing at her from the inside out. She knew she was a victim, as much as she hated the term, but now her father could not hurt her anymore. The healing came slowly, and the nightmares still reminded her that the darkness of her experience could only be peeled back slowly because each layer removed brought new pain and feelings from which her body and soul could not be easily purged. Her father-hero had become her nighttime horror. The antiseptic of tears had helped as she cried out in the dark of night to God in words similar to those of the psalmist of old.

Oh God, why aren't you here?
Why don't you save me?
It seems all I can do is groan
and feel the pain.

She thought about the family who had later taken her in and renewed her in love and caring. She had "found religion," as her dad would say, but no, she had found more than religion. She had found life, a living God.

Her life had been turned inside out and back again, and she looked for the beauty again and sometimes saw it with great clarity. She had spent many hours in therapy, both as a teen and even now, although now it was less traumatic. It was more like "life maintenance," as her current therapist put it, and it was also less often.

Now, despite the heaviness of her work, there was more laughter and love than she had ever known before, and that came from children with cancer.

She loved them, and they loved her. As she walked up the street, passing familiar storefronts, she knew she was not the teen who had fled from here. She was someone else. It was this new person her dad would meet, an adult woman, and whether he had changed or not didn't really matter.

She was a grown woman now, and her personality embodied her name— she was a person of faith. She was "marked" by it. "Faith Marks," she said out loud to herself. Yet part of her was still a little girl, and she knew it. She longed for a daddy's love and to feel his strong arms around her. Yes, he had done terrible things, but she had come to believe that creation was not a one- time event but rather an ongoing process, and that God breathed new life into people and circumstances. She thought of it as a rebuilding of the soul, but it was more like waking from a deep sleep in a dark place and slowly being caressed by light as it soaked deeper into your soul, giving you a new vision of the world without the lens of yourself in the way. She knew who she was and had painfully, not easily, forgiven him. She prayed that her dad had changed as she took this step of faith toward this unknown and, for him, unexpected reunion.

She could smell bread from the bakery on McKinley Street and was glad it was still there. Nothing in the world said "welcome" like the smell of fresh bread. She recognized the shadow of the Odd Fellows building and suddenly realized that even with the coming morning light, there were many dark spaces lingering throughout the town. She felt chilled, though it was warm, and a foreboding feeling began to nest in her mind. She saw a few people she recognized. Mrs. McKenzie was putting her cat out. Thirteen years ago, she had thought Mrs. McKenzie was an old lady. She hated to imagine how old she was now. Mrs. McKenzie glanced at Faith like small town folk do to strangers, especially as night fades and a new day brings new events. But the old woman paid her no mind and went back inside, although Faith could swear she saw the edge of the curtain move to one side. A guy in a red pickup slowed down and craned his neck to gawk at her as he passed by. "Men who listen to brokenhearted country music all day think they're every girl's savior," she thought to herself. "But to be fair, most men think that about themselves anyway. You can't blame it on the music."

The mailbox post was still standing outside the house, but it looked more like a victim of war than a receptacle for the daily mail. The rainbow she and her mother had painted was barely recognizable. Weeds grew all along and through the fence, and her tire swing was on the ground, covered with mud and weeds. The shredded rope hung from the tree like a dead snake. The porch light was off or out, but there was a light on inside.

Faith stepped up to the screen door and knocked, but there was no answer. She looked at the rusted handle of the screen and whispered to herself, "What happened to Miss Confidence?" As she pulled the door, the squeak was a voice from the past. She didn't knock again. She knew the door would be unlocked. As she turned the knob, she thought, "Thirteen years and counting."

"Dad. Dad, are you here?" There was only silence and a sound she knew well, the gentle sound of steam rising from the kettle on the wood stove. But it was the odor that hit her first. There was the expected smell of old wood and worn furniture with generations of dirt and sweat, but there was also the sweet scent of an aromatic candle that had burned earlier. Her eyes surveyed the room, and nothing seemed in disorder; there was no clutter. It did not look like a widower's house. "Maybe he remarried," she thought to herself. To her surprise, the kitchen was absolutely clean except for a coffee mug in the sink. There was the distinct aroma of bleach. She glanced onto the back porch and saw that her dad's boots were gone from their warming place. It confirmed what she already knew. She would not have to look in the bedrooms, which she had told herself she would not go near.

The sound of the screen door and the "Hey, who are you?" all came so quickly that Faith jumped when she turned toward the sound. There was a bearded, young man covered in grease standing in the doorway. He looked more concerned than threatening. Before she could answer, he said again, "Who are you? And what are you doing in Lou's house?"

"I'm his daughter, Faith, and I haven't been home in a long time. Who are you?"

"Well I'll be a baked hog at a Jewish barbecue! We all thought you'd never be back. I live across the street; moved here a year after you done took off. Your daddy didn't tell me you was comin' or that you was so pretty, that ol' rascal."

"He couldn't tell you. He didn't know. In fact, it was kind of a last-minute decision on my part. Would you happen to know where he is?"

"Yeah, he's at the Sunshine. In fact, he's doing my shift cuz I had to go to St. Maries for a birthday party, and my truck broke down again. I didn't think I would get back in time, so he took my shift. Your dad had already left for the mine by the time I got home early this morning. He won't be back 'til the end of the day shift, which is three o'clock. You're going to wait for him, aren't ya? I know he would love to see ya. Say, I know it's none of my business, but why did you run away? Your dad is such a great guy and all. I know your mama died, and that must have been hell on a kid. It had to be rough."

"I don't want to be rude, but you're right, it's none of your business. It was a long time ago, and I was just a teenager."

"Yeah, I did a lot of crazy stuff when I was a teen, too. I gotta go work on my truck while I can. Nice to meet you."

"Yes it was nice to meet you, too, Mr . . . ?" Faith said to the empty doorway. "Well, if my dad's going to be gone all day, I think first I'll take a nap on the couch and then bake him a pie. Won't that put a sugar coating on his surprise!"

She looked at the spot on the floor where her mother's vase had broken and thought about how she had fled this place. She knew she was far from healed, but she also knew God had done much to heal her over the past 13 years. She thought about how she had escaped from this place, this very room. All the king's men of the nursery rhyme couldn't put Humpty Dumpty back together, but the healing hand of God was slowly putting her back together. She smiled as she punched the pillow on the couch and let her head sink into it. Soon, she was fast asleep.

The noise awoke Faith, but it took her a moment to realize where she was. She almost tripped over her shoes as she hurried to the door, but before she reached it, the greasy neighbor came crashing through with a look of desperate alarm on his face.

"There's a fire at the Sunshine, and your daddy's there!"

As she tried to grasp his words and the shock of his intrusion, he turned and headed out the door toward a truck waiting at the curb with its engine running.

"Wait!" She turned, scooped up her shoes, and ran toward the truck. Her mind was a blur as they raced through town, but when they reached the highway, her mind went to her mother's accident and death. "It was on this road, just a few miles from here," she thought to herself. "Now I've come to see my father, and he may be in danger." The thought brought a sense of fatigue. She was glad the man driving this pickup—Jason, he said was his name—was concentrating on the road and not talking. She had thought that at the worst, her father might reject her completely. But the idea of him dying or being in trouble just as she arrived had never occurred to her. "No, he's probably fine," she thought and pushed the worst out of her mind. "There are accidents in mines all the time, and they have procedures to bring aid. But this was a fire, and fires played by their own rules."

CHAPTER TWENTY-ONE

A Wandering Shepherd

Pastor Mason Chalice was in his study thumbing through the church hymnbook trying to find something upbeat. The organist always played every hymn like a funeral dirge. He heard that the Catholics had a young woman right out of college who played organ, but he knew there was no chance of getting her. Mason looked around the room. They called it the pastor's study, but he thought it looked more like a custodian's closet. One window leaked in the winter, and the desk looked like it had been run over by a snowplow.

The ringing phone jerked Mason out of his rumination. He was so startled that he dropped the hymnbook on the floor. Reflexes told him to pick up the book, but the irritation pounding in his ears told him to answer the phone. He did, although forever after he wished he hadn't, and he wished he had never come to this place.

"Pastor, there's a fire at the Sunshine, and uh, uh, I thought you should know cuz you're bound to be needed."

"What do you mean, needed?"

"Well, gosh, there are still some men trapped in the mine. Some are dead, we know, but not who, and them families will be hanging around wanting comfort and all, Preacher, kindness and stuff. Oh, and lots of prayer, yeah, lots and lots of prayer. You know what I mean?"

"Who is this?"

"Wally Hanks. You know me. We met at the Christmas bazaar. I'm Mabel Cottonwood's cousin. In fact, I'm calling from her house out on Big Creek Road, close to the mine."

"Oh, yes, yes, I remember now," although Mason had no idea who Wally Hanks was or Mabel Cottonwood, either.

"Tell me, Wally, are there many people, I mean families there?"

"Pastor, I've never seen anything like it. Cars, trucks, police, fire trucks, TV crews—just about everybody who is anybody. That's why I called you, but I have to get back to the mine cuz Mabel is a frightful mess worrying about Henry, that's her husband. He would never let us call him Hank, no way, or he would . . ."

"Wait! Hank, no, um, Wally, did you say TV crews are there?"

"Yes sir. I think I saw at least two. There were over a hundred men in that mine. This is gonna be big news all over the country."

"Okay, Wally, you take care of your cousin, and I'll be right there. Yes, I know my responsibility."

Mason reflected on what he had just been told. "TV crews, big story, national story, this is my moment. I can be like Peter Jennings who reported on a train wreck in the middle of Canada and was recognized for his talent and good looks and became a national reporter for ABC. Now the Bishop will take notice of me. Let's see, should I wear my clerical collar or just a tie and jacket? No collar. When the Bishop sees the news, he might not pay attention to me if he thinks I'm a Catholic priest. Oh my gosh! That little priest is probably already there."

Mason stood and stepped in front of the spider-webbed mirror on the back of the door to his study. The glass was not cracked, but the silver paint behind it had seen better days. He straightened his tie, checked his hair, grabbed his jacket, and exited through the back stairway so he could avoid the rummage sale people. He was amazed that the parking lot was empty. "I guess the ladies got done early."

He started his car and was about to pull out of the church's small parking lot when he realized he didn't know where the Sunshine Mine was. One of the deacons had given him a tour of several mines last fall, but he couldn't remember which were which, nor did he care. "He thought I should understand how my parishioners lived and worked. What a crazy idea."

He started toward the main highway and then remembered the man on the phone said something about Big Creek Road, and before he could reach the highway, there was a train of cars and pickup trucks, and Mason decided to follow the pack. Sure enough, as they came to Big Creek Road, everyone began exiting. He looked at the small houses to his left and remembered his shock when he had passed by here last fall. He figured they weren't much bigger than some of the tenements in New York, but they looked a lot less sturdy.

When he got closer to the mine, there was a state policeman directing traffic and telling people where to park. Rather than follow the officer's directions, Mason pulled to a stop at the officer's feet, so close that the officer stepped back to save his toes and looked at Mason with both a personal and professional frown.

"Sir, you'll have to pull in over there and walk in from here. We have to keep the road clear for emergency vehicles."

"Yes, Officer, I know, but I am a clergyman, and I've come to bring comfort and encouragement to the families of this community."

"Glad to have you, Pastor, but I'm afraid you will have to walk from here. But you're sure needed up there."

"Well, then, maybe you could consider me an emergency vehicle and let me get closer. I have a bad leg, and walking is difficult."

"Okay, there may be some room, and since you are handicapped, I guess I can make an exception. When you get stopped up ahead by my partner, just tell him I said for him to find you a place to park and not send you back."

"Nothing like a little fib to get you what you want," Mason thought. He absentmindedly rubbed his leg as if he believed his own lie, wondering what he should do to get before the cameras. "Handicapped, ha!" he said to no one. As he pulled up toward the mine, he saw a crowd and a number of emergency vehicles. He wasn't sure where he would find room to park, but before he could make a decision, he realized that someone was tapping on his driver's side window. As he rolled the window down, he noticed the officer was much older than the other one and probably had more authority.

"Excuse me, but you're not supposed to be up here, Sir. You will have to turn around and go back."

"Yes, Officer. Your partner let me through because I am a clergyman, and I have come to bring comfort to the anxious members of my community in the midst of this terrible tragedy. I also have a bad leg and have trouble walking any distance."

"Okay," he said in an irritated voice. "Park over there by that TV camera truck, but leave them enough room to move easily back and forth along the side of the truck."

"Thank you, Officer." Mason thought of limping when he got out of the car, but he decided if either of the two policemen said anything, he would just tell them about the pain and how he has learned to bear with it, how he is a suffering servant. The TV truck seemed to be abandoned, so he scanned the crowd for any sign of a camera crew, but there were too many people milling around. He didn't remember where the entrance to the mine was, but it didn't matter now because bright spotlights were shining on it. He could see a few men going in and out of what must be the office because they were dressed in suits. There was another group standing near the front of the entrance. They were obviously miners, and they were arguing with each other. He couldn't hear what they were saying, but he knew it was not where he wanted to be. Mason decided to work his way toward the suits.

"Pastor Chalice! Oh, am I glad to see you. I'm glad they let you drive all the way. I guess they knew to give priority to a minister."

"Hello, Father. You're already here, I see."

"Yes, like you, I came as soon as I heard."

"And they let you drive all the way, too?"

"Yes, they were very gracious. What do you know about what's happened, Pastor Chalice?"

"Only that there has been a fire, some are dead, and they are waiting to hear about the others."

"That's correct as far as we know. About a hundred men got out alive, and almost another hundred are still in the mine. They don't know whether they are dead or alive. Some supervisors went in to assess the situation, and word is that they are dead now, too." The priest quietly crossed himself as he delivered this news and emitted a great sigh. "But we are here to bring Christ into this tragedy. Let us go together as brothers in Christ and bring whatever hope and comfort we can." The priest reached for Mason's arm, but Mason recoiled slightly.

"I'll be there in just a minute, Father. You go on ahead. I need to gather myself together first."

"I understand. You need a quiet moment. I will see you soon, then."

Mason thought, "The last thing I am going to do is let that little Italian lead me around like his pet puppy and be the spokesman for the press. I need to find out what's going on so I can present myself to the press as a compassionate authority." Taking in the entire scene, it seemed to Mason there was both chaos and order, with both trying to find their place. There were those who were working a Red Cross station, unloading coffee urns and water bottles. There were men trying to organize and make decisions about rescue, he presumed, and what appeared to be rescue crews arriving in trucks. And then there was chaos, people moving across the area, back and forth, looking for information, for their husbands or sons. A few women were huddled together hugging and crying, but it seemed no one knew exactly how the fire started, who was still in the mine, and whether or not they were alive. It was not the settled kind of setting Mason felt comfortable in, and he knew these people expected him to somehow bring hope to them. Then it occurred to him that it could be worse. He could be in Vietnam with bullets flying over his head or into him. "At least here there are TV cameras, and I might receive some kind of recognition for my sacrificial compassion, which might enable me to get out of here and back to civilization." Mason straightened his tie and moved toward the Red Cross table. It looked like a safe place to begin and gather some information he could offer the TV people. It was less crowded, and at least the people around it appeared to be clean.

CHAPTER TWENTY-TWO

Morning News

"**G**ood morning, Mr. Petroli."

"A good morning to you, Miss Agnes. You are later than usual today. You okay, not sick?"

"No, nothing like that, Petroli. My bosses are on the West Coast, and I have a few hours head start, so I can take it a little easier today and they will never know, unless you were to tell, of course."

"Not me. No tell on a pretty, nice lady like you. They in California? I hope not. We went to visit Maria's sister, and California rocks and rolls like Maria's hips. I'll never go there again, I told her. You go if you want, but I'll stay home in New York where there is no rock and roll. The ground knows where it belongs. What you want today, Miss Agnes?"

"I think I'll have a poached egg, wheat toast, small orange juice, and a cup of the best coffee in New York."

"Yes, Ma'am. I'll get your best coffee first, and here is your free paper, compliments of your friend Petroli."

"Thank you."

Agnes noted there really was nothing new in the news. Nixon was unveiling plans for getting out of Vietnam, while 30,000 anti-war protesters protested in Washington, DC. Speculation was that the North Vietnamese offensive in March might speed up the ending of the war. That same month, Congress sent the Equal Rights Amendment to the states for ratification, much to the delight of Agnes's sorority sisters. Helen Reddy was on top of the charts with "I Am Woman." In April, 70 nations signed a treaty banning biological weapons, there was fear of a coming cholera epidemic in Bangladesh, and the Yankees were talking World Series already.

When Agnes reached the office, it was quieter than usual. She was typically the first one there except the many mornings Mr. Bartlett came in early to make calls to Europe or get a jump-start on the day. She started the coffee and looked at her clean desk with the financials sitting on top. The peaceful morning made her realize how much she enjoyed her job, but Crystal's question kept resonating in her mind—*Couldn't we be doing more?* When the coffee was ready, she poured herself a cup and stood at the skyscraper's window and gazed at the Manhattan skyline. She could see the Hudson River, the tugs and barges navigating their way toward the docks or moving farther out toward the large ships waiting to be guided alongside a vacant wharf. What an amazing place, New York, a hub of so much activity. She decided she could cull some old files and do a little market analysis of her own.

Agnes had been so busy she hadn't noticed the time slipping away. She discovered she really enjoyed being there by herself. She even pretended for a few brief moments that it was her company and she was the boss.

She was opening her yogurt when the phone rang. "Agnes, this is Conrad. There's a fire at the mine, and it's really bad. Mr. Bartlett wants you to pull the safety reports from the federal inspectors and send them to our lawyers at Roscoe, Moorman, and Gardner. We may have to defend ourselves. Also, if anyone calls for information, say, 'The company is cooperating in all rescue efforts, and will do all it can for the benefit of its workers and their families.' Otherwise, don't say anything to anyone, and for God's sake, don't allow yourself to be interviewed."

"So, Conrad. Are there still men in the mine?"

"About a hundred. Nobody knows for sure . . . yet."

"Do we know if they're alive?"

"That's the critical question, and no one knows the answer. Gotta go. Bye."

She sat there for a moment trying to imagine the scene of frantic workers escaping a burning mine, people hurrying to the scene to help, and women trying to find out if their men are safe. She looked down at her yogurt and fruit on her desk and realized that she had no appetite. Agnes rose from her desk and stood at the west-facing window. She wanted to pray for them, but it had been so long since she had prayed at all. Then she decided if God heard prayers and it wasn't for or about her, it might be something God would care about. She closed her eyes and prayed for those people in Kellogg, Idaho, so far away in what seemed like another world. When she opened her eyes, she saw a pigeon on the ledge outside the window. No, she quickly realized it wasn't a pigeon—it was a white dove. She remembered the stained glass piece her grandmother had hung in her kitchen window, and she remembered asking her why she kept it there. "The dove, Agnes dear, is a symbol of God's spirit, God's presence. It reminds me he is always near when I need him the most."

Agnes thought of the time she asked her grandmother the worst thing that had ever happened to her when she was a child. Her grandmother had scolded her for asking such a question and then cried for a moment and told her. "When I was a little girl, just over six years old, there was an accident in the mine outside our village. Almost all the men in the village worked in the mine except the butcher, the pastor, the ice man, and the dairy man. The accident killed all those who worked in the mine that day, and only a few who were upside lived. Fortunately, my father was upside, but he was never the same afterward. We took all we had, which wasn't much, and came to America and joined our relatives who were already here. My father worked on the docks until he was too old to work. It's not just the miners who suffered, Agnes. We all suffered, the entire village."

Agnes glanced down at the dove, and it suddenly turned toward the window and looked up as if it were looking at her. Then it turned and flew away, lost in the Manhattan skyline. She found herself saying, "Thank you."

She realized it had been about an hour since Conrad's call, and she didn't remember returning to her desk or pouring herself more coffee. She let herself into Mr. Bartlett's office, picked up the remote, and turned on the TV.

Authorities have released little information about the source of the fire or its location in the mine. This mine has more than 100 miles of tunnels, and because of the size of the toxic cloud, mine operators have not been close enough to determine where in the mine the fire is exactly. We do know just over a hundred miners escaped safely, but at least that number, or close to it, still remain in the mine. It is believed if any are below the fire and could reach air vents, there is a chance they are still alive, but no one seems to know. Ironically, the mine owners were attending a meeting in Coeur d'Alene when news of the fire broke, reviewing, among other things, mine safety. Both owners and opera-tors of the mine are on the scene, but as I said earlier, they are not yet releasing the names of the missing men, or even of the known dead.

Things here are quite chaotic, as you can see. There are of course, firefighters and rescue team miners. The Red Cross has set up a station, mostly for families. There are press communications and many, many people from the surrounding towns. This just released, "There were 173 men in the mine," and we are unsure how many got out unharmed. We will try to see if we can get closer and perhaps talk to one of . . .

There was a flash of black, and the reporter disappeared. Agnes turned to another channel and heard a similar report. She muted the sound and watched the scene. She could see women huddled together, some obviously in tears, and some miners who had managed to escape, milling about appearing to be in shock. Agnes could see that there were some people sitting on the tops of trucks trying to get a better view of things like they would at a baseball game in a city park. It all seemed so unreal, yet she knew she was connected to it by pen and ink and financial and production reports. But she had a sense she was more connected than she had ever thought possible. Watching those women and remembering her grandmother's words—*We all suffered*—somehow made her feel more connected, and her heart hurt for these folks. "These are my people," she said to herself.

CHAPTER TWENTY-THREE

The Wait

Penny leaned against the door jamb of the boys' room. Even Cable had finally fallen asleep after they had asked Penny so many questions she couldn't answer. Then came their prayers, which tonight were from their frightened hearts. She was frightened, too, for Butch, for all of them. Tonight there was no giggling or rough-housing or pillow-tossing. They all laid there, each one alone with their thoughts about their dad. Cable was on the single bed; Kelly and Michael were on the bunk beds. They all had on their Christmas pajamas from Butch's mom, each one with a different machine. Cable had bulldozers, Kelly had dump trucks, and Michael had road graders. When they opened the boxes on Christmas Eve, they were all ecstatic and, of course, had to argue about who had the coolest piece of equipment.

Penny thought back to when each of them was born and where Butch was at the time. He was right there for Cable and almost drove her crazy. He kept saying, "Breathe slow, breathe slow" until she finally told him that if he said it one more time, she would take the baby as soon as it was out and leave him. When Kelly was born, Butch was fishing down by St. Maries but got back just in time. But Michael came early, and Butch was at work in the mine. Penny remembered Butch coming into her room while she was nursing Michael. He was covered with dirt, and a red-faced nurse was right

219

behind him yelling, "You can't come into a hospital all dirty like that." She remembered the tender look on Butch's face when he took his finger and touched Michael's cheek as their new son vigorously sucked her milk. Butch kissed her on the forehead and whispered, "You okay?" When she nodded, he turned and thanked the indignant nurse and left. Penny found out later that Butch went home, cleaned up, and took the older boys out for ice cream to celebrate. Then they all came to the hospital to see the baby. He brought both the nurse and Penny a rose. He never went out and celebrated with his men friends or got drunk when any of the boys were born. He just nested in with his family.

Her thoughts went to Butch in the mine, and she closed the door quietly and tiptoed to the kitchen, not that she actually thought the boys would wake anytime soon. She glanced back at the laundry area and saw the dirty clothes she was going to do today when the boys were in school and she and Sybil got back from Coeur d'Alene. "How suddenly things change," she thought to herself. She looked at the stove clock and realized her mother-in-law was a little late, but who could blame her? Her son and youngest brother were both in the mine. Penny thought about the families she knew who had more than one member of the family in the mine. "Come on, Louise, I need to get there," she said quietly as if getting to the mine would bring Butch out any faster. But at least she might know what had happened to him, and she wanted to be there when he did come out. He would wonder why she wasn't there.

Her eyes drifted to the deer antler hat rack by the back door. It held most of Butch's hats. "Men collect hats like women collect shoes," she thought. One of the loudest disagreements they ever had was when she wanted to get rid of two of his hats. "They're just broken in," he kept saying. All she could see was grease, holes, and filthy looking caps that covered her handsome husband's wavy black hair. There was his USA hat with the American flag across the front and his Boston Red Sox hat because he said they needed all the help they could get.

Whenever she said, "So you're wearing Boston today," he always said, "You watch. Someday they will break the curse and win the World Series." Then, of course, he had his Green Bay Packer's hat just to irritate his dad who was a Chicago Bears fan. She realized she was wringing her hands and wondered when she had breathed last when she heard a car on the gravel driveway.

"Have you heard anything?" Penny asked as the couple came in the back door and dropped at the kitchen table like labored hikers after a long trek across rugged mountains.

"Everything was about the same when we left, except they're talking about drilling from the other side of the mountain in order to get to the fire without having to confront the smoke. As soon as it's out and the exhaust fans clear all the air, they can go in and hopefully get to everyone." When Butch's father finished speaking, he put his head on his arms on the table and wept. His wife rubbed his back and pulled a tissue from her purse with her other hand and handed it to him.

"The boys are asleep, Louise. If you two get tired, go lie down on my bed. I'll be home as . . . well, before dawn."

"I'm sorry, Penny, I shouldn't blubber like this."

"Cliff, you don't have to be sorry. Besides, Butch got his tenderness from you and Louise, and I love you both for it. I'll let you know if I hear anything."

"That reminds me," Louise said. "The phone company set up a temporary phone line near the Red Cross table, mostly so reporters can call in their stories, but people can update their families, too. The way I understand it, no one can call in, but anyone can call out." Louise took Cliff's hand and put it against her cheek. "But if too many people want to use it at once, you might as well come home rather than wait."

"I'll try to call if I know anything at all. Oh, I almost forgot. There's some leftover spaghetti in the fridge, and there's still some of the bread you brought in the breadbox. I'm sure neither of you has eaten, and we all need our strength."

As she drove to the mine, Penny thought of all the families who were going through a vigil like hers. A hundred miners meant their immediate families, then parents and grandparents, brothers and sisters, uncles, all their children, and most miners' families were large with grown children in some cases. Miners competed for jobs and fought one another when things got heated at union meetings or sometimes a bar, but they were all family, and they would hang together, especially against outside influences like the government or owners as the sometimes violent history of the valley had proven. But when something like this happened, they all rallied to help each other. Earlier, she had noticed two women she knew from Osburn bringing food to the Red

Cross table, and miners from Burke and Murray had volunteered to be part of the rescue effort. She heard that a team was flying into Spokane from Colorado. "No matter what, the world was still filled with good people who cared," she said to herself.

Penny thought a moment and remembered it was Tuesday evening. She couldn't focus enough to recall what they usually did on Tuesday evenings. There wasn't bowling or her quilting group or Butch's American Legion Hall meetings. "I guess we just put the boys to bed and read or watch TV or work on our projects," she thought. That reminded her that Butch had bought all new parts for the barbecue and was getting it ready for summer. She pulled over before she reached the highway, hung onto the steering wheel like it was a life raft, and sobbed. After a few minutes, when the chills stopped and her body stopped shaking, she reached into her pocket and pulled out a small package of tissues. "The always-prepared mom," she said to herself. "I wish I had a dollar for every nose I've wiped, including my own." Penny wiped her face until she knew she could drive again. "Dad always told us kids, 'Know your destination before you start.' I know where I'm going, Dad. It's what I'll find when I get there that worries me."

Penny couldn't believe how many vehicles and people were at the mine. She counted four TV vans, several state police cars, two fire trucks, and three ambulances. There were several unmarked vans but not one hearse. She didn't think it reasonable, but she was willing to take that as a good sign. The first thing she did was head for the Red Cross table to see if they had a list of the men still in the mine and the names of the deceased they had not released earlier. She saw Amos Hamilton talking to a man she didn't know near the table, and he turned toward her as she approached.

"Your boy doing all right?" he asked.

"Yes, as best he can," Penny answered. "Thank you for watching out for him today. I really appreciate it."

"Nah, I didn't do anything," Amos said as he looked at his weathered boots. "Hell, excuse me, Ma'am, but he took care of me."

"It was good for him that you were here. Do you know if they have released the names of the men who died? Earlier, they said they couldn't identify some of them and were waiting to notify us. Have you heard anything?"

"Yes, Ma'am, it's just like you said. No names yet."

Penny sighed and turned toward the crowd. "What about the union people? Do they know anything?"

"I doubt it," the man said. "Reynolds is running for reelection, but to his credit, he is trying to find out all he can as fast as he can, but the owners are being very hush-hush. We just had a meeting about the safety issues a few weeks back, as you probably know. The mine received a report that they were not responding to recommendations from the Bureau of Mine Safety. We all know the safety officer, and he is one of the best. He just cares about the safety of the men, so the owners must not be listening to him. But frankly, Ma'am, all that is wind right now. The important thing is getting those men out alive."

"Yes, it is," she said as she wiped a tear from her eye and looked for a familiar face in the crowd. Penny realized as she moved toward the crowd that she missed having Cable with her. It was best he was at home, but she knew now how much comfort she had actually taken from him. "But no child should be at a mine disaster where his father might not survive," she decided. She felt a vile taste in her mouth as the thought parked itself in her mind.

CHAPTER TWENTY-FOUR

Winston's Lament

Winston Hitchcock couldn't believe his luck. One of the biggest stories to ever hit the region was now international news, and he was short personnel at the *Times*. He had been watching the news on TV when he heard about the fire at the mine. Between the printers' strike, an unusual lingering flu season, and the usual absences, he was short-handed. Worst of all, his best reporter was in the wilderness somewhere. And then there's Christina Mayberry. She's a little inexperienced, but so far, she's done good work. Besides, she's very attractive with that long, blonde hair and those beautiful, blue eyes. A little naive, but miners and all the men involved will fall all over themselves to talk to her. The more he thought about it, the better he liked the idea. Pete Webb got too much attention and was getting too big for his britches anyway.

Winston dialed Christina Mayberry's number, and a male voice answered with a flat "hello." Winston was taken aback and cleared his throat.

"I wish to speak to Christina Mayberry. This is Winston Hitchcock."

"Christie, your boss is on the phone."

Winston grimaced as the voice on the other end shouted. He tried to picture the appearance of this male by his voice, but he couldn't. Obviously, Christina wasn't as naive and puritanical as he had thought. After a moment or two, he heard her answer in a very professional but slightly nervous voice.

"Hello, Mr. Hitchcock. What can I do for you?" Winston was still processing the existence of her male companion and hesitated. He was tempted to ask who had answered the phone, but even he knew better.

"Have you heard the news about the mine fire in Kellogg, Idaho?"

"Yes, we saw it on the news. It sounds horrible."

We? There was that guy again. "I want you to cover it for us. Stay on top of all the developments, do some interviews—wives, miners, owners, and so on. Do you think you can handle it? I may send someone to help later in the week if this thing goes on very long, but for now, you're our presence there."

"I'm flattered you thought of me. I'll get ready and get on it first thing in the morning," she said with great enthusiasm.

"No, you'll get on it tonight . . . now . . . Tuesday night," he said firmly. This is a rescue operation. They'll be working around the clock. The weather is good. Drive like you're going to a fire because you are. Mayberry, this is a major story, and I mean major. We need to be on top of it. Now that I think about it, I'll send Simpson and Hackwith, but not until tomorrow. Any questions?"

"No, sir. I'm on it. Goodbye."

"Sorry to ruin your evening, buddy boy, whoever you are," Winston said to the phone as he hung up. He looked out the window at the lights on Mercer Island where the Mercer brothers kept the brides-to-be when they brought them from the East until the men of Seattle could afford the bride price. Winston walked into his study and looked at models of Boeing aircraft dating back to the first single-engine canvas and wood two-seater float plane built in 1916. He gently picked up the 1920s BB-L6, the first plane to fly over Mt. Rainer. "What a thrill that must have been. Now we fly over it all the time and think nothing of it," he said out loud to no one. Winston always wanted to fly, but his eyesight doomed that dream. As he prepared for bed, he thought of Christina Mayberry. And where in hell was Pete Webb?

Christina drove into the night, stopping in Moses Lake to refill her coffee thermos, use the restroom, and get some gas. Her brother had put her sleeping bag in her car and thrown together some food items. She looked at them on the seat next to her and thought, "He's a guy." There was no way she was going to eat Italian salami all the way to Kellogg. She had picked up a sandwich at an all-night grocery in Ellensburg, but she was too excited to be hungry. She had only been at the paper a year and a half, but she had tried really hard at everything she did. She only had one story, which had been edited to pieces, so she figured she was doing okay. But this . . . this . . . was a huge story, and she figured Hitchcock assigned it to her because Pete Webb was on vacation somewhere.

She really liked Pete Webb. He was always kind to her and didn't treat her like she was an idiot because she was younger and new at the newspaper. He showed a real interest in anything she was working on and always gave helpful suggestions without being patronizing. When she reached the top of Fourth of July Pass, she looked for any sunlight that might be peeking over the mountains farther east, but it was still too early. Although she was tired of driving, her adrenaline was high and her excitement was beginning to accelerate. She had never been to Idaho before, but she had heard that its beauty was amazing. If she had not been in such a hurry to get to Kellogg, she would have stopped to watch the sun come up in full bloom. But even in the dark, the trees and mountains seemed to be making a glorious statement.

Christina was not prepared for what she would soon see when she arrived. She was a good student and a fast learner, but she had never been around death or even seen someone who had died. Winston Hitchcock could not have sent a more naive reporter to cover this horrendous tragedy. She had caught sight of the rescue operation on the gas station's TV screen when she stopped in Moses Lake for gas. But the small screen couldn't capture the enormity of the event, even with the incessant commentary by a man who truly appeared out of his element. The radio had been her constant companion on the trip and had informed her of some of the developments.

> *Authorities are saying they neither know the cause of or the location of the actual fire. Rescue attempts have been thwarted due to the toxicity of the smoke that rises into the sky like an untamed serpent, killing everyone in its path. Nearly a hundred men are believed to be in the mine, and there is no word whether or not any are still alive.*

Christina wasn't sure what angle she should pursue first. Maybe just the facts of the matter and then some of the human interest aspects. She was feeling the anxiety of a new challenge but at the same time telling herself that she was up to the task. She noticed old equipment and blackened stumps as she approached Kellogg, but she didn't exit because the radio said the mine was east of the city on Big Creek Road. When she turned onto Big Creek, she immediately saw an Idaho State Police car with its red lights flashing. The officer, who had been leaning up against the car, stepped onto the road with one hand raised. She stopped and lowered the window.

"Are you headed to the Sunshine Mine, Ma'am?"

"Yes, Officer. Here are my press credentials," she said as she handed the State Trooper her credentials and gave him what her father called her Scandinavian smile.

"*Seattle Times.*" You didn't waste any time. Go up the road until you see the next patrol car, and then park. Do not drive past it," he said in a rather commanding voice. "Ma'am, this may be a little out of line," his voice suddenly sounding gentler. "I know you have to do your job, but there are a lot of tender souls up there. Try to remember that, okay?"

"I will, Officer, and thanks." Christina began to ponder his words as she drove closer to the mine. She thought a comment like that might change one's perception of the police.

Suddenly, she heard a horn and quickly pulled to her right only to see a car with two men fly past her going back down the road. "Why would they be in such a hurry going away from the mine?"

When she turned the corner, the first thing that caught her eye was the twisting cloud of smoke rising into the sky. "Toxic smoke," she said out loud to herself. Then she took in the patrol car, news vans, and the Red Cross banner and table. There were crowds on each side of the yellow tape, and some of the women were crying. Christina was surprised at the number of children she saw. Most of them were clinging to women, and others were standing mute near the Red Cross table with what looked like older siblings.

Then, with no prelude or warning, Christina had a revelation like few experience. She would never forget these few seconds because they changed her view of life. When she looked at the women and children, she realized this event wasn't about a fire in a mine but about them and their lives, or at least the future of their lives. She began calculating how many children may be losing their fathers if every miner only had two children and there were no survivors. This just wasn't a temporary crisis event; this was an event that would be felt for generations to come. She thought about her own father and how important he was to her life. Suddenly, her body shook with some undefined tremor. She felt cold as she thought about the potential of how many widows and fatherless children there could be. With a new resolve, she knew it was time to go to work. There was a story to be told—in fact, more than one.

*****

EXTRA! EXTRA! READ ALL ABOUT IT.
IDAHO MINE FIRE, 100 MEN TRAPPED—
ARE THEY ALIVE?

J. EDGAR HOOVER DIES. READ ALL ABOUT IT!

Oscar had been standing on his wooden platform yelling this at the top of his lungs for hours, and he was just beginning to feel the little tingle in his throat that comes just before your voice gives out.

"Oscar, give me a paper, please," DJ said in a rather mellow voice.

"Boy, you're sure quiet this beautiful morning. Why so glum?"

"Beautiful? Oscar, it's raining again. What's so beautiful about that?"

"In case you haven't noticed, I'm selling papers out of both hands, and not just to the regulars. This mine fire is big news, and ol' J. Edgar kicking the bucket last night makes for a double-dipper. Big news. I'm all for big, *big* news," he said with great enthusiasm.

"Here you go. Thank you, sir."

"I haven't sold this many papers this fast since D. B. what's-his-name jumped with the cash last November. Do me a favor, and take these 20s and go to First National around the corner and get me more quarters."

"EXTRA! HEAD OF FBI DIES! MINE FIRE DISASTER IN IDAHO!"

"I'll buy you one of Wally's breakfast hot dog specials."

"Yes, Ma'am, here's your paper. Thank you. Yes, it is awful."

"EXTRA! EXTRA! MEN TRAPPED IN FLAMING MINE!"

"Thank you, sir."

"Just tell the girls at the bank that Oscar needs more quarters. They're my lunch girls. They take good care of me."

"J. EDGAR HOOVER DIES. READ ALL ABOUT IT. EXTRA! EXTRA! MEN TRAPPED IN IDAHO MINE!"

"Sure, I'm glad to help, but I'll pass on the hot dog. What do you mean they're your lunch girls?"

"Nosy, aren't you, Mr. Pretend Investigator. They come here every Thursday, sit on my box, and eat their lunch from Wally's. They all happen to be soft on the eyes, so they attract a number of young gentlemen who work nearby. It has boosted my sales on Thursdays, which is usually a slow day. Then once a month, I buy all the girls lunch. Wally wins, I win, and the girls win. I'll probably be invited to more than one wedding. But hurry up and get those quarters. I'm running low."

"EXTRA! EXTRA! FBI HEAD DIES! MINERS TRAPPED IN MINE. READ ALL ABOUT IT!"

DJ wondered if Pete knew about the mine fire and if he was covering it for the paper. He could call a friend at the *Times*, but he decided to go to Pike Place Market and see what, if anything, interesting was going on.

CHAPTER TWENTY-FIVE

No Man's an Island

Pete enjoyed being by himself and removed from the clamor of his daily life and problems, but he found himself yearning for some human contact. He replayed in his head the conversations with Faith and realized he missed the sound of her voice, her teasing smile, her laughter, and even her tears. More importantly, she had given him much to think about. He and Brindle had fished, and he had visited the newborn mule, but he longed for some company, for some noise apart from the quiet hum of nature and the occasional rumble of a train in the distance at night. He found himself looking longingly at a plane in the sky earlier that day, wondering about the people in it. "Maybe I'm not a hermit in the woods kind of guy," he said as he walked back to the cabin.

It was now Wednesday, and he was pretty sure he would have to touch civilization soon. It was his fourth day to be alone, and he was tiring of the sound of his own voice. He went into the small bedroom and picked up the red and white plastic radio he had noticed earlier. "The batteries are probably dead," he mumbled to himself. He carried it out to the porch where the reception might be best. When he turned it on, it squawked. The static sounded like scratching glass with a sharp object. He turned the volume down as fast as he could. Finally, he heard a clear voice:

J. Edgar Hoover died at his home last night . . . (static). . . . He was 77 years old and had served as director of the Federal Bureau of Investigation since its inception in 1935. During this time . . . (static) . . . organizations, Hoover served under eight presidents . . . (static) . . . .

"The paper must be abuzz with Hoover's death," Pete said to the red and white radio. "People were beginning to wonder if the old guy would ever die," he informed the wilderness around him. He stared at the radio, disbelieving what he had heard.

Pete could feel the vastness around him, and he knew he was a small piece within a much grander scene. He thought for a moment about the fleeting nature of life. "While 77 years seem like a long time, the years pass by quickly. You see them coming and going, but you have no brakes. The people who try to stop it get caught up in a cauldron of distorted perceptions. You can start a day looking at the hours before you, and suddenly the month, the year is gone," he said to no one. Then Pete remembered what Brindle had said. "When you find your mystery girl, don't wait." Pete began to wonder if he had been given an opportunity he shouldn't pass up.

Before Pete could turn the radio off and mull over what he had just heard, he heard this:

In other news, the Sunshine Mine fire in North Idaho is still burning, and more bodies . . . (static) . . . were removed this morning, which still leaves . . . (static) . . . miners trapped inside. Rescue efforts are continuing around the clock, and it is . . . (static) hoped the remaining are alive.

"In Los Angeles today, it was announced . . ."

Pete held the knob and turned off the radio. There was no question in Pete's mind what he would do next.

Pete drove up Big Creek Road as he had been directed by the giant of a man at the gas station. The man was crying as he told Pete how to get to the mine, wiping his face with his greasy hands on his ruddy cheeks. Pete couldn't remember if he had ever seen a man that big cry before. But then he remembered Sean McDonald after a firefight in Nam. They had won, at least the officers thought so. The Viet Cong were either dead or had fled back into the jungle. But as they went through, clearing the village, Sean came to the last hut and heard a noise, a whimper. When he looked in, there was a young woman holding a child who was about three years old. The young boy had been shot and was dying. Sean fell to his knees and started crying large sobs. One of the guys said, "What's he crying for? He doesn't know if he shot the kid." But Pete remembered that Sean had shown him a picture of his three-year-old son just before they went in-country.

Pete knew this mine disaster must be bad, but how bad he was yet to discover. He first noticed the long line of old cars and pickup trucks parked randomly along the road, some very far off. When he got nearer, he saw media vans, a Red Cross station, and a police barricade. Beyond it, he saw a large crowd milling about and a few cars close to what he guessed was the mine operation's office. There was no sign of Faith. He had come to a complete stop before the barricade, and an officer was moving toward him.

The policeman glanced at Francis with what Pete took for a look of disdain. But he smiled when the officer said, "If you back up a little bit, I think you can squeeze between that Chevy pickup and that Ford sedan. But be careful not to hit anyone," the officer said with a chuckle, like Francis would fall apart if Pete casually bumped another car. He realized if he did park where he was told, he wouldn't be able to get his door open. Just as he was contemplating his next move, a car on the other side of the road pulled out and began moving slowly away. Pete quickly shifted and darted across the road before anyone else could take the space. As he walked past the officer, he grinned as if to say, "See that, smart guy?"

After showing his press pass, which he always carried with him, Pete stepped around the barricade. His eyes went to the media cars, but he didn't see any that looked like they were from the *Times*. He knew there was a big story here, but right now, he was only interested in finding Faith. He approached the Red Cross table, which was no more than a sheet of plywood over two sawhorses. As he walked up, he saw two women talking, and one kept wiping tears from her cherub-like cheeks. The other was saying, "You have to get yourself together, Maude, or you won't be able to help anyone."

"I know, Pearl, but there are so many men still in the mine, and who knows if any of them are alive?"

"Yes, but our job is to make these families' wait a little easier, and your crying won't help." In an attempt to disengage herself from her tearful friend, the woman turned toward Pete. "How can I help you, young man?"

"I'm looking for a friend. Her father is a miner."

"Was he working in the mine, do you know?"

"No, I'm afraid I don't."

"If he was, they'll have him listed, but they haven't released a complete list yet. Sometimes, miners trade shifts like waitresses do, and they don't always list themselves. So it's hard to know who is and who isn't in there. The fire started yesterday, but we still don't have a list of injured or dead."

"I'm sorry, it's my friend I'm looking for, not her father, but if he was in the mine, she'll be here. In fact, she may be here anyway because she's a nurse."

"What is your friend's name or her father's name? Maybe we know them."

"Her name is Faith Marks, and her father's name is Lou, I think."

"Oh, my gosh! Faith returned?" the scolding one gasped.

"You know her, Ma'am?"

"Well, I did, but not really. She was a teenager when she ran away, I mean, left here. One of my neighbors was the librarian, and she spent a lot of time with Faith. It was so tragic, her losing her mother like that. Why do you think she's here?"

"I brought her part way, and she may be here by now."

"Oh my!" the woman kept saying. "My, oh my! Did her father know she was coming?"

"No, she didn't tell him."

The woman was holding her chin and shaking her head, and her words became mutterings the more she seemed to think about the idea of Faith returning. Pete decided these two couldn't help and left. It seemed to him that no one here had a normal posture. They were either standing on something to see over the crowd, they were stretching to see, or they were hunched over hoping the news of death would pass over them and their loved one would come home today. He scanned the crowd looking for Faith. He spotted a woman who seemed to be reassuring others while at the same time carrying her own burden and anxiety. Pete stepped up.

"Excuse me, Ma'am."

"I'm sorry, I don't want to be interviewed," she said with some irritation as she looked down at the press pass hanging from Pete's neck. "Please, go away." She turned and began to leave.

"I don't want to interview you, Ma'am. I just want your help," Pete shouted over the noise of machinery being moved about, which, he guessed, was part of the rescue. The woman had already taken a few steps, but she stopped, not in response to what Pete said but to the tone of his voice. She turned, squeezed her hands together, and took a deep breath.

"I'm sorry, young man, we're all tense. My name is Emma Reed. How can I help you? You aren't from around here?"

"No, Ma'am, my name is Pete Webb. I'm from Seattle, and I'm looking for Lou Marks. Actually, I'm really looking for his daughter, Faith. She came to see him, and she was not at his house, so I figured she might be here."

"Faith has returned? Oh, what a mercy. I don't think I would know her if I saw her. She . . ."

"Pete!" Her voice carried beyond the noise of the machinery and the fire trucks with their engines running continually. Both Emma and Pete turned as Faith ran up and threw her arms around Pete. Then she stepped back and held his hands in both of hers. "I'm so glad you're here. Did the paper send you?"

"No. I came looking for you. They don't even know I'm here," he said as he caught his breath. He noticed her hair was all out of sorts, and he thought there were expressions of both stress and relief on her face at the same time, if that were possible. She looked very tired, but not the kind that comes from lack of sleep. She stepped toward Pete with her winning smile and hugged him again. He could feel tension ease from her.

"Excuse me, Faith. You may not remember me, but . . ."

"Emma Reed! Oh no! Is Charlie in there?"

"I'm afraid so, but I don't think you need to worry about your father. He doesn't work this shift, Dear. Oh, you look so good. I'd forgotten how pretty you are."

"Thanks, but one of his neighbors told me that he and my dad had switched shifts so the guy could go to a family event. I'm afraid he's in there, Emma, like a lot of other good men. As Faith spoke the last three words, there was a hesitant tremor in her voice, and a tear began to fall from the corner of her eye and slide down her cheek. Emma reached out and embraced Faith with a hug that only a woman who has had her heart torn apart can do. Then Emma whispered in her ear, "Lord, deliver our men to light and life, and if not to us, to your tender embrace. Amen." Faith looked at Emma and mouthed, "Thank you."

"Em, Em." All three of them turned at the sound of the woman's voice. Pete realized she was one of the women from the Red Cross table, the non-blubbering one. "Sis, Charlie's not here."

"What do you mean he's not here? Then where is he?"

"They just gave us a list of three men who were the first out of the mine yesterday. They were taken to the airstrip and then flown to the hospital in Coeur d'Alene by members of the air rescue team. It happened so fast that few knew they had even left. But Charlie's name was on the list."

"If they took him to the hospital, it means he's alive or at least has a chance. Thanks, Pearl, I'm going to Coeur d'Alene to be with Charlie. You can watch after Greg."

"Greg's a big boy, no, a young man. Don't you worry about him. You sure you're in a mind to drive yourself?"

"I'm in a much better mind than I was a few minutes ago. I'll be careful now that I know my Charlie's alive and being taken care of. I just hope he's not hurt too bad. Enough talk, I'll call you at the house." She started to leave and then turned back to face Faith. "I'm glad you came home, Dear. Your father is a changed man. I think God worked a quiet miracle in him. I hope he's okay."

"Thanks, Emma. You go be with your Charlie, and you can tell him I still remember him giving me peppermint sticks when I was a kid."

"I will. Bye."

Pete and Faith watched Pearl accompany Emma to Charlie's truck and hug each other. Pearl gave a hesitant wave to her sister and then returned to the Red Cross table, which had a flurry of people around it.

Emma's drive to Coeur d'Alene felt like the longest she had ever made. She wished she could turn her mind off and not think of so many things, but a freight train of ideas was running through her head, never stopping to unload. Normally, she would have enjoyed the scenery, especially around Cataldo with the wildlife habitat and water fowl, but not today. She was intent on one thing—getting to Charlie as fast as she could. She thought about Charlie lying there in the mine, the ambulance ride to the small airport, the rescue plane, and their dream home. Would the property stand empty if Charlie died? If he died, she would sell it. No, she would give it to Greg. "Stop! Listen to yourself. Charlie's not dead. Oh Lord, let my Charlie live, please. He's such a good man, but you already know that, and he is a humble man, and you know him well. He talks to you all the time, and he doesn't ask for things like most. He just thanks you for embracing us in Jesus. Please don't take him now. It's selfish of me, but please."

Emma pulled hastily into the Kootenai Hospital parking lot and hurried toward the emergency entrance. As she approached, the automatic doors opened, and she knew the rest of her life would be determined by what she found inside.

CHAPTER TWENTY-SIX

Jammed Up

W hen Christina awoke, it took her a moment to remember where she was and how she had gotten there. She looked around the room and saw the painting *Haymakers* by Homer on the far wall. She realized for the first time as she gazed at the painting that both the men and the women worked in the fields gathering hay, unlike mining, which seemed to be exclusively a man's world. But when the mines had trouble, it wasn't only the men who suffered and maybe died, but their women and children suffered as well. Christina had never been around such sorrow before. When they carried out the dead men, all conversations stopped. Everyone waited within a shared fellowship of tension. Who is he? That's all they wanted to know, but because it was a fire, identifications weren't immediately known.

The soft pastel colors gave Christina a warm feeling, and she rested a moment before she lifted the handmade quilt off her legs. She went into the adjoining bathroom and stared at her face in the mirror. "Oh, how frightening! You could star in any monster movie," she said as she turned on the tap. "It's Thursday. I wonder if they have cleared the mine of the smoke, put out the fire, and gotten all the rest of the men out." She had spent all day Wednesday trying to get information for the *Times*, but no one was sharing much. She happened to run into, literally, a guy from the Associated Press, and he was willing to share some information he had overheard. She phoned it in after getting back to town and finding a pay phone. Now she knew why that car had been racing away from the mine earlier. It was the press, and they were trying to find a phone and meet a deadline on the East Coast.

She was surprised how caring and sensitive the state police were to everyone. "Another stereotype destroyed," she thought after her interviews yesterday. She had worked well into the night and was exhausted when she asked at the Red Cross table where she might find a room for the night. She found out that the town was already filled up. Pearl Shields overheard the conversation and invited her home to the house she shared with her sister and brother-in-law. She explained that her brother-in-law had been taken to the hospital in Coeur d'Alene and her sister had gone to be with him. Pearl fed Christina some leftover pork chops, and then Christina went right to bed. She was so tired that she just kicked off her shoes, threw the quilt over her, and buried her head in the down pillow.

Now it was morning, and Christina could smell fresh coffee. She was more than ready to eat before she headed to the mine. Because she knew her expenses would be covered, she thought maybe she would just get some coffee here and then find a place to eat where she might pick up some news from table chatter. When she entered the old-fashioned country kitchen, she saw a young man with blond hair sitting at the table reading a book. He didn't notice her at first, but with her next step, the floor creaked, and he looked up.

"Oh, hi. Did you sleep well? My name's Greg. There's fresh coffee, and the mugs are in the cupboard above the coffee pot, and if you need sugar, it's there, too. The cream, real cream, is in the fridge. In that warming pan are some fresh muffins my aunt made before she went back to the mine, and there is some homemade raspberry jam on the counter. I was tempted to eat all the jam with a spoon, but I knew they wouldn't be too happy with me if I did. Let me move these books so you can sit down."

"Thank you for all this hospitality," Christina said with a smile, all the time thinking how wonderful it is to wake up to all of this—homemade food and a very handsome host. She would forget about table chatter for now. "You say Pearl is your aunt?"

"Yeah, both Pearl and Emma are, and my uncle Charlie lives here, too. He got a faraway look in his eyes and seemed to choke out the last few words. "Sorry, they took Charlie to the hospital in Coeur d'Alene on Tuesday. He was one of the first out of the mine, and Emma didn't even know he was gone until Wednesday when Pearl found out as she was working at the Red Cross table. He's alive, but his lungs are damaged. I'm doing an internship for the University of Montana, and this is my last term. They're letting me stay here until graduation."

"Do you know anything more yet?"

"Charlie's in intensive care, alive, thank God. But they're concerned about the damage to his lungs and maybe his brain. No one knows what the lingering effects of the fumes are going to be for the survivors."

"I'm glad he's alive, and as you know, you have to take each moment as it comes," she said with a slight smile while picking up a muffin. "What are you studying?" Christina asked as she took a generous bite of the warm muffin and tried to keep the jam from spilling down her chin. While she licked her sticky fingers, she watched Greg watch her, and he chuckled. Christina wiped her chin with a napkin.

"My emphasis is in corporate management," Greg said, "but it hasn't been what I thought it would be. Now with the fire, the mine will be shut down after they get everyone out, for all kinds of inspections."

"For how long?" Christiana asked as she reached for another muffin.

"It could take anywhere from several months to as much as a year. I'm hoping the school will waive the last few weeks when they know that the fire is the reason I can't complete the term."

"So do you work in the mine office?"

"Yes, I work for crazy Mr. Nims, but don't quote me on that or he will be sure to give me a horrible report. Frankly, he may anyway, but I don't care anymore. I just want to get away from him."

"What makes you say he's crazy?"

"Have you ever heard of the term *obsessive compulsive*?"

"Sure. Is Mr., what his name? Nims, obsessive compulsive?"

"He sure is, and about important things like how a piece of paper lines up on his desk or whether pencils in a container are sharp all the time and the points are always up. I could go on and on, but it just makes me crazy."

"You don't think Pearl would mind if I ate another muffin, do you?"

"Actually, it's Emma's recipe, and don't worry, she takes great pride in her muffins. She is a very humble woman, so you'll be in the clear. Besides, nobody eats less than three. I guess you heard about J. Edgar Hoover? It's been all over the TV."

"I heard, but right now, the Sunshine and its people get all my attention."

Greg looked at her and smiled. "Aunt Emma thinks watching television before dark is a violation of the Lord's command to be fruitful. Uncle Charlie has a hard time fighting for football time. He says, "Monday night football was a gift of God himself." Greg hesitated and wiped his eyes. "I should be at the mine now, doing whatever I can, but I just can't face it," Greg admitted. "I'm mustering up my courage. Funny, I was always known as the big tough athlete, but I'm afraid of facing the possibility of all those men still inside being dead and the possibility of my uncle's death, too. At least he got out alive, so he has a fighting chance. I keep thinking Aunt Emma will call with good news."

"It's hard for everyone, Greg. The closer it hits home, the harder it is. I talked to a woman yesterday whose husband, son, and brother are still in the mine. It's amazing that she can hold it together at all. I was praying for the men as I drove here. They were nameless, but now as I meet these women, I'm praying for their men by name. I have written their names in my book. Your uncle will now be at the top of my list."

"He's due to retire, and then they're planning to build a house on the Clark Fork River. They've been planning on it for as long as I can remember. I guess death interrupts everyone's plans when it comes like this."

"Probably more than you and I can imagine because we're young. I think it interrupts life no matter how it comes, which is why it's called a curse. It alters the present and the future and ends our dreams in ways we can't ever know. Right now, we can only hope and pray," Christina said and thought to herself how tender this young man seemed.

"Forgive my curiosity," Christina continued, "but you look older than a college senior."

"I'm older than most collegians. I spent two years in the Peace Corps before going back to school."

"Where were you?"

"Tanzania, helping put in water systems and educating people on basic hygiene. It taught me a lot about the value of people, regardless of their nationality or culture. I've thought about going back someday, but first I need to finish my education. I have also thought about going back to ranching and forgetting this corporate stuff. I'm one of those guys who just hasn't figured his life out yet. What about you? Aren't you a little young to be covering such a big story? No offense meant."

"None taken. Yes, I am, but it so happens that the newspaper is short-handed, and the lead reporter is on vacation and can't be reached because he's in the wilderness somewhere. Funny thing, when my boss called me to assign me to this story, he called me at home, and my little brother answered the phone. He is only a year younger. He attends the University of Washington and lives with me. I think Mr. Hitchcock thinks I have a live-in boyfriend," she said, laughing.

"So there's no boyfriend?" Greg asked as he glanced down at his empty plate.

"Not for now. There's no one I'm interested in, and no one seems interested in me. The job keeps me really busy with odd hours. And that reminds me, I have to get back to the mine. Thanks for the muffins and the news about Hoover. Guess I'll see you later, if Pearl lets me stay another night."

"Oh, she will," Greg said with a conspiratorial smile. I'll be in and out, too. Things are pretty strained right now."

Christina stood to leave, thinking, "I wonder how Hoover's death is being handled at the paper. My breakfast was sure more than I ever expected. Nice company, too."

Greg was thinking how wonderful it had been to visit with Christina and watch his aunt's raspberry jam almost drip off her chin.

CHAPTER TWENTY-SEVEN

Angel on the Move

"It's time to get a little rest," Hollis whispered as he sat down in his recliner and opened his worn, black Bible. He knew he probably wouldn't get much out of it on this lazy Saturday afternoon, but it was sometimes like that. His thoughts drifted to that load in Shreveport and not wanting to head back with an empty truck. And he remembered the kid in the Shreveport cafe—in the so-called New South—who called him a disgusting name and then went after him with a broken ketchup bottle. Hollis wondered how the kid felt when the wrath of his large black fist went through his little jaw that day.

Hollis was reaching through the layers of canvas that kept turning into spider webs that clung to his arm . . . he was reaching . . . he heard a bell. He had to stop the bell before the spiders heard it . . . and came. Hollis hated spiders. No, it wasn't a bell . . . it was the phone. Hollis's mind shouted at him, and he knew he had to answer the phone. He sat up from his comfortable position on the couch, realized his Saturday afternoon nap was over, and reached for the phone. "Yo!" Hollis croaked out of his dry mouth as he pulled himself up on one elbow.

"Hollis, wake up! This is Merle."

"What time is it, Merle?"

"It's six thirty, buddy, and I'm sorry to bother you on your weekend off, but it's an emergency."

Hollis knew Merle was not one to be easily alarmed, and he didn't use the word *emergency* to enhance his sentences like some folks do. If he used the word, Hollis knew somebody was bleeding at his feet or Merle was in deep need of help. "What do you need me to do?" Hollis asked as he tried to wake up and clear his head.

"What do you do better than anybody I know? Drive truck. Did you hear about that mine fire in Idaho, in the Coeur d'Alenes?"

"Yeah, but that was several days ago. Haven't heard much lately. Don't they have 'em all out by now?"

"That's just it. They don't, and there's a possibility that some of those poor guys still down there could be alive. Over at the base, they got this thing they use to clean missile silos, and they think they can lower it down a shaft to get down and see if anyone is alive and maybe get to them if they are."

"Where do I go?" Hollis said as his feet hit the floor.

"Go to the base, Gate F. It's on the south end about a quarter mile off Presidential Way. The rig is loaded, ready, and fueled. At the county line, you'll get a police escort to the state line and then pick up another one in Idaho. You got red flashers all the way to the mine. If you get low on gas or have to pee, tell the Smokey in front of you, and they'll arrange a refuel ahead, even if they have to jerk some grease monkey out of bed to open a station."

"Weather?" Hollis grunted as he pulled on his boots and reached for his flannel shirt. He noticed the pocket was torn. He was going to fix it, but he hadn't gotten to it yet. "Maybe when I get back," he whispered to himself.

"Good until Idaho, and then some rain. Might be a few flurries on the peaks, but it won't be sticking, and it's nothing to slow you down."

"What about shotgun?" Hollis grabbed his keys and waited patiently for the answer, knowing his bladder was screaming at him that he had to pee.

"I couldn't find anybody, and there is no time to lose. We might drop one on you along the line; otherwise, it's all you, ol' buddy."

Hollis grinned. "We could end up violating the eight-hour rule, and the Feds might squawk," not that Hollis cared much about regulations or regulators when a job needed to be done.

"Anybody gets in the way of this trip is gonna have to answer to a lot of angry miners, and I wouldn't want to be around. Besides, somebody with heavy clout planned this trip. Need me, beam me up on the CB. Oh, Hollis, I don't have to tell you how important this may be. Those men have been stuck down in that dark hole with no food or water for four days. You may be their only way out. Good luck."

Hollis hung up and headed for the bathroom. "No, you don't have to tell me how important this is," Hollis thought. "I stood outside that coal mine in West Virginia for two days 'til they brought my daddy out. No, this is one man who knows how a miner's family hurts."

Hollis splashed some water on his face hoping to wash some of the spider webs away. In the kitchen, he opened the fridge and pulled out two Cokes, a banana, and an apple and dropped them all into a fishnet bag he had picked up in Tijuana. He grabbed a bag of chips from the top of the fridge and headed out the door. When he stepped into his old pickup, he wished he had a dog. "Maybe that's what I'll do after this run, get myself a hound."

When he got to Gate F, two sentries stood at the entrance, and Hollis rolled down his window and started to say, "I'm the trucker . . . ," but before he could, the gate opened, and the sentries were shouting, "Go! Go! Go!" He saw the rig backed into the loading dock. It was a red Peterbilt and looked almost new. He could see the load on the back and could make out the shape of a round dome under the canvas. As he stepped out of his pickup, he realized the truck was idling and making the purr only a fine-tuned diesel could make. An Air Force officer flanked by two others came forward and greeted him.

"I'm Lt. Colonel Evans, and your truck is ready, Mr. Washington." Evans grasped Hollis' hand and shook it. Hollis could tell this man thought a lot of his handshaking, but he wasn't interested in a pissing contest right now. Any other time, he might have thought about teaching this man how to kneel.

"Good," Hollis grunted as he threw his bag into the cab and turned to examine the tie-downs on the load.

"I already said everything is ready," the officer said with an edge of irritability in his voice. Hollis knew this man was not used to either being doubted or opposed.

"I know exactly what you said, Sir," Hollis said with a little impatience of his own. "But this rig is now my rig, and I'm responsible for it." Hollis never looked at the officer. He just continued to check that everything was good, and it was. When he was done, he approached the officer.

"You can thank your men for me, Sir. They did a good job." He knew the emphasis on the work others had done would grate on the officer, but he also knew a bunch of airmen had done all the work. It was always the guys you rarely see who do the work, and others wear the medals. Hollis tipped his cap at the two men behind the officer as he climbed into the cab, and there was no mistaking their pleasure at the exchange. Hollis looked at the instruments, the leather seat, the air conditioner, the stereo radio, the small fridge, and two thermoses of black coffee and thought to himself, "If this wasn't so urgent, I could enjoy myself." Ordinarily, he would have checked the oil and the brakes, but he knew the mechanics had this rig ready, and it would be fine. "Besides, sometimes ya gotta have faith in people. Yes, Mama." He pushed the clutch and grabbed the gear shift. Hollis felt the transmission shift smoothly as he played it like a musical instrument, and the giant rig eased forward. As he passed through the gate, the two sentries saluted, and Hollis pulled twice on the horn. He was on his way.

It wouldn't be long before darkness would set in and give Hollis a clear night lit up by a full moon—the kind deserts are famous for. It was the kind of night where country western songs try to fill in the loneliness of the dark, but all they do is remind you how small and alone you really are. Hollis loved the roar of the engine, the hum of the wheels on the road. The load was light, and the trailer felt as if it weren't even there. That would help with the climbs, but if he ran into slick conditions, a light trailer would not have much traction. He would have to watch himself on some of the mountain corners, especially going downhill. He began to calculate how long it would take to get to Kellogg. No one had said anything yet, but if he had an escort, he didn't figure he had to worry about the speed limit, just keeping the rig on the road. If he could average 65 miles per hour the whole trip, it would mean hauling like crazy through Nevada and Idaho. He could make up for the slow climbs that might drop him to 35 or 40 miles per hour, but he figured he would no doubt make it in record time and arrive Sunday morning. He knew it wasn't about trip speed bragging rights; it was about saving lives. Then he realized it was an answer to the prayer he had prayed a few weeks ago about carrying a load that could help somebody.

He was coming to the county line and could see two sets of taillights ahead about a quarter of a mile. "Well, boys, it's about time we decided who's gonna be in charge of this here haul." Hollis pushed the pedal and could feel the truck engage its power for additional speed. As he passed the police cars, he could clearly see the emblems on the sides and the bars on top. Hollis pulled on the air horn and hollered, though they couldn't hear him. "Let's get our asses in gear, boys. We got some folks waitin' on us." He glanced down at the speedometer, and he was doing 76 miles per hour as he roared past the idle State Troopers. Suddenly, the CB squawked, "Mr. Washington, we are on your tail, but as soon as we get our heads back on, one of us will get in front, at least if we can catch you." Hollis chuckled at the response. He could see the red lights flashing in his rearview mirror, and he felt like he was part of something important.

"You can call me Hollis, boys, and I think you can stay in front easily enough, but the guys in the next state may want to hang back on the downgrades. Fortunately for you, Nevada is flat and straight here."

"What's your handle, Mr. Washington?"

"Sambo."

"You gotta be kidding. Like little black Sambo of former restaurant fame?"

"That's me, boss. I'm black, but nobody ever called me little. And the name is really from a book. The restaurant copied it because it was a popular children's story; that is, until people got so sensitive. Now they can't tell the important from the ridiculous."

"I'm afraid if we call you that over the radio, we might get busted by the brass. How about just calling you Hollis?"

"That's fine with me, and it would sure please my mama. I do have one question for you boys. What is our situation here? I understand the speed laws are going to be overlooked, but what about truck lanes, inspections, and such?"

"Well, Hollis, that's an interesting question. Our orders are to escort you to the state line and not let anything impede your way. I'm sure it will be the same with the officers on each leg of your trip. I would assume when you get to Kellogg, the last officers to escort you will give you a ticket for every violation along the way and fine you enough to put you behind bars for the rest of your days."

Hollis could hear the officers laughing and thinking it was a cute joke. But he also realized that some state governors and the Feds had gotten together and decided they were going to pull out all the stops so the men down in that black pit might have a chance. Hollis knew right then that he would do the same. He glided through a curve bordered by a dry wash and pressed the accelerator farther toward the floor.

CHAPTER TWENTY-EIGHT

Leaving the Scene

Early in the morning on Friday, Pete had met up with Mayberry, Hackworth, and Simpson at an area created for the press to gather. He wasn't sure whether it was created by the press out of a desire to keep a distance from the tragic reality or if it was an attempt by the locals to cage the hyper-hungry cats who seemed more interested in their stories than in lives.

"So Winston is putting you in and pulling us out," Lester Hackworth said to Pete with a slight sneer in his voice.

Puzzled, Pete looked at all their faces. The two men were staring at him with a look of challenge, and Christina was staring at her feet. "What are you talking about?" Pete asked, disturbed by the looks he was getting.

"He wants almost all of us back at the paper to help cover the ramifications of Hoover's death and some new D. B. Cooper angle. He's sending me to DC," Simpson offered, "which, I have to say, after being here will be a welcome change. Sleeping in a real hotel and having a salad with more than one choice of dressing is something I'm looking forward to."

"But you're in the middle of covering a major mine disaster," Pete said. "If all the missing are dead, it will be the worst hard rock mining disaster in American history."

"We know, and all of us agree, but Hitchcock says it's old news and nobody cares anymore except the locals, and we can print stories about the fire from the news services. The Associated Press guy here has unearthed some great stuff, so Winston may be right. He said the fire has gone from page 1 to page 17 of the *Los Angeles Times*. Besides, if he's putting you in, why are you talking like he's pulling everyone out? He's not pulling you out, is he?" Hackworth asked.

"Winston doesn't even know I'm here, and I wasn't going to tell him, but now I think I need to," Pete said with a tone of disgust.

Pete shook his head in frustration, looked up at the mountain that overshadowed the mine, and let out a breath that could be seen by all in the early morning air. It seemed to have a life of its own until it mingled with the floating breath of the others. "Doesn't he realize what this means to hundreds of children and women? It will have an impact for generations if all they do is keep pulling out dead bodies."

"You don't have to convince us, Pete," Simpson interjected. "We've seen what's happening here. I talked to a lady yesterday whose father, husband, and son are all still missing. Frankly, I don't know how she keeps it together."

"Well, you guys do what you have to, but I'm calling Winston to see if I can get him to at least leave one of you here with me."

Simpson put his hand on Pete's shoulder. "If I don't get to go to DC because of your call, I will forgive you, but you'll owe me a steak dinner at one of Seattle's finest," he said, grinning as he turned away with Hackworth following, shaking his head slightly. Christina didn't move. She looked around at the mountains and then the people. Then she turned and looked at Pete with a sadness in her blue eyes.

"I doubt anything you say will change Mr. Hitchcock's mind," she said. "I don't think wisdom is a frequent companion of his."

"You're pretty wise for your age," Pete said as he matched grins with Christina's. "You're right about that, but I'm going to try to get him to leave you here. I've observed you, and you're not only a good reporter but you're a good human being." Christina blushed slightly at the remark, and before she could say anything, Pete continued. "As you probably already discovered, the story from the top will be formed in favor of the owners and management. They will be 'doing all they can to help families,'" he said as he curved his fingers in the traditional quotation marks, "and discover the 'error'—meaning, 'what did a stupid miner do wrong?'—that caused this mess. You will see all responsibility will be moved away from them. But the real story is all around the people. Most of the stories written so far that I've seen are about statistics, not about lives, despair, loss, hopelessness, or faith and courage—except for yours. They're doing the same as they did with Vietnam—body counts. There is an abundance of important stories here. Just look over there." Christina cast her eyes across the road to the crowd of women who huddled outside the official tent, waiting for any crumb of a word about their men.

"See the woman on the left wringing her hands, shaking her head, and saying no over and over?" Pete continued. "She already knows her brother is dead, and she is waiting to hear about her husband. See the lady in the red coat nearest the fire truck? She has two sons in the mine, and she is doing all she can to comfort the others. You need to get alongside these women and tell their stories so the real tragedy isn't buried in statistical reports and sterile news accounts. Another thing, months from now after the inspection as to what actually happened and what caused the fire, there will probably be a congressional inquiry. Convince Winston to let you follow that story. You're good enough to do it well."

"Thanks, Mr. Webb, but . . ."

"Pete."

"Okay, Pete, but aren't you going to write about all of this?"

"Maybe someday, years from now. But right now, I'm working on some changes in my life, and I need to be with Faith. Outsiders would say she needs me right now because her dad is in the mine, but the truth is that I think we need each other."

"I think I understand. I saw you two together yesterday and how you were reaching out to people. I'm understanding a lot of things for the first time in the last few days. Thanks, Mr. Webb . . . I mean, Pete. Thanks again for the advice and especially the affirmation. I'm supposed to meet one of the rescue supervisors in a few minutes, so I gotta go. If I have to leave here, I think I'll do it slowly, if you know what I mean," she said with a conspiratorial grin. "I hope it all works out well for you, and I hope Faith's dad is alive."

"We all do," he muttered under his dancing breath. Pete watched Christina leave. She walked with a determined stride toward the official tent, and he thought to himself that some young man is going to be the envy of many when he marries her.

"Mr. Hitchcock, Peter Webb is on line two," said Mr. Hitchcock's personal secretary. Winston grabbed the phone. "Where in the hell are you? There's a huge mine fire in Kellogg, Idaho. J. Edgar Hoover died, and the FBI thinks it has a new lead on D. B. Cooper. I need your ass in here now! We're swamped with good stuff, and you're prancing through the wilderness like Davy Crockett."

"I was fishing, not hunting like Crockett. I know about all of that. I'm at the mine. Simpson, Hackworth, and Mayberry brought me up to date."

"Good. You're already there. You can give it your take today and then get back here. I'm pulling everyone out, and then I want you on Cooper. People are fascinated with him. They're making D. B. Cooper T-shirts that say 'Come Fly with Me' or things like 'Jump for Cash.'"

Pete stared at the bulletin board in the gas station as he waited for Winston to finish. He noticed a pink flyer for a rummage sale at the Methodist Church on Saturday and wondered if such a thing would still go on given the disruption the fire had caused everyone. He doubted it would.

"Winston, the story here is too big and important. The impact on so many people's lives is beyond comparison; it's beyond comprehension. If you need to pull Simpson and Hackworth, do it, but leave Christina. She's become trusted among these folks. They don't see her just as another reporter. She has empathy; they relate to her. The story is, after all, their story. If you neglect the impact of this on real people, you'll be making a big mistake."

Winston listened to Pete with an impatience bred of privilege and then emptied himself into an outburst. "Look, Webb, I'm the owner-editor of this paper, and I call the shots." Winston thought it interesting that Pete was all too willing to let the men go but wanted to keep Christina there. He also referred to them by their last names but her by her first name. He figured there was more behind it than Pete's appreciation of her reporting ability. "Pete probably doesn't know about the live-in she has in Seattle," he thought.

"I'll run the paper, and you just work on what I tell you. Now get back here so you can follow up on the Cooper story."

Pete closed his eyes, pinched the bridge of his nose, and said very calmly and slowly, "Did you forget? I'm on vacation, and I have more than a week left." There was a pregnant silence on the other end of the line that penetrated the miles between them.

"I'm cancelling your vacation. Get back here now!"

Pete could hear the frustration and tension in Hitchcock's voice, and he could picture the veins on the man's neck appearing with his face bright red. When Pete responded, he spoke with such a gentle authority that even he was surprised at the tone of his own voice.

"Winston, ol' buddy, while I was alone in the cabin and out fishing, I did a lot of thinking about life, about my life. I have a different perspective than I had when I left. I encountered something on the way that set my mind down an unfamiliar path. I now view things differently than when I left Seattle."

"I don't care about how you view life, damn it! The only path I want you on heads straight back here, pronto! I need you here, now!"

"If you'll let me finish, I was about to tell you that I've met someone, and after much thought, I've decided to give . . . *you* . . . a raise—I quit."

"What? You can't qu . . . quit!"

Winston suddenly found himself talking to an obnoxious dial tone that kept buzzing in his ear. He stared at the phone, feeling very alone. He gently placed the phone on its cradle like it had just been hurt by something said and turned to the side. He removed a bottle of scotch and poured himself a drink. His hands were shaking, and he spilled some. His bewilderment was so great that he didn't notice. He wondered if Christina was Pete's "someone." Despite his very expensive private education, Winston was unaware that most jealousies are the fruit of self-created fantasies. His fantasies, coupled with his ego-inflamed imagination, left him ripe for the picking.

* * *

"DJ, this is Pete. You awake?"

"Hi, Petie. Stupid question. You know I'm allergic to sleep. You at that mine fire?"

"Yeah, I'm here, and it's horrible."

"It was all the talk until Mr. FBI croaked, and now it's all about the secret files and who's going to get scandalized. Oscar hasn't sold this many papers since JFK was assassinated. How did Winston get hold of you? I thought there was no phone at the cabin. Did he send out an Indian scout?"

"He didn't. I got here on my own because of someone."

"Someone?"

"Never mind that. It's not why I'm calling. I need your help. I need you to call Tom Stockwell at the *Post*. Winston is pulling everyone out because of Hoover's death, and this mine fire is too important and bigger than anyone even imagined. It's more than the number of men. It is the number of women and children, too. It's like a meteor crashed into Lake Washington, affecting more than the folks on shore. Besides, there are still men in the mine, and even though they haven't found any alive, that doesn't mean there aren't some down there waiting to be rescued. Reporters need to be here. This is going to have an impact for generations of folks."

"I assume you told all this to Winston and none of it penetrated his over-privileged plaster of Paris brain. I thought you had more influence with him, being his number one guy."

"No, he's obsessed with Hoover and D. B. Cooper. He has no clue what he's neglecting. I tried, but I don't have any influence with him now anyway. I quit."

"You what?"

"Just listen, DJ. Look, call Stockwell, and tell him I'll be at this number at 5:00 p.m. your time today if he has any questions. You got it?"

"Yeah, but who's the someone, and what do you mean you quit?"

"I'll tell you later. I got to go now."

"Wait! I've got to tell you about Gwen."

"What about her? She okay?"

"That would depend on your interpretation, but most would say she is more than okay."

"DJ, what about Gwen?"

"All right, I don't want to break your heart, but my half-awake intuition says your heart is elsewhere for some reason. Gwen has moved to London."

"London?" Pete shouted.

"Easy, writer guy. Evidently, your girl had her eyes on this Brit while she was supposedly with you. He's a biggie at Barclay's. He put a shiny on her left hand, and I guess wedding bells are warming up to compete with Big Ben."

"That's wonderful. Gotta go. Later, DJ."

DJ heard the sound of the receiver drop. "That's wonderful? That's wonderful?" he repeated out loud to himself. "Your girl gets engaged and leaves the country, and it's wonderful?" DJ decided his friend Pete must finally be ready to give his heart away. He just hoped the "someone" was ready to receive it.

CHAPTER TWENTY-NINE

Shadowy Memories

Hollis was focused on his driving, but even so, his mind could travel across timeless landscapes at the same time. Sometimes they were familiar, and other times they were new and perilous. But it wasn't the landscapes that posed a threat, bore caution signs, and made him uncomfortable. It was the scenarios played out on the landscapes and the actors who played them. The shadowy figures that moved across the geography of his imagination and memory could be far more frightening than anyone he really encountered. He figured it was that way with most folks.

Hollis remembered the time out behind Slandstone's grocery back in West Fork, West Virginia, on a Saturday afternoon. It was July, and the sun was somewhere beyond the top of the sky shining straight down on them with blazing white heat. He wanted to go to Bixby's farm and swim in the hole and swing on the rope, but the others said they did that all the time. Today, they needed some real excitement, something daring. Grant Tucker decided they should steal something from old man Slandstone. He said the grocer had so many things in his store that he would never miss whatever they took, but Hollis also knew it was wrong, and he wasn't anxious to begin a life of crime. If his daddy found out, it would be a trip behind the lean-to that covered their wood supply, and he could already feel his butt burning.

But what would be even worse would be the silence at supper. His mama and daddy would say "please pass this" and "please pass that." If he or Everett or Sissy started to say a thing, they would get "the look." Those cold, black eyes of Daddy's would turn a keyhole in their souls. Their will to speak would shrivel like a plum on a tin roof in August. And Mama would stare at you, meaning, "Don't you speak, child. You done brought shame on this house." Hollis had seen it the time Everett had "borrowed" the strawberry flat from the back of Jason Turnipseed's flatbed while he was in Slandstone's buying some beer. After that, it was quiet at supper for a time longer than tomorrow.

Freddy White had broken the sticks and held them in his clenched hand so nobody could tell which was the shortest. The fat on Freddy's chubby little hands engulfed the sticks. Hollis knew if he picked the shortest, he would have to go into Slandstone's and steal something. But he hadn't decided which was worse—facing Mama and Daddy or being called "chicken" by all his friends. Hollis could remember knowing he would get caught. Mama told him the good Lord always revealed the ways of the wicked. So no matter what Grant said, Hollis knew stealing was wicked work.

The sun was so hot that Hollis wondered if the good Lord was already preparing him for hell. Willy Sharp took the first pull, and it looked real long. When Grant pulled his, it was the same. Then there was only Freddy and Hollis left, and Hollis knew he would lose if he was last because that's the way it was in a movie he saw once in Anderson. He reached for the sticks, but Freddy pulled his out first, and his was long. Freddy just opened his hand and let Hollis stare at the short stick in his dirty, chubby hand. Hollis looked at the stick and then at the hole in the left knee of his pants and wondered if he could crawl through it and disappear. When he looked up, they were all looking at him, grinning. Grant took the short stick out of Freddy's hand and held it up to Hollis's nose. "Go in there, and get something worth having."

"Like what?" Hollis remembered asking. His daddy had told him that sometimes if you're in a tight jam, just ask questions, and sometimes the other guy's answer will give you a way out.

"How 'bout some gum?" Freddy always wanted gum.

"No, that's too easy. How 'bout a ginger ale from the cooler?"

"Slandstone will hear the ice moving. It always makes a slish slosh noise, and he'll catch me."

"Yeah, they chorused together, ginger ale."

Hollis approached the front of Slandstone's and saw the clock on the courthouse across the street. It was moving toward two o'clock. He would never forget that sight or that time. He was hesitating, waiting for the clock to chime when the town's quiet was shredded by the siren from the mine. He realized for the first time that he never heard that clock chime that day. Something was wrong, and everyone knew it at once. Everyone was moving toward the mine. Hollis remembered Slandstone coming out of the store and jumping into his Ford pickup with the missing rear fender. He yelled at the boys to get in the back. Hollis took three steps and was over the tailgate. They all made it except for Freddy who was too slow, and Slandstone wasn't waiting for anyone. Clem McBride hopped on the running board as they passed the Shamrock Cafe and held onto the open window. Pace Renfrew jumped on the other side as they cleared the edge of town. Hollis was glad Pace was there because his daddy said if he was ever in a bind, he would want Pace at his side. Hollis didn't know yet if his daddy was in a bind, but he knew he was at the mine.

The entrance to the coal mine was a mile up the road and hundreds of miles beneath it. When they turned off the county road, they could see a cloud of black dust drifting just above the trees. They were among the first ones there. Men were running everywhere. Hollis almost pitched out of the truck when Slandstone stopped just below the slag heap. Slandstone and the other men ran toward the office, but Pace Renfrew grabbed a man who was headed toward the equipment shed. Hollis couldn't hear what he said, but the man kept shaking his head, and Pace lowered his like he was saying his prayers. Hollis saw commotion by the mine office and could see people bending over men lying on the ground. Hollis didn't want to go over there, but he knew he had to for his mama. She had to know if Daddy was hurt, dead, or still in the mine. He could tell that some men were still in the mine because so many were putting on gear and running toward it. Hollis squeezed between a post and a pile of cable and looked carefully at all the faces.

Some of the men were moving an arm or a leg and coughing a lot, but the others didn't move. The man closest to him was motionless, and Hollis noticed a fly walking across his forehead, first one way and then the other. If Hollis didn't know better, he would have thought the fly was making the sign of the cross. He stepped forward and brushed the fly away and glanced at the other faces. They were all black with coal dust like black chrysalises awaiting their transformation into butterflies. He knew none of them were his daddy, but they were somebody's daddy. He recognized some of them and began to feel a tear for the kids who wouldn't have a daddy anymore. Noise came from the mine, and Willy grabbed his arm. They looked toward the mine entrance where a crowd had gathered. Mr. Dixon, the mine supervisor, was standing on top of a backhoe shouting about a rescue team.

"How many are still down there? Do you know?"

"About 30. We know some are alive because they have been sending signals up by tapping on a pipe. We're trying to get a count, but they are not all in the same spot. We got some out who are already dead, so we can assume that there are probably others dead as well. But now we got to do everything we can to get everybody out alive. A crew is coming up from Anderson to help, but that will take about an hour. We can't wait that long. Let's get to work. Hanson over there will divide you up and tell you what to do. Slandstone, we need lots of water, food, and blankets. Keep a tab; you'll get paid by the company later." Hollis turned to watch Slandstone go to his truck, and that's when he saw his mama climbing off the back of a flatbed and Jason Turnipseed helping her down. He ran to her, shouting, "He ain't here, Mama, he ain't up here with those men over there."

Wrapping him up in her arms and swallowing him up in her breasts, she said as her chest heaved, "He's down there, Honey. He's down there in dat black hole. Then she prayed, "Oh Lord, deliver my man from the pit, deliver his soul to the light of day. Oh God, have mercy." Hollis could remember the hot day turning dark; the smell of coal dust, coffee, and baked beans; the sounds of men shouting; the grinding of machinery; and Dr. Halldime giving quiet instructions throughout the night to volunteer nurses. Hollis didn't sleep that first night. They pulled out eight more men. Six were breathing, and they rushed them to Anderson to the hospital. The other two were taken down the hill in a pickup to the funeral parlor. "Funny thing," Hollis thought, "West Fork wasn't big enough for a hospital, but it had a funeral parlor." He had never thought of it in all those years.

His mama sent him home and to town on stupid errands, but he always raced back to the mine, not poking along and throwing rocks and taking his time like he usually did when she sent him on errands. The day seemed to last forever, and for all the activity, nothing seemed any different. It was almost like this is the way life had always been. He remembered being at the mine with everybody in town, all talking about the same thing like some unseen force was pulling them together with an unseen magnet. Hollis thought he would stay up again the second night, but he couldn't find the strength to stay awake. He slept and then was awakened by a great silence. It came with the dawn. As the yellow-orange sun silently rose above the mountains, all the machinery stopped. The shouts had transformed into whispers. Everyone stopped whatever they were doing, and all eyes turned to the mine entrance.

The men marched out of the mine two by two like ants in formation, each pair bearing a stretcher. Their heads were bowed, and they watched where they put their feet, careful not to meet anyone's eyes. Each pair carried one man, and it was clear that these miners were now pall bearers. Hollis remembered his mama's arm over his shoulder, and when the third pair emerged from the dark shadow of the mine's entrance, she grabbed him so tightly that he thought she was going to snap him in half. She stepped past him and walked up to the stretcher. The man in front looked up and stopped. Hollis recognized Pace Renfrew and saw trails of black mud draining from the corners of his eyes and down his cheeks. Hollis' mother touched Pace on the shoulder, and whispered something, and he nodded. She bent down and kissed his daddy on the forehead. Then she turned and walked toward Hollis, her face looking as if the cast of old age had come over her in that single moment. She took his hand and said, "Let's go home, Son. Your brother and sister be needun us."

Hollis snapped out of it and reached over in his swift-moving semi with its precious cargo to grab the thermos and pour himself some coffee. He was glad it was hot and black. Any other kind just ain't coffee. He couldn't help but think some things just stay the same. Here he was, racing to a silver mine thousands of miles from that other disaster that always plagued his memory and reminded him of his daddy and West Virginia where folks had prayed that their man was alive and hoped he would come out of that mine like Lazarus had walked out of that grave.

The radio squawked. "Hollis, there's some construction up here," the State Trooper said. "They've been resurfacing one side, and the road is a little rough. You may want to take it easy through here."

Hollis set the coffee aside and spoke to the radio. "I'll tell you what, Officer. You hit the road at 80, and if you're still in one piece, then I can do 85, copy that?"

"Copy, but it's a dumb ass idea. We're already slowing down to 45."

"Are both sides bad or just ours?"

"It looks like only the northbound lane. They only do one side at a time."

"Well, boys, I mean officers, I guess this is when we find out how good you are at your job. I recall you said you're not supposed to let anything be an impediment to our trip. Well, you better clear the southbound lane cuz I'm moving over." Hollis pulled on the air horn and moved into the southbound lane to head north. He knew it wasn't as reckless as it sounded because he could see for miles, at least if a car had lights. And besides, with a patrol car running interference, he felt safe. "You let me know when we've passed the rough road, and I'll get back where I belong." He could see the patrol car hesitate but then pull into the left lane and accelerate. "It ain't like we're in the middle of commuter traffic, gentlemen."

When Hollis crossed the Nevada-Idaho border, he was picked up not by two State Troopers but by four, two in front and two behind. He could feel the adrenaline overcoming his fatigue. Crossing the border into Idaho was like being on the five-yard line when you don't have any push left in you, but the adrenaline makes you feel like you can move a mountain. So you move a mountain of men and score. Hollis had made one rest stop, but otherwise he was planned to make a straight-through drive of almost 800 miles. The four cruisers with their lights flashing made it look more like a parade than a long-haul run. They had to slow down as they weaved their way through the narrow streets of the small town not far from the mine.

It was early Sunday morning, but plenty of people were standing on the sidewalks watched the flashing cruisers and Hollis's rig pass by. No one waved as you might expect. They just stood in silence. On one corner, Hollis saw two ladies holding hands and crying. In front of City Hall, a man made the sign of the cross and extended his hand as if he were blessing the caravan. Looking up one side street, Hollis saw a line of cars and realized he was looking up the hill toward a cemetery.

Lord, may what I am hauling today help keep someone alive, even if it is only one. Amen. Amen. Amen.

Hollis followed the cruisers that eventually left the main highway and started up a gulch where he figured the mine was located. As he approached, his pathway was cleared of a few stragglers who hadn't gotten the word that a big truck was arriving. Men with safety vests guided him to the correct spot. He hadn't even turned the rig off before a crew was disassembling his load and a large crane was moving into position.

He opened the door and stepped down to stretch his legs and see if the rest of his body was still attached. He could see fatigue on every face he saw—miners, women, bystanders, Red Cross workers. "A crisis has become an endurance contest," he thought to himself. As he turned around, a State Trooper approached him with a smile on his face. "Here it comes," Hollis thought, "the end of the joke." But rather than pretend to cite Hollis, the officer simply put out his hand, and Hollis did the same. They were both big men, each with an air of confidence and a heart of compassion. They stood there for a moment sharing their strength, not as a contest but as if they wanted to give whatever they had to the other. No one took notice of those two strong hands bound together for a brief moment, one white and one black. The hands were only an extension of their hearts.

"Thank you, Sir, for bringing this. We hope we can find the last few alive."

"I was glad to do my part, Officer, but like you, I just pray it helps."

"Amen to that," and the officer turned and left. Hollis was about to step back up into the cab when he felt a jerk at his sleeve and turned. He looked down. There was a young boy standing there holding a cup of coffee.

"You want some coffee, Mister? My name is Cable, and my dad's still in the mine. They're going to use that thing you brought to get him out. Mom had to take my brothers to Grandma's, but I got to stay cuz I'm the oldest."

Hollis looked at the boy and thought about a day in West Fork so many years ago. "It don't matter if we are white or black," Hollis thought to himself, "we have one common enemy—death. It robs children of their daddies and sometimes their mamas. We may have our problems with each other, and we often don't understand each other, but we'll come together to fight this enemy. The Lord sets us free," Hollis thought as he looked at the hopeful boy.

"Thank you, Son. I'll take the coffee, and I'll pray for your daddy."

Hollis could see a man approaching over the top of Cable's head. He had seen that look a thousand times. It was time to move out. Lifting himself into the cab, he heard the boy say, "Pray for my mama. She and my dad have been in love forever." Hollis swallowed, but not coffee. He almost choked on the thought of what this boy's mama must be going through. It's been nearly five days, and she doesn't know whether her husband is alive or dead. He gritted his teeth, shook his head, and shifted the empty truck into reverse.

CHAPTER THIRTY

Stormy Weather

Now that his job was done, Hollis could give his attention to the message his stomach was sending him. He suddenly realized he had a hefty hunger as he slowly drove back down Big Creek Road. When he reached Kellogg, he saw a neon red cafe sign and pulled the rig to a vacant spot on the street around the corner. When he entered, there were no customers, but the place was clean, and he could tell by the aroma that good food homesteaded here. Just as he settled himself at the counter, the kitchen door hit the wall with a dull thud, and a waitress nodded at Hollis as she came through the door with a tray of coffee cups.

"Coffee?" she asked with a smile that would make anyone feel welcome.

"Please, Ma'am," Hollis sputtered, surprised by how awkward he felt in the presence of her smile. He had seen a thousand waitresses in his time, but there was something different about this one.

"Can I get a hamburger and French fries this time of morning? And some water, please. Oh, and a large glass of milk, too, please."

The waitress nodded and said to Hollis, "You want me to pour the milk into your coffee? Just kidding. If you're tired of French fries, we got real fresh onion rings, not the frozen kind. They're really good, too."

Hollis thought as he looked at her face that if she were selling used cars, she would sell everything on the lot. "That sounds good," he said with a sudden shyness.

She disappeared for a moment and was back cleaning and straightening things. Hollis heard a bell. She pivoted and went to the window and grabbed his order. "Want any ketchup with that? You're not from around here, are ya?" she asked as she placed his food in front of him.

"No, I'm just passing through. No, thanks, I'm not a ketchup guy. Umm, these are good onion rings. Hot, too. Now, Ma'am . . ."

"The name's Stormy, like the song "Stormy Weather." My real name is Rachel, but no one calls me that. Stormy comes from my personality," she said and winked. She returned to her back counter work. "You're like in the Bible, Rachel?"

"Yeah, my parents said I'd be worth waiting for."[9] She half turned and blessed Hollis with her radiant smile again. "I'm still waiting," she laughed.

Hollis laughed, too. "I think your parents got it right. How come there's nobody here? This is good food."

"Like I said, you're not from around here. We had a huge fire in the Sunshine Mine with 93 men trapped inside. That was nearly a week ago. So far, everyone they have found is dead, but there are still some inside. People are either at the mine, waiting word about the last few, or consoling those women whose men died. People don't want to look like they don't care by coming out, or they're afraid they'll run into someone who has just lost their man, and it's as awkward as can be, especially if you are one of the ones whose man got out alive. Some families lost more than one man, too. I think by now most folks know where they stand, except for the ones still waiting. I think the town wants to come out of the gloom, but with daily reminders of death and loss, it's hard. Folks have been coming out more, but it's early yet. This is a hard place to scratch out a living when things are good, but right now, just being here is hard."

"Yeah, I know about the fire. I just brought a piece of equipment from Nevada to help them get deeper into the mine without messing with the smoke, I guess."

Stormy stepped closer and leaned on the counter. "You're the truck driver they all said was coming with that missile silo thing?"

"Yes, Ma'am. I guess I am."

"Well, bless your soul. You sure got here fast. You got jet engines on that truck of yours?"

Hollis laughed. "No, but I had State Troopers leading me all the way so everyone would get out of my way. Most folks were in bed most of the trip, and the weather was good. You mind, Miss Stormy, if I ask you a personal question?"

"Well, that depends on how personal, and I don't even know your name yet."

"Hollis, my name is Hollis Washington."

"Well, Mr. Washington, now that I know who I'm talking to, you may ask your question. But be careful, because I'm not far from a very sharp knife," she said with a teasing grin.

"I'm surprised to find a black waitress in this part of the country. How did you get here?" he asked in almost a whisper, even though the cafe was empty.

"Well, there was some mine worker problems earlier in the century—shootings, explosions, and a terrible rift between the miners and the mine owners. To keep the peace and settle things, the governor of Idaho, Steunenberg I think was his name, called in a regiment of the National Guard, and they happened to be all black. Well, at the time, there were fewer than 300 blacks in the entire state, so to the locals, it looked like a foreign invasion. Anytime you got young soldiers around young women, no matter what color anyone is, there's bound to be trouble, and I guess there was more than enough. Anyway, some of those soldiers liked it here, just like the Navy ones who were at Farragut on Lake Pend Oreille during World War II. They came back or never left. My grandpa was one of those soldiers. That's how I got to be here, apart from my mama being in a family way from my daddy. The mining problem was settled, at least for a little while, but the governor was assassinated after he was out of office for what he had done. There was a big trial in McCall, and Clarence Darrow was one of the attorneys. Some famous people from all over the country came to watch it."

Hollis stared at the remaining onion ring, took a healthy bite of his hamburger, and just thought as he ate.

"I think Rachel is a better name for you. It's from the Good Book, and it tells the story of a woman loved desperately by a man. That's a good sign for any woman."

"Mr. Washington, I think we are done with the personal items. Here is your check." With that, Stormy went into the kitchen, and the door thudded again.

Hollis wiped his mouth, shrugged his shoulders, and watched the door as he reached for his money. He looked at the bill. He sat there for a moment into eternity, and then he dropped the 20 on the counter. The kitchen door didn't move, so he slid off the stool and left.

The next day, Hollis woke up in a cheap motel on Sherman Avenue in Coeur d'Alene. There was "no room in the inn" in Kellogg, and he only managed to get this one because folks had been leaving. The Sunshine was still news, but old news. He usually didn't sleep in, but he realized as he stared at the cigarette smoke–stained ceiling that the road race had stressed him out more than he thought, even with police escorts. That particular big rig carried a heavier load than anyone could see, and it was on his shoulders and heart, not the axles. Hollis padded across the not-too-clean floor and peeked out the window. He knew it was going to be a nice day and picked up his worn, leather Bible. It had been his daily companion since Harriet Greenwood, his neighbor, had given it to him before he went into the Marine Corps. She said to him, "Hollis, life is not fair, nor is it always pleasant. Pain can be a hard companion, but this living Word will be a friend who will never let you down because the good Lord lives and breathes through it."

Hollis slowly opened the pages and closed his eyes. "Lord, I don't mean to be a bother, but I pray you will get anyone out of that mine who is still alive, and be with all of those families who have lost their men. Especially be with Cable and his ma if it turns out to be the case for them. Amen." Hollis opened his Bible to Jeremiah 29:11–14 and read:

> *For surely I know the plans I have for you, says the LORD, plans for your welfare and not for harm, to give you a future with hope. Then when you call upon me and come and pray to me, I will hear you. When you search for me, you will find me; if you seek me with all your heart, I will let you find me, says the LORD.*

Hollis sat in the chair by the window for a long time. "To give you a future with hope." He thought what that might mean, and he prayed with his chin on his chest, his large hands in his lap. Finally, he said, "Well, Lord, if you're going to give it, there isn't much I can do but wait, and it sure seems like life is full of waiting."

"Merle, this is Hollis. It's delivered."

"I know. I saw it on the news this morning. You did real good, Buddy. Where are you now?"

"I'm in Coeur d'Alene, Idaho. But I was wondering if I might get a few days off before I head back."

"It turns out the company name was mentioned three times on every morning news show, so the big boys said you should get a two-week paid vacation starting now. How does that sound?"

"It sounds great, but what about the truck? What do I do with it?"

"I've arranged for you to leave it at the truck stop at the Broadway exit in Spokane, just off I-90. Rent yourself a car. The company's picking up the tab. But don't get any ideas and pick out a Maserati."

"I wouldn't think of it, but thanks for the idea, Merle."

"Very funny. Oh, I almost forgot. There will be a check for your vacation at Western Union in Spokane."

"Thanks again, Merle." Hollis heard the click at the other end and knew Merle would be watching his little black and white TV stuffed in a corner of his dusty, cluttered office with a broom and toilet plunger hidden behind the door. He knew the broom was rarely used. It was Merle's little kingdom where he handled dispatch of the trucking fleet like a little general sending out his troops.

Hollis walked a few blocks to a small diner. He enjoyed the chance to stretch and move about, and his muscles yearned for some exercise. The maples along the street and in the yards were fully leafed, and the sky was a robin-egg blue. Somewhere in the distance, he heard a dog bark. It made him think again that maybe he should get one. "Your muscles need a little more exercise than butt sitting," he said to himself. "Maybe after I cash my check, I'll find a place to run."

Hollis looked at the steak and eggs in front of him and felt guilt knowing the pain and helpless hurt roaming around and settling into the mountain valley he left yesterday. "But the living have to keep living, and I did what I was asked to do." And Miss Mercy always said, "A hungry man is no good to anyone." And she worked hard at keeping everyone fed back at her little cafe in West Fork.

There were few in the diner because the breakfast crowd had already gone. One young couple had a child—he guessed he was about one—in a high chair. They were feeding him scrambled eggs as fast as the little guy could chew. He was like a baby bird awaiting the next bite. The parents were taking turns so they each had a chance to eat. Hollis couldn't help but smile at the scene. The mother caught his look between bites and smiled back. "Nothing brings joy like new life," he thought to himself. He could hear some of the chatter and occasionally picked up talk about the mine. When he finished, he spoke gently to the waitress as she passed his table. "Ma'am, could I have a cup of coffee to go, please? I wanna go sit by your beautiful lake and sip some good coffee."

"Sure thing. Most of us drift down there during the day if we get a chance, just to sit by the lake and let it calm our souls." As he left, Hollis smiled at the young couple. They both smiled at him, and the open-mouthed baby had a bewildered look on his face as the distracted father held a spoonful of eggs midair beyond his reach.

"The waitress was right, Lord. You made one beautiful lake here, and the sun shining like that must be like angels dancing on a mirror." He began to quietly sing to himself a song he had heard in a big church in Colorado Springs.

> Praise to the LORD, the Almighty, the King of creation! . . .
> Let the Amen sound from his people again;
> gladly forever adore him.[10]

From where he sat, Hollis could see the boat launch, the big motel, the city park, and the beach, and to his left was the place the locals called Tubbs Hill. He watched some mallards swim south along the hill's shore, occasionally dipping their heads beneath the water and then lifting them toward the sun and shaking the water loose. The males with their green feathers seemed to glow as the sun hit their wet heads. Hollis stared south down the lake, which seemed to disappear on the southern horizon. Just then a thought hit him like his mama's palm on the back of his head. He could hear her say, "Don't you got no sense, Boy? It's right there in front of you! Nothing changes if you just sit on your butt!"

He spent some time thinking about the last 24 hours and decided he had nothing to lose. Hollis had mixed emotions about going back to Kellogg, but he knew he would, even if it proved he was a darn fool.

He parked a block from the Kellogg cafe, and when he stepped inside, his first thought was how different it looked and felt after he'd gotten some rest. It was almost full of people. Most of the customers took a good look at him when he walked in like people always do when someone is coming in where they are. Then there is the second look that white folks take when a black person they don't know shows up. But Hollis knew the drill, and he had seen the opposite in more than one jazz club when some white folks showed up. You can almost see the recording of everything folks have ever heard, good or bad, about another kind stirring in their heads. He never knew whether the prolonged looks were because of his size, color, or good looks.

"It's your good looks that you get from me, as well as your beautiful black skin that you get from both your folks," he remember his mother saying. "And it's your size from your daddy. He's one big fella, just like you're going to be, Hollis."

The noise was from wall to wall, everything from whispers, laughter, and the clink and clank of dishes and silverware. You could tell people were trying to move on. Just then the kitchen door swung open with its thud, which added to the audio chaos, but it was a different waitress, a woman with bottle-blonde hair, and Hollis knew instantly her life had been tough. She had an abundance of makeup, trying to project a youthful appearance that had been left on the side of the road a long time ago. He'd seen many like her decorating the highways of America, from one diner to the next.

"Hey, April, how 'bout some more coffee?" someone hollered from the rear of the cafe.

"Hold your horses, Abbot. Can't you see I got four plates here full of hot food for some of the *nice* customers?" Everyone laughed at that, and the man named Abbot said nothing. As she put down the last plate of what appeared to be pancakes, Hollis approached.

"Excuse me, Ma'am, but is Rachel here today?"

"We got no Rach . . . Oh! You mean Stormy?"

"Yes, Ma'am."

"She's off today. Why?"

"Do I get my coffee, or do I have to go down the street?" the voice in the back bellowed.

"Go on down the street, and while you're at it, catch a ride to Missoula and don't come back." The waitress said it loud enough for everyone to hear and then poured the demanding customer his coffee in the midst of chuckles and laughter. All the men in Abbot's booth were staring at Hollis.

"Ignore them," she said, "Why do you want Stormy?"

"I'm her cousin, and I was passing through. Thought I would stop for a little bit and catch up." Hollis was not about to tell anyone what he really had in mind.

"She's at the grocery store next street over. She was just in here to pick up her check on the way."

"Thanks, Ma'am," Hollis said over his shoulder as he moved toward the door. He headed in the direction she had pointed and found himself running down the sidewalk. "Slow down, big boy. You know what happens when you get in a hurry. You make some big mistake and end up eating a full plate of regret. A big black man running down the street might mean trouble to some of these folks. You may not be in the South, but you are still in America."

He didn't really know why he grabbed a shopping cart on his way in, but his mind went to snacks, lunch, Rachel, and back to the idea of being a fool again. A pimple-faced box boy stared like Hollis was carrying a gun, and Hollis reminded himself that not one white person had said an unkind word to him since he left Nevada. "Don't reverse-stereotype," he told himself.

He passed by two old-timers leaning over their shopping carts like they were on a rail fence at the edge of a pasture. He heard one of them say, "Don't you remember the Gold Hunter Mine near Mullan in 1919? Those two fellas were trapped in that mine for two weeks and came out ready to dance a jig. Hell, there may be more than a dozen left alive down there. We just have to wait until the last man is accounted for and the cage comes up for the last time." Hollis saw the man's friend nod his head in agreement.

Rachel was standing over the meat counter. She was wearing jeans that accented her figure and an Idaho Vandals sweatshirt with the sleeves cut off just above her elbows. Her legs were long, tapered nicely to her ankles. Hollis noticed she was wearing a gold anklet that stood out against her brown skin. He quietly slipped behind her and off to one side. He noticed the light fragrance of her perfume. He watched her pick up, pinch, and put down several cuts of meat.

"I prefer the short ribs over a good barbecue with corn on the cob and lots of butter." Rachel jumped at the sound and proximity of his voice.

"My lands, you almost scared me to death, Mr. Washington! What are you doing here?"

"Shopping, just like you," he said, grinning and pointing at his bag of potato chips and some sandwich meat.

"I don't see any ribs or corn. Now, just what are you shopping for?"

"Well," Hollis stammered, "I was hoping maybe I could spend some time with you."

"Oh, you did, did you? And just what was you planning to do during this, uh, time with me?"

Before Hollis could answer, a group of women who had been chatting quite loudly down the aisle all stopped at once. Both Hollis and Rachel looked toward the women, and Hollis noticed a short man coming down the aisle. All the women scattered but one. On her face was a horrific look of fear. She looked like she felt trapped. Hollis realized that the short man was a priest, and his eyes were glued to the woman. As he approached, he put out his hand and must have whispered something. The woman screamed, "Nooo!" and fell to her knees as her cry echoed throughout the store. She wrapped her arms around herself and began rocking back and forth. The sobbing poured out of her as if she had never cried before in her life. Her entire body trembled, and raw groaning sounds rose deep from within. That's when Hollis realized she was a relatively young woman. The other women, all older, now returned to her, gently lifted her to her feet, and guided her out of the store, followed by the priest.

"They must have found and identified her husband's body," Rachel said in a whisper. "Whenever anybody who has someone still in the mine sees the Methodist pastor or the Catholic priest coming, they know they have identified another body. They say it's driving Pastor Chalice crazy having to be the angel of death. Her name is Penny, but I don't really know her. She has three boys. When the third one was born, her husband brought the two older ones into the cafe for ice cream to celebrate. He seemed like a good guy, always speaking softly to his boys. He never yelled and screamed like some men do. And . . ."

"How would you like to go to Coeur d'Alene and stand in the sunshine, look at the lake, have dinner, and get away from here for awhile?" Hollis interrupted.

"Right now, Mr. Washington, that sounds like the best thing that could happen today. Yesterday I served three families—or what's left of them—and they were all like zombies. There is nothing you can say or do. Grief is everywhere like low-hanging fruit ready to fall all over this valley, while hope is hiding in the shadows, praying."

CHAPTER THIRTY-ONE
Birth of a Pilgrim

Most of the mine's executive team would return to New York, but Bartlett and Conrad would stay in Idaho in hopes of mitigating some of the negative publicity and finding men alive. Conrad had informed Agnes that Bartlett had hired a security service to provide bodyguards around the clock because of an air of hostility toward the mine owners, and they were fearful because of the Silver Valley's violent history. While Agnes had some things to occupy her time in her New York office, there also was much time to think and, more importantly, reflect. She found herself asking what she had accomplished in life that was significant beyond making money. What was it that made life meaningful?

Agnes found herself drawn to Celtic music and began listening to the ancient songs of her ancestors. As the days passed, things were becoming clearer, and now they knew that most of the men had escaped the fire the first day, but 93 miners had been trapped in the mine. They had extinguished the fire and cleared some of the air in the mine, but other areas had to be sealed and declared safe before rescue could continue. It had been almost a week, and none of the trapped men had been found alive. Conrad assured her that every widow would receive a $10,000 life insurance payout, but it meant little.

Agnes prayed for the men still trapped in the mine. Praying for the people in Idaho had renewed something long buried, and she found herself praying often and about more than the Sunshine fire. Her real interest was in the women who kept their vigil, going in and out of a makeshift tent, the mine manager's information tent. She watched TV coverage of the women crossing the road to the Red Cross station and mingling with each other, hoping for a word of assurance, a word of hope. Agnes realized, unlike everyone else, that these women were living in a state of suspended animation and shock, not knowing if their worst fears or their dearest hopes were true. As the days went on and more and more of the dead were identified, the number of women keeping vigil became smaller. It seemed to Agnes that the ones who remained looked more and more desperate. But she knew as they waited that they had to care for their children, answer a child's unanswerable questions, and hold themselves together at the same time. Most of them were probably on a financial ledge with debts they barely managed before and now realized that the main source of their income may end. Agnes knew it was in one way a calloused way to think, but she also knew the reality of it all was pressing down on these women.

When Agnes arrived home, the first thing she did was turn on the TV. Most people probably didn't notice, but while the Sunshine fire had been covered almost continuously since the first TV crews arrived in the afternoon of that fateful Tuesday, now it seemed like all the news was either about Vietnam or the life and death of J. Edgar Hoover, the FBI director, who had passed away that same Tuesday evening. News now became updates of every aspect of Hoover's life. Of course, the real and unknown news was what would happen to Hoover's alleged "secret files" on some of the most powerful people in Washington, DC. The media were either telling Hoover tales or speculating on the damage that might come to some in the Capitol. She had no feelings one way or the other. Hoover was an old man, but most of the men down in the Sunshine weren't. She knew the youngest was only 19. She couldn't get the women out of her mind and awoke several times in the middle of the night wondering about them.

She asked herself if it was possible that any of those women were sleeping. The time difference seemed irrelevant; they were all aching for the same thing. She would close her eyes and imagine herself as one of the waiting women and tell herself she must rest so she could help her children. Then she would remember that she wasn't really one of them—or was she in some mysterious way?

Agnes was at her desk. It was Tuesday afternoon, May 9, a little more than a week since the fire started. She was reviewing some contracts Bartlett wanted updated when her phone rang on her private line.

"Agnes here."

"Honey, you watchin' TV? Turn on your TV. It's me, Beth. The mine is on. Big news!" Agnes rolled her chair back and hurried into Bartlett's office. As the screen flickered, she saw a crowd of people jumping up and down and two men bent over, emerging from the mine. They were pale and obviously exhausted, but they were alive.

A reporter was standing before the scene, his fashionable hair blowing in the mountain wind and some raindrops obscuring the camera's perfect view.

> *After lowering a capsule used for cleaning missile silos, which arrived by truck from Nevada, rescuers were able to bring out two men who survived by lying next to an air vent and eating lunches left behind. The two men appear uninjured but will receive medical attention. We think that if our numbers are correct, most of the miners have been accounted for. But even if there are more alive, this is the worst hard rock mining disaster in US history. Back to you, Diane.*

Agnes stared out the window at Manhattan's skyline. The tears came slowly at first, but then she found herself bawling. When she stopped crying, she turned off the TV. The last word she heard was "Hoover."

Agnes went to her desk and began typing. When she finished, she took her fountain pen and signed it, put it in an envelope, returned to Bartlett's office, and placed it on the top of his desk. She put on her coat, put her fountain pen in her purse, looked around one last time, and locked her office. She said goodbye to the girls on the fourth floor, gave the guard at the security desk her keys to the office suite, and left the building. Agnes didn't know exactly what she was going to do, but she did know one thing—she could do more. But first, she had to find herself.

When the girls gathered next, there was the usual chatter as they waited for everyone to arrive. When Crystal arrived late, looking a little harried, Julio took her drink order and disappeared. When he returned with Crystal's drink, he was carrying a white envelope. "Now that you are all here, ladies, I have been instructed to give this to you."

"We're not all here, Julio," Beth corrected him. "Agnes isn't here yet."

"This I know, Senora, but Senora Agnes instructed me to give you this because she won't be here." The sadness on Julio's face was unmistakable.

"It probably has something to do with the Idaho thing," Rosalyn said as she sipped her drink.

"At least they found someone alive," Rachel commented.

"Two. It's a miracle," Beth said as she handled the envelope.

"Open it, Beth," Donna said as she tried to stare through the envelope to its contents.

"Hold on, hold on. You women are like cats in the back of a Chinese fish market," Beth said as she tore the end off of the envelope. Before pulling out the letter, she reached into her purse, put her glasses on, and then began reading.

My Dearest Friends,

I treasure the time we have spent together, both for the laughter and good times, but mostly for the friendship. I am sorry I did not come to each of you individually, but once I put certain things in motion, there was no time. Crystal's question, "Can't we be doing more?" and the events accompanying the Sunshine Mine fire have made me reevaluate my life and what I am doing. While I do not have answers yet, I'm making changes that hopefully will enable me to find some answers and find myself.

I have sold the condo, resigned from the company, and, as you read this, I will be on my way to Ion, Scotland, to spend time with the Abbey community. Then perhaps I will hike through the Hebrides, visit Mull, and then go to the village my grandparents emigrated from. Who knows what after that? I certainly don't. I will think of you often and with gratitude. I have recently discovered a lost language called "prayer," and I will speak of you often in it.

All my love,
Agnes, "the Pilgrim"

PS I've already paid for tonight's drinks.

Beth set the letter on the table, grasped her purse, and without a word rose and hurriedly left the room. None of them sitting there spoke. Their eyes drifted from each other to the table and around the room. Julio, for the first time, seemed to be nowhere. They sipped their drinks in silence and one by one left the room. Crystal, the last to leave, looked at the letter on the table and carefully folded it. For a moment, she held it against her chest. Then she placed it in her purse, and as she rose from the table, with only their silent drinks remaining, she began to cry.

CHAPTER THIRTY-TWO

Pizza Revelations

The music sifted through the pizza parlor, infecting customers who unknowingly tapped their feet on the floor or their fingers on the table. Some more consciously nodded their heads to the beat.

Henry Hyde was about to cross over to the other side of the room and say hello to "Mr. Robinson" when he realized the man sitting with him was the same policeman who had released the body of Mr. Scott to him. "Well, maybe they know each other," he thought. But he was careful to slide back behind the partition where he could not be seen. As he was ordering another beer, he saw a young lady walk in who went straight to their table and give Mr. Robinson a peck on the cheek as she sat down. She smiled at the policeman, and Henry could tell they obviously knew each other. He slid further back into the corner. He wished he knew what they were saying, but the music and chatter were too loud.

Henry and Franklin had been close all their lives, but lately Franklin seemed more distant, and Henry didn't think he was always telling the truth. He had to keep reminding himself that Franklin was, above all things, a con man and always had been. He himself had been conned when they were kids, but he didn't think Franklin would do that again, would he? He pondered it for awhile and then chugged down his beer as fast as he could. He wiped his mouth with his sleeve and gruffly called to the waitress. "Another beer here," making sure he was well out of sight of the policeman, Mr. Robinson, and their female companion.

"Do we know anything yet?" DJ said as he looked at Betsy, thinking to himself, "I love this woman" as he hummed the lyrics to "Pretty Woman."

"Well, I could keep you in suspense, but that might be hindering a criminal investigation. Right, Michael?" she smiled.

"You bet. I might have to lock you up. You too, DJ, as a coconspirator," he said, smiling, as he sipped his beer.

"Me? I don't know anything yet. Come on, Betsy, what's up?"

"My, my, the disc jockey is being impatient. Like I told you on the phone, we've been watching for receipts with Mr. Scott's signature for the false cards. Today we received a charge from Universal Travel. One of the cards was used to charge two tickets for plane fare to Caracas, Venezuela, plus hotel and rental car reservations for one month. My boss, Mr. Benton, said I could tell you tonight, and tomorrow we will take all the evidence to the Fraud Investigation Unit."

"If you don't mind," the policeman said, "I would like to be there to bring some clarification to what has taken place so they know you weren't all out there by yourselves chasing criminals."

"You mean, like we were?" DJ said with a smile.

"Do you think we have to tell them how the Hydes got the cards?" Betsy asked.

"No, it doesn't really matter. They're not their cards, and they're making purchases with them. Besides, the bank made the phony cards to catch them. So as far as the police are concerned, the bank baited and caught fraud in action. For the trial, it might be necessary, but I doubt it. Besides, this will only be one case among many."

"So Franklin and Henry are planning a vacation to Venezuela," DJ said as he picked up the last piece of pepperoni between his fingers and blew on it before he put it in his mouth.

"No, that's the funny thing. I'm not sure Henry is going, and the man's name on the ticket is Franklin Able. It's obviously a fake name, but his companion's name is Fan Kim. The name sounds Chinese to me," Betsy offered.

"Oh, my God! This gets better and better!" Michael blurted out. "Hers is no fake name."

"Who is she?"

"Fan Kim is the leading Madam in all of Chinatown. She has been linked to a number of criminal activities, gambling, drugs, smuggling, and, of course, prostitution. She is a very sly lady, sly and deadly like a snake. The entire Seattle police force as well as the FBI would love to see her locked up."

"There is another thing," Betsy said, after dipping a bread stick in the red sauce and taking a bite. "Mr. Scott—uh, Franklin Hyde, alias Franklin Able—also placed a money order with the bank to be sent to a bank in Venezuela to be drawn on by a real estate firm for a down payment on a house in Barquisimeto. Because it was such a large amount, Mr. Benton handled it himself. He didn't send it through but notified both the real estate firm and the bank that they were being caught up in a fraud and if they heard from "Mr. Scott" to pretend they had received the money, notify him, and he would keep them informed."

"When do they leave?"

"The day after tomorrow."

Before anyone could digest this information, the waitress, whose name tag said Shelly and whose dark hair seemed to constantly invade her forehead, came to their table. "Could I have a beer?" Betsy asked. "A pale ale from the tap, please."

"Sure thing. Any of you gentlemen want more beer? Pizza?"

"No, we're good. We still have some in the pitcher."

"Seeing as how these gentlemen, as you call them, ate all the pizza before I got here, could you bring me a small pepperoni, mushroom, and olive?"

"It's two dollars extra for the third topping. Is that okay?" Shelly asked as she checked out Michael admiringly.

"That's fine. Thanks." Both Betsy and DJ smiled.

"Do you get that a lot?" DJ asked after Shelly left. He looked at Michael with a large grin.

"What are you talking about?" Michael responded, looking down and blushing, pretending he hadn't noticed.

"I'm talking about young women ogling you because you fill out the shoulders and sleeves of a shirt with pure muscle."

"Nah, she just likes my taste in shirts. Besides, you forgot to mention my handsome face."

"There is that," Betsy said as she put another bread stick in her mouth and poked DJ with her elbow.

When Shelly returned with Betsy's drink, Michael did a little ogling of his own. He noticed she had a good figure and a smile that could lift anyone out of depression.

"What do you think Henry is going to do if Franklin takes off to South America with his lady friend?" DJ asked, glancing at both of them.

"Maybe he doesn't know about it," Michael said, "and Franklin is going to leave him high and dry. My guess is that from what you have told me, Franklin controls the funds, and I'll bet Henry doesn't even know where the money is. Remember, they've been running a legitimate business for several years, and it doesn't look like they've spent much of it on themselves or the business. I'll bet my badge that if Franklin is linked up with Fan Kim, he is either tied to some more serious crime or she's taking him for a ride, and I would love to know."

"Didn't you say she was known for being involved with smuggling? What if she and Franklin are involved in it together? Why would she use her real name but a fake name for him?" Betsy asked.

"What about him buying a house? How does that figure in?"

"Maybe they need a base of operation, DJ," Michael said as the waitress approached.

When Shelly set the pizza on its stand in the center of the table, she leaned in and began to whisper. "This may be nothing, but on the other side of the partition, across the room, is a bald guy in an ugly polyester suit who keeps peeking out at you three. There's no one else back here, so he has to be looking at you. He's also on his fifth beer, which may mean he may do something stupid. I just thought you should know. He gives me the creeps."

"Thank you, Shelly," Michael said. He handed her a $10 bill and opened his wallet in such a way that she could see his badge." Her cheeks flushed red, and she quickly pocketed the ten-spot and walked back toward the kitchen without looking toward Henry.

Watching Shelly leave, Michael was able to get a glimpse of the man behind the partition. "It's Henry, folks. He obviously recognizes DJ and me," Michael said. "And it's making him suspicious that we're together. We can't afford to let him tell Franklin, or they could disappear tonight. But I have an idea. As far as you know, Henry drives, right?"

"Yeah, I saw him driving the hearse when I was checking out the funeral home," DJ nodded.

"Then as soon as Betsy finishes her beer and pizza, you two will leave and go home and wait to hear from me. I'm going to leave now and wait for our inebriated friend."

"What if he follows us? I don't want him knowing where I live," Betsy whispered.

"We'll go to my place and wait to hear from Michael, okay?"

Betsy put her hand on DJ's. "Did you get the Miles Davis record you were bartering for with that guy? If you did, I think I could be persuaded to come to your place." DJ looked at Betsy and smiled.

"Yeah, I got it. Eat up."

"If he follows you, take main roads and drive five miles below the speed limit until you don't see him anymore. He's my problem, not yours. Go home." Michael stood, left a $20 bill on the table, and walked out the door without looking toward Henry. He tipped his baseball cap toward Shelly as he left. She nodded and blushed. Betsy and DJ looked at the $20 bill and smiled to themselves. They resisted the temptation to look toward Henry as they left.

CHAPTER THIRTY-THREE

The Right Fit

L arry Frost was a contradiction, but few people knew it. He had been an orphan as a child during the Great Depression. While many who experience even less disappointment and difficulty become hardened, encrusted, and bitter, Larry Frost became caring, open, and joyful. On this day in 1972, he was the cheerful manager of J. C. Penney's men's department in Coeur d'Alene, Idaho.

Everyone knew about the Sunshine Mine fire. It was in the local news daily, and they were still waiting to hear how many would get out alive, if any. Larry had lost count how many they had found dead and how many were still missing, but there seemed to be more bad news than good. News crews, reporters, members of the Bureau of Mines, union leaders, lawyers by the dozens, and the mine owners themselves came through Coeur d'Alene. Some stayed at Templin's North Shore on the lake. All motels along Sherman Avenue were full. There were even people camping in tents to be part of it all, at least in the beginning. The locals eavesdropped in the coffee shops and restaurants, catching news as it fell from lips between coffee and toast, or beer and a burger. Rarely did anyone ask directly because it was usually met with a silent stare or "We don't know" from a troubled soul. The locals knew that most of these outsiders looked down on them. People all over Idaho felt a bond with the miners and their families. These were "their people, their neighbors who were suffering." As people moved about this paradise on the lake, inside they ached, waited, and prayed.

Larry joked with other employees, like always, teasing Melinda about her new boyfriend as they folded shirts and arranged the new pants on the rack. The morning had been routine with little business, but mornings were usually slow. Larry had just come back from Hudson's Hamburger across the street where he had coffee with "the boys." It wasn't as pleasant as usual, though, because all they could think to talk about was the Sunshine fire. Anything else sounded frivolous and insignificant. Larry kept thinking about the kids who now would have no fathers, and as much as he tried not to, a memory of a moment he thought he had long forgotten kept coming to mind.

His back was to the door when they first came into the store. He was trying to figure out how to best display the new polo shirts that had come in for spring and summer. He didn't notice them until they were in his department. The woman had a ponytail and was holding the hand of a cute boy with a wild cowlick and a bruise on his chin. The other two were standing perfectly still, their feet anchored next to their mother, but their eyes were roaming all over the store. Larry took a deep breath, and although he did not know this family, he knew enough just by looking at them. He smiled his generous smile and started to say something, but before he could speak, she did.

"I need suits, shirts, and ties for my two oldest boys. For Michael, a shirt, tie and slacks," she said in a flat voice void of emotion. Larry realized the woman wasn't smiling like a mother who was delighted because she was going to show off her sons at a special event. He took time to carefully measure their sizes, but as he did, he noticed the bib overalls and faded shirts. Their shoes were well worn, but everyone was clean, and Larry knew this mother cared about her boys.

"What's your name, young man?" The boy looked over at his mother, and she nodded.

"I'm Cable. I'm named after a mine hoist cable."

"Cable. I like that. It's a very strong name, a good one to grow into."

Larry glanced at the mother, and she smiled at his comment. He noticed some of her tension begin to ease.

"My brother here is Kelly. He's only six. I'm 13, and I'm the man of the house now, cause . . ."

"Cable!" his mother sternly addressed him, and he fell silent with his eyes on his feet.

Larry looked into her eyes and could see the sadness. He could tell she was straining to keep her composure, handle her children, and do what needed to be done. Her eyes became moist, and quietly and gently, like the father he was, he said to her, "Ma'am, are you coming here from Kellogg?" She nodded and whispered yes.

"Well, we'll find what you need so your boys will be dressed like the fine young men they are." Turning to the middle boy, whose face was spattered with freckles, he said, "Your brother says you are six, but you look much older. Are you really six?" The boy looked at his mother who was now grinning. "Yeah, I'm six, and I've lost one tooth." He proceeded to show Larry the gaping hole where his tooth had been.

"And did the tooth fairy bring you anything?"

"Yeah, I got a whole dime!"

"Well now, that's pretty good." Larry smiled at Kelly and continued to measure the boys. He didn't really need to, but he knew it would give them something to do and feel important. When he turned his attention to the youngest boy, the boy blurted out, "I have all my teeth, but I got a bruise. See here?" and he put his finger on the spot.

"Wow! That's a big one. Did it hurt?"

"Just a little. I took the training wheels off my bike and fell, but now I can ride without falling."

"Why, that's quite an achievement. You should be very proud," Larry said with his affable grin.

While Larry was ringing up the sale, he noticed two women with four boys and two girls enter the store and come directly to his department. The older woman with gray hair approached the mother of his three customers. Two teenage boys followed closely behind. The others pretended to be looking at clothes while all the time watching the woman.

"Penny," she said in a strained, muted voice.

"Hello, Doris. I got the boys done early. We had to go by Yates for the funeral stuff."

Larry Frost knew Gilbert Yates, and he knew these families would be treated well. Gilbert would probably absorb some of the cost by the time

284

this was all over. It wouldn't be the first time, he knew for a fact. The small gathering of families was now obvious to all in the store. It was a sight that became common as mothers and grandparents made the pilgrimage to Coeur d'Alene to buy clothes for their sons and daughters so they would look nice at their father's, brother's, or uncle's funeral—in some cases, all three.

The locals began to recognize the signs—pickup trucks or older cars driven by fatigued women followed by children who came for haircuts and clothes. Their faces were unfamiliar. Coeur d'Alene was still small enough that even though you didn't know everyone in town, an unfamiliar face was easily recognized. These women and children were victims of this horrendous tragedy. Their lives would be forever changed, and everyone knew it. These were their neighbors, even if they lived on the other side of Fourth of July Pass, and they reached out to them with small, quiet kindnesses. Discounts suddenly appeared where none had existed. Desserts and ice cream cones were free. The locals knew they couldn't reverse the disaster, but they could let their neighbors know they cared. Each night, Larry Frost walked home to his small house on 15th Street feeling more tired than he had in a long time. In the face of each child, he saw some of his past, but with each new child, he smiled again and spoke in his soft, caring voice, calling each of them by name.

CHAPTER THIRTY-FOUR

Burial

Penny knew some of the folk were upset because they were taking Butch to the cemetery in the back of a pickup. She knew Butch would rather be in his truck than in a hearse anytime, and this was his time. Besides, with the burying of so many men, there weren't enough hearses, even though they had brought some from St. Maries, Coeur d'Alene, Spokane, and even as far away as the Tri-Cities. "At least I didn't have to buy one of those fancy caskets," she thought to herself. Butch's uncle went into his wood shop as soon as he heard and started making Butch's casket. It was the most beautiful one she had ever seen with all natural wood. It was fitting for Butch who loved to work wood with his uncle.

Penny wore her hair down at the sides with a slight curl on the ends, the way Butch liked it. "The boys look so nice in their new suits and ties," Penny thought to herself. Cable was carrying himself like he had just been initiated into manhood, and I guess in one way, he had. Kelly kept wiggling like everything itched and pulling at his tie every few minutes. It was surprising that he still had it on. Even though Michael didn't have a suit because they didn't have any for four-year-olds, his white shirt and slacks made him look as dressy as the others. "Your father would be so proud," Penny told them.

They walked out of St. Rita's Catholic Church, first Father Toraselli and then Butch carried by his closest friends and his brothers. Roger Benson,

Butch's partner, wasn't there. He had died with Butch. Then came Cable, Kelly, Penny, and Michael.

As they left the pavement and began the final climb to the cemetery, Penny remembered the first time she had been there. She and Butch were in high school, and it was their senior year. He asked if he could take her to a movie, and Penny's daddy made it very clear that he expected Butch to behave himself. Penny laughed at the thought because Butch was so shy that it had taken him months to get up the courage to ask her out. She had all but given up hope. Long before, she had made up her mind who she wanted to share her life with. The movie was so bad that they left early, and he drove her up here on cemetery hill overlooking the valley.

"I come up here when I want to think," he told her. "What are you thinking about now?" she said, and he turned all red and didn't quite know where to look, so he just stared out the window.

"How much I like being with you," he said, blushing.

"Well, that's a good start, Mr. Butch Megivern, but you're supposed to tell a girl how pretty she looks. Or don't you think I'm pretty?" She laughed at the remembrance of how flustered he got when she said it. He was not used to being teased by a girl. He only had brothers. She had slid over next to him, put her head on his shoulder, and held his arm. "Look, Mr. Megivern, you and me are going to be a pair from now on. Is that what you've been thinking about all these months, how I could be your girl?"

"How did you know that?" he had stammered.

"Let's just call it a mystery, Butch. It's just a mystery." They sat there for a long time saying little, feeling each other's warmth, and listening to their breath. Penny thought of all the times she awoke in the night and watched him sleep and listened to his breath. But now there was no breath. She lifted her chin and took Kelly's and Michael's hands and took a step forward.

As they walked toward the freshly dug grave, Penny glanced down at the area below where a family was lowering another miner into a grave. She knew his name—Al Cross. He used to bowl with her dad. Her dad said he would be a better bowler if he could keep his anger in check. The teenagers were Al's sons. She saw the widow lift her head toward her, and their eyes met. It was a blink of time, but in that slight moment, a bond of sisterhood was sealed. They had joined the women who had through all the yesterdays buried their children and men. Women, Penny knew, are the fountains of life, but they are also the bearers of grief, frequent travelers in the valley of the shadow of death. Penny felt the weight of the shadow pressing against her heart. Sara Cross nodded slightly, and they both looked away. Penny thought about something her mother had told her about being a woman. "We bear children in pain at birth. We raise them in worry and fear and pray we will never see their death, but it is our sons who go to war. We usually outlive our men and grieve for them. If we are lucky, we may have them until we, too, are old. A woman's life is destined for pain. It is the price of love."

Penny thought of her mother's love and wished she were here. "Take care of him for me, Mom," she whispered beneath her breath.

Penny's thoughts turned to the joy Butch had brought into her life. She closed her eyes and heard him laugh the way he did when he teased her. Father Toraselli's words called her back to the moment, and she felt as though there was a rock in her stomach. "Why did Butch die?" she thought to herself. "Why did any of them die? For what? So some woman in Florida could have a silver necklace? So we could have a bigger barbecue or a new couch? They all think they're so smart, these young men who walk out of high school and into the mines. They have more money than they have ever seen and think they are so smart. Then come the mortgage, car and truck payments, hospital expenses, and just the cost of life. We had a good life together, hard times, but lots of laughter and love. It was too short, Butch. These men gamble their lives every day. There must be a better way to live."

While others were lowering their loved ones into the grave because they had no alternative, Butch's brothers and friends were doing it because it was what Butch wanted. He had told Penny when his grandpa died that it was a family tradition. "We bury our own," he had said. "Keeps us tied to life, being close to death, staring it in the face." As they lowered the casket, Penny made a promise to herself. Her sons would never work in the mines, even if it meant moving out of the valley. "Never, never, never," she mumbled to herself as others tried to smile and console her as they walked back toward the road.

Before they reached the road, her maternal instinct kicked in, and she realized she was missing one of her pups. She stopped, turned, and saw Cable still standing at his father's grave. He stepped to the side and folded back the artificial turf covering the dirt that had been removed from the grave. He walked to where the cemetery workers were waiting by a front end loader and spoke to one of them. The worker went behind the loader and returned with a shovel. He nodded as he handed it to Cable. Penny watched as Cable carried the shovel to the dirt pile and then scooped up a shovelful of dirt and dumped it on top of his father's casket. She could tell he was taking deep breaths, but he had that determined look on his face that he had whenever he set his mind to something. It was the same look Butch had. He did it three more times, spilling dirt on his polished shoes and new slacks. When he finished, he jammed the shovel into the remaining dirt. Cable walked slowly toward her with his head high, tears covering his face. Penny felt her own tears flowing down her cheeks as she watched her young son walk toward manhood.

CHAPTER THIRTY-FIVE

Court Amor

Hollis and Rachel spent the day in Coeur d'Alene relishing the sunshine and warm spring air. They walked Sherman Avenue, peeked into the shops, and enjoyed each other's company. They rented a boat and cruised around the shoreline starting at Silver Beach and heading east into Wolf Lodge Bay. Rachel told him how the bald eagles came down from Alaska and Canada to fish in the bay in the winter. The majestic birds nested along the southern shore in the trees on Mineral Ridge and came out over the bay, circling through thousands of years of evolution and suddenly propelling themselves straight downward and, with a quick thrust, turning with talons extended and grabbing an unsuspecting salmon, lifting it high into the air for its journey to the feast where it would be the honored guest.

It was time to go back to Kellogg. As they approached the town, their laughter, kidding, and chatter melted into silence, and neither one said anything until they saw a hearse and a long procession behind it. All the cars and trucks had their headlights on, following slowly. "I probably served him coffee or breakfast more than once, whoever it is this time. Lord, be with the wife and family and any children who have now lost their daddy. Be with them in the hard, lonely years ahead. Amen." Hollis reached out and touched Rachel's hand and then took it and swallowed it up in his own hand.

Hollis decided not to take his bonus vacation just yet and took his rented Mustang and headed back to Reno. He had a few short runs up and down the state and one over to San Francisco. He also had one to Austin, Texas, and all of them combined gave him a lot of time to think. He knew the mine disaster had changed a lot of lives, but it also made him feel things he hadn't felt in a long, long time, like the heavy sense of powerlessness to change events, the reminder that death brings finality unlike anything else. It ends who we are and stops plans we have made for ourselves. He thought about his mother and how she raised her head high and said the Lord would provide for them and not to worry about his father because she was sure he and Jesus were swapping stories and laughing so the clouds shook. The memory brought a smile to Hollis's lips.

The more Hollis had time to think, the more Rachel came to his mind. He knew that sometimes God turns and twists bad things and even people's evil intentions to bring about good, and he knew in his heart that Rachel might be his good. He felt guilty because so many people only got grief and loss from the Sunshine disaster, but through it, he might have received a gracious gift he didn't deserve. "Isn't that how it is with all of God's gifts?" he reminded himself. He had written Rachel one letter, and it had taken awhile for her to write back, but he could tell she was thinking of their time together, too. He wasn't sure he should write again, but one night as he was mulling it over, his phone rang, and it was Rachel. Hollis was speechless, but it didn't matter because she had some things she wanted to say.

* * *

A week later, Hollis walked into the Kellogg cafe, took Rachel's hand as she put down a cup of coffee, and pulled her through the kitchen and out the back door.

"Hollis, I missed you so much, but what are you doing pulling me around away from my work? I'll get fired."

Hollis cleared his throat and looked out at the street and then back at Rachel. In almost a whisper, he said, "The Lord and I have been wrestling these past few weeks, and . . . well . . . I just . . ."

"Speak up, man, and don't be so wordy. I do hope the Lord won your little match, whatever it was about. I've got to get back to work before I lose my job."

"What I got to say is . . ." Hollis cleared his throat for the second time. "Will you marry me?" Rachel stood there with her eyes wide and her lips pursed, but she didn't say anything. She just looked at the man in front of her and reached down into her intuition box, grabbed hold of its contents, and brought it back around to her brain. From there, she dragged it across the landscape of her heart. She thought about all the widows in the valley and knew if she gave her heart to this man, someday hers could be broken, too. But she already knew this man was the treasure she had dreamed of and prayed about.

"Hollis, my mother told me someday I would meet a man who was a rock and all heart at the same time. I could never figure that out until I met you. But what kind of man proposes to a girl in a dirty alley?" she said with her smile he had come to love. It said everything and more. She put her arms around him, and they embraced and kissed. First, it was a long, powerful, don't-you-ever-leave-me kiss and then a you're-fun-to-be-with short little kiss."

"You could have waited until I finished my shift and then proposed in some romantic spot, but you would have had to wait to kiss me," Rachel said, grinning.

"I couldn't wait any longer. Besides, I'll be kissing you a lot more than today." She smiled again as he said it.

"Yes, you will, Mr. Washington. Yes, you will."

Rachel turned in her apron and walked out the front door with her arm in Hollis's, and they drove to Coeur d'Alene to the Kootenai County Courthouse. They got a marriage license and skipped across the street to the Court Amor Wedding Chapel. In 15 minutes, they were husband and wife with a legally signed marriage certificate and even a photo.

On their honeymoon, she asked him if there was anything he would like to do for a living other than drive truck. He took a stick, drew a big circle in the sand, and made a happy face. "I've always dreamed of opening a barbecue joint with outdoor tables, a big deep pit barbecue, and a play area for kids. Maybe we would have a special time for kids to learn how to cook, just a few kids at a time, and their mamas and daddies could sit and eat, drink coffee, visit with each other, and just have time together."

"Well, Mr. Washington, I think we ought to see what we can do about making your dream come true. I know a good waitress who would love to work by your side, and she's pretty good at baking pies."

"Is that a fact, Mrs. Washington?"

After the honeymoon, Hollis and Rachel bought a small house with a big yard. There was room for a vegetable garden, a large patio, and even a horseshoe pit. Then they went looking for a Chocolate Lab puppy. When they found one, they named him Magnus Miner the First.

CHAPTER THIRTY-SIX

The Arrest

Franklin was seated at the airport bar with his ticket in his pocket and his passport in front of him. He was mulling over his new name, Franklin Able. He liked it. Fan Kim was smart enough to keep the first name the same so she wouldn't mistakenly call him by the wrong name at the wrong time. He liked Able, which he thought was a compliment from her. He only wished they had come to the airport together. It made him a bit uneasy, not that he didn't trust her but because she kept much to herself, maybe too much sometimes, he thought. But he knew she would be here shortly. After all, she loved him, and there was still plenty of time for them to have a celebratory drink together before their flight. He looked around the room and wondered what stories all these people carried. "I wonder how many are traveling with fake passports." The thought had never occurred to him before, and he laughed to himself.

He looked up at the TV screen and noticed that a baseball game was on. The Giants were playing the Dodgers, the eighth inning, and the Dodgers were ahead 3–1. The Giants were up with a man on first and third with only one out. Franklin wondered if Seattle would ever have a Major League Baseball team. The Giants' hitter had two strikes on him, but he connected on a straight fastball and hit what might end up being a double. The man on third came in easily, but the man who had been on first base was making a run for home. Everyone at the bar was shouting as the runner slid safely into home plate when the throw went wide.

Franklin was so caught up in the game that he took no notice of the two men who entered the bar wearing dark suits, white shirts, and military-style haircuts.

If he had noticed and thought about it, he might have considered it odd that neither had any kind of carry-on luggage or even a briefcase. They glanced around the room, looked in his direction, and then moved straight for the bar. One stood on Franklin's left, the other on his right. Just as Franklin felt his personal space being invaded, one of them reached into his vest pocket and pulled out a wallet with a badge showing. "Mr. Hyde, we would like you to come with us." There was no introduction, just the badge and the statement in a calm, authoritative voice, which made Franklin suddenly uneasy, anxious, and confused. Out of the corner of his eye, he saw some of the customers turn their attention from the game to him and his visitors.

"But I have to catch a plane soon. There must be some mistake." Trying to sound calmer than he felt, Franklin continued. "I'm sorry, but you have the wrong person, Officer. My name is Able, Franklin Able. See, my passport is right here," Franklin said with a tremor in his voice that even surprised him. He slid his fake passport across the bar so the man on his left could see it clearly. The man never even glanced at the passport, and the number of people taking notice that something unusual was happening had increased significantly, which made Franklin all the more anxious.

"There is no mistake, Mr. Hyde," said the man on his right. "We were advised that you would be traveling under the name Franklin Able. Now will you please come with us?"

"Advised by whom?" Franklin sputtered.

"I will take your passport for now," said the man on his left, "and you can come quietly with us, or we can put you in handcuffs and lead you out."

Franklin felt like he was falling down a dark shaft with no sign that the fall would stop. He looked at both men. Neither blinked. Franklin pushed his glass across the bar. He slid off the barstool and turned in the direction of the exit. He continued to look around for Fan Kim as they led him out of the airport. They handcuffed him at the curb and placed him in the back seat of a black sedan parked in a no-parking zone. He had passed hundreds of faces as they led him out of the airport, many of them Asian women, but Fan Kim was nowhere to be seen. As they drove out of the airport, Franklin wondered, "What could have happened to her? How did they know my fake name?"

CHAPTER THIRTY-SEVEN

Where the Wind Blows

Faith was sitting on top of the concrete wall at the Third Street boat ramp in Coeur d'Alene. The lake was calm and still, glass-like, with the sun shining across it mirroring a few white clouds above. It was peaceful, and she was, too, in a partial sort of way. She could feel the sun on her face and knew the day would get warmer. It might be an uncomfortable drive back to Seattle, but she didn't know how she could be more uncomfortable than she had been the last two weeks. People always say, "Waiting is the worst," but it's not. It's the finality that is the worst—the finality of death, the heavy conclusion that one is impotent to reverse what has happened. Suddenly, the mesh of ideas, relationships, hopes, dreams, frustrations, regrets, and the entire future are decimated by this one reality. One comes to understand within the time of a single breath one's own frailty. Some quickly deny it with everything within them, while others stand in awe, viewing life through a new lens. Others remain in shock and mentally anesthetize themselves from reality and live with everything off-kilter.

Faith thought about taking her shoes off and standing ankle-deep in the water, even though she knew it would be cold. When they had brought her father's body out of the mine, she was flooded with a mixture of emotions—relief for not having to confront him, regret for not being able to tell him she forgave him, and later, relief that he had not been horribly burned like some but simply went to sleep from the poisonous gas the fire had created. She was grief-stricken that he was no longer alive. She would never be able to tell him what had happened to her after she ran away or have any kind of future with him. When she learned from others that her dad had actually saved Charlie Reed's life by dragging him to safety, she suspected that perhaps her father had changed since she saw him last. But then, maybe not. After all, miners are a kind of brotherhood, and they will do all they can in a time of danger to save others, regardless of the risk to themselves. But after talking to Emma, she knew he had changed.

Emma had told her about the first Sunday in March when Faith's father came to church. Emma remembered the date because it was her month to prepare things for communion. She was surprised to see him, of course, because he rarely came. Oh, he might come to a rummage sale looking for a shirt or a pot for the kitchen because he had ruined one. But this Sunday, he came in late and sat in an empty pew in the back. Emma could tell he was beaten down. He sat with his head bowed, turning and twisting his hands in and out. He didn't stand for the singing of the hymns. He just sat there with his head bowed, looking like he had been in a rough fight and lost.

At first, Emma thought he was there trying to do penance for a bender the night before, but getting drunk had never bothered him as long as she had known him. Besides, he was too alert to be hung over. She glanced at him as often as she dared without making him uncomfortable, and of course, she prayed for him that whatever was going on the Lord would bring him not just peace but would bring him to himself. The entire time, she kept thinking of the story of Jacob wrestling with God and how he was given a new name, Israel, one who wrestles with God.

"Don't we all at one time or another?" Faith said out loud.

The account might have left Faith with a lot of questions except for what Emma said happened afterward. Lou Marks was never what you would call a quiet man. He was far from it, but he was a private man. Whatever went on inside of him stayed there. Emma had witnessed his grief from afar those years after his wife, her mother, had died; and then Faith left. For some reason, Emma held a place in her heart for the man and couldn't bring herself to judge him. "I couldn't exactly remove the speck in his eye until I had removed the log in my own," she had thought many times to herself.

The very next week, Emma noticed Lou walking down the street past the McConnell Hotel. She remembered he was standing tall, no longer bent, not carrying a Don Quixote defeated look as he had before. He was smiling and whistling. She hadn't seen him smile since Claire died. Later, she heard he had gone to the family of an injured miner, chopped wood for their stove, and done things the man couldn't do himself. Oddly, he had hardly known the man. Charlie told her that Lou had brought a couple GIs off the highway who were headed for Bozeman to say goodbye to their folks before going to Vietnam, and he had bought them breakfast. He had become a caring, outgoing man who was now looking out for others instead of being a hardened, grizzled old man who wore his bitterness like a sign around his neck in order to keep others away. It was why he was in the mine. He was taking someone else's place, and it cost him his life.

Faith couldn't help feel she had missed something wonderful by not getting to see him, being able to tell him she had forgiven him long ago. But the more Emma shared, the more Faith felt at peace. "I will never know in this life the new man my father became. I lost my father years ago to an insipid evil, but Lord, you gracefully defeated the evil in him, and he became an even better man than the one I knew."

Faith knew her life had not been turned upside down like the Sunshine widows. She was returning to a job and her home with no loss of income. And now, she had good memories of her father that she would always cherish and nurture. "Life is quirky," she thought. "I went to Idaho to reconcile with my father, to bury the past, and on the way I may have found my future."

A gentle breeze was now coming across the lake, and a small sailboat was coming around Tubbs Hill. Faith could see it was piloted by two young boys. She could hear their laughter as it skipped across the water like smooth stones. She wondered what kind of men they would grow up to be and if their failures and mistakes would teach them wisdom or if they would simply join the fellowship of foolish men that seemed to be growing more each year. She hoped their mistakes and heartbreaks would make them strong and that they would become wise men who blessed others with their lives. As a gust of wind filled the sails, the boys cheered, and Faith remembered Jesus's words: "The wind blows where it chooses, and you hear the sound of it, but you do not know where it comes from or where it goes. So it is with everyone who is born of the Spirit."[11]

"We spend so much time indulging ourselves, adorning our bodies with what we think will make us beautiful and happy, yet it really is what we allow inside that brings truth and joy to our lives. It's what determines the course and content of our lives." Faith thought of the cocktail party in Bellevue and all the people who, while nice, seemed empty. No one said anything of substance about themselves. The conversations were like tiny pebbles bouncing off a sheet of glass. Nothing stuck, but there was a lot of clatter.

The boys were moving farther away toward the City Park beach and were in front of the arcade that had closed down. As she watched the sail flutter in the wind, her mind went to Pete. She realized the thing she liked about Pete from the very beginning was that he listened, not just with his ears but also with his heart. He was flippant at first, but they were strangers then. She had shared more than she ever intended to, and so had Pete. She realized they had reached a level of honesty that she had never had with any other man. She felt almost from the beginning that he was safe. She was concerned about his cynicism, but ironically, the entire experience of the mine seemed to bring something long buried inside of him to the surface. When he showed up at the mine, not as a reporter but as her friend, her heart was so filled with joy despite the situation that she couldn't help but embrace him. She had suddenly felt less alone and less afraid. She took comfort from his presence. Her reaction surprised her, but there was no doubt that she wanted him beside her, especially when the news of her father finally came. When they carried her father out of the mine in that black body bag, she only wanted to be in Pete's arms, and he was there—silent, strong, understanding—and he had hardly left her side during the entire ordeal.

"Why don't you admit it and stop beating around the bush?" she thought to herself. "Admit you're in love with him." A smile crossed her face as she watched the boys bring the boat around and head back where they had come. She was headed back, too, but even though it was to the same place she had left, nothing would be the same. A burden had been lifted from her soul, and an adventure awaited her with a man she was sure God had put in her life just at the right time. She smiled when she thought of herself riding back to Seattle with a "serial killer" carried by a saint.

Epilogue

The year was 1974, and Richard Nixon, fearing impeachment, had resigned in disgrace over the Watergate scandal. The nation was still reeling as Gerald Ford tried to bring calm to the "troubled waters" after pardoning Nixon. There was no "sound of silence" when it came to Vietnam. Almost everyone wanted out except the "Hawks" and those who had something to gain financially. More than a million men would die before it would be over in another year. But like the feeding of the 5,000, they didn't count the women, children, and other civilians. Statistics often cover rather than reveal the truth, especially in war. While there were loud, violent voices occupying the national stage at almost every major university campus and federal building in the country, in a narrow valley in North Idaho, folks were paying tribute in a weighty, somber quiet, to the 91 men who died in the Sunshine Mine fire two years before.

Many of those present had come hundreds of miles, some because they had watched, some because they had read reports of the rescue drama as it unfolded, and others because they were part of the mining community and held a kinship with those who had died and the women who had had their lives derailed in this catastrophic disaster. Others came because their lives, too, suddenly without warning, had been shredded and torn asunder. They knew that the presence of someone who had also walked with them through the ragged, shattered remains in the valley of the shadow of death brought a small measure of comfort.

Everyone knew the monetary compensation didn't go very far. For most, it was now probably monetary history swallowed up in bills, mortgage payments, and even moving expenses as part of the widows' exodus from Silver Valley. But it would never replace a loved one who grinned at you across the breakfast table while the fragrance of bacon and coffee filled the room, or gently slapped your butt while you stood at the sink and maybe put his arms around you and whispered something in your ear that made you giggle, and you knew you were loved. Now there were children to be cared for without the support of a father, and your bed was too big and too cool at night. Those private, familiar moments had been thrust into the realm of personal history, a pile of memories that would never be experienced with your man again.

Penny glanced around and took in many familiar faces, and she was glad she had finally decided to come. She had wrestled with coming from the time she had heard of the memorial until yesterday. She slept little last night with the memory of that terrible time, the waiting, and every day since replaying it over and over in her mind with a cacophony of voices echoing inside her head throughout the night. She hadn't wanted to come. She knew it would bring back the pain she was trying to free herself from, but it also reminded her of all she and Butch had had together. It brought back good memories and blessed her with a sense of gratitude for her years of marriage. It was the boys who insisted on coming, especially Cable. He said he would go even if she didn't. She came to realize it was something her boys would appreciate for years to come. Their father had been a hero to them, and he always would be. His death in the mine just solidified it forever. They each had on one of Butch's caps, and even though Michael's was a little big and pressed down over his ears, they were all so proud. She was heartened that so many people who were not from the valley were there to pay tribute to the miners. She had heard of one woman who came from Portland to pay tribute to the wives and children. It was good to know someone understood, at least in part.

Cable said he saw a woman at the bakery who was telling Mr. Giovani she had come all the way from New York. Her family had been coal miners in Scotland. She said she had changed her life because of the fire. She wanted to see this place and be with the women she had only seen on TV. "Did she say anything else?" Penny asked. "No, but Mr. Giovani came out from behind the counter, hugged her, and said, 'May God bless you, and thank you.' Mrs. Giovani, instead of getting mad and shouting at Mr. Giovani like she usually did, stood behind the counter and cried." When Penny thought of Mrs. Giovani not clobbering her husband, she thought, "At least the world still has small miracles." It brought a quick but brief smile to her face.

Penny could see several mine owners, but they looked especially uncomfortable, and none of them ever held eye contact with anyone. The safety violations and the breathing equipment that failed and burned men's lips so they cast them aside left the men especially vulnerable and was the cause of death for some of them. The safety officer had tried to upgrade the equipment and do a review of the mine's safety prior to the fire, but he had been ignored. The safety officer had heard that Nims tried to make him the scapegoat, but he had documented everything he had ever recommended, so Nims looked like the crazy fool he was. Nims had left the country, and rumor had it that he was working for a mining company in South America somewhere, but no one except maybe the mine owners cared. His intern from Montana had shared enough to verify what everyone suspected—that Nims was a crazy man. Butch had always told her that. Word was that Mrs. Nims had returned to her people in Connecticut and changed her name back to her maiden name. Penny knew there were still lawsuits in the courts, but those things meant little to her. Her course had been set, and now she knew she needed to navigate it as best she could for the good of her boys.

After the move to Coeur d'Alene, she was able to pick up some classes at North Idaho College while she waitressed at the Iron Horse. Her aunt and uncle had moved to Coeur d'Alene years before, and they helped with the boys. She was glad the boys loved Coeur d'Alene because she didn't want any of them to mine. Cable had already said he was going to become a civil engineer and learn how to make mines safer. The idea didn't frighten her like mining itself, and she thought Butch would be pleased.

Penny looked at State Senator Phil Blatt, the main speaker for the event, and realized he was fighting back tears. Blatt had seen to it that a capsule be brought from Nevada as quickly as possible to get down to the lower levels and reach any men who may still be alive. Surprisingly, two men had survived. It was a miracle they were alive, and all the bells, horns, and sirens in Kellogg went off when word came that the two men were pulled from the mine alive. It was a glorious end to the darkest tragedy of their community's life.

Death had borne too much fruit—too many lives lost and too many lives uprooted, exposed to the elements and hardships of life. Ninety-one men had died, and 82 had survived. Seventy-seven women were widowed or lost sons, 200 children lost their fathers, and many lost uncles and brothers as well. Penny closed her eyes and felt the warm tears forming. She could feel her heart beating and whispered, "I miss you so much." She listened as Blatt read:

> *We waited in spirit at the mouth of the pit, ached in unison at the news of the dead, joined in jubilation at the rescue of the living, marveled at the poise of the little community, and we became strong. The flux of widows' tears welded their strength into our bodies, and we were all Idahoans. We were all miners. We were all proud.*

Penny thought to herself, "The larger world forgot them long ago, almost before anyone knew how bad it was. One man dies, a man who holds the secrets of many powerful people, and all eyes of the world turn toward him, but almost a hundred miners die, and the world treats it as a sneeze. The statistics bury their lives, their families, and all the pain and loss that roam up and down the valley and beyond for generations to come."

Penny knew J. Edgar Hoover's name would be in the history books and studied by her grandchildren, but the names of these men would be forgotten, filed away only in the official reports and what would become historical newspaper accounts. Below this statue being dedicated were their names— names that would greet the days they would never see. She thought about the unfairness of it all. Now she and Louise, Butch's mom, were the only adults left of their clan. Poor Louise was paralyzed with a stroke, lying in a Coeur d'Alene nursing home waiting for her heart to stop. Penny thought about Cliff, Butch's dad, who, hearing of his son's death, simply sat down in his chair, and his heart stopped beating. Cable said, "It was because Grandpa wants to be with Daddy, so he left." Penny knew it was truer than merely a child's wistful explanation. She noticed there were only two TV vans at the memorial, one from Boise and one from Spokane. She guessed the dedication of a monument was not as important as the fire had been. Penny felt Michael lean into her, and she put her arm around him and pulled him closer.

Emma let go of Charlie's hand and handed him a Kleenex so he could dab his tears without too much embarrassment, although this certainly was a time when tears were more than appropriate. Charlie had barely made it out alive, and if it had not been for Lou Marks, he wouldn't have. The doctor said Charlie's lungs had suffered some permanent damage, but as long as he didn't smoke, he should be fine for many more years. But his mining days were definitely over. "Many more years are all I want," he once said. Emma was grateful for those who had rallied around and helped them build their house on the river. It allowed Charlie to be totally away from everything that reminded him of that day, although he still had nightmares. Emma's thoughts turned to the osprey she had seen gliding over the river this morning before they left, and she whispered a thanks to God.

Emma looked at Greg and Christina who had gotten married last summer. They had come to the memorial from over the hill, from their ranch in Montana. Christina had gotten a job at a small Montana newspaper, and they were raising Black Angus cattle. She knew they had plans to support a community in Tanzania and were gathering people with a variety of expertise to aid them. Emma wasn't sure, but her female intuitive sense told her that Christina was pregnant. She wasn't actually showing, but Emma knew the signs were there, especially if you watched Greg's care of her.

"It's ironic," Emma thought. "We're here honoring the dead, but I'm thinking of new life. Life seems to have its own pull forward. God won't allow us to remain mourners forever. 'A time to mourn, and a time to dance,'[12]" she recalled from Ecclesiastes. As Father Toraselli led them in prayer, she thought of Pastor Chalice and how he had left Kellogg shortly after the fire. She heard that he left the ministry to take a job in government. Emma was sure it was good for him, but she wasn't sure it was best for the country. She looked to the end of their row and saw that Brenda's two-year-old was asleep in his stroller. She smiled.

Pete and Faith sat near the rear of the gathering. Faith knew that many of the folks thought her an outsider because she had left only to return when it was too late. Faith understood, and it mattered little to her. She knew in her heart that her father had found peace with himself and with God.

After Emma Reed had shared all she knew about Faith's dad's changes in behavior prior to the fire, it was not difficult for her to see her father as the hero she had adored as a small girl before he lost himself to an evil darkness within him. She had learned in her own healing that God is both the giver and the sustainer of all life, a mysterious spirit who cleanses and forgives us, who gives all people worth. Faith kept thinking of her father as the lost prodigal who had finally returned and received the loving embrace of his own gracious Father.

Pete held Hope, his baby daughter, on his lap and was glad she was finally asleep. He knew this ceremony was important for his wife. Faith had grieved, but as she said, she had borne her grief years before the fire and her father's death. She was assured that he knew God's forgiveness, and that was all that mattered to her. Pete thought about DJ and Betsy and how DJ had always talked about the power of names. He looked at Faith and was thankful for the depth of her faith and how it had "marked" his life, bringing him out of his cynicism and into an appreciation of life as a gift. Faith Marks was now Faith Webb, an entangled woman of faith. Pete put his hand in his pocket and felt his compass. "I have found my way," he thought.

Pete felt little Hope's warmth against his body and could smell the fragrance of the baby shampoo in her hair. He smiled as he thought of the ride in Francis two years before, how beside the highway, while Faith cried on his shoulder, he had smelled the shampoo in her beautiful, blonde hair—something she and Hope now shared. His mind went to the two pictures on his desk at home—the original one of the cabin with his parents that he had found broken when he returned home, and the new one with him and Faith and Hope, the picture Brindle took. He thought of his old chipped bowl that he wouldn't let Faith give to Goodwill. It was full of fresh fruit now, sitting in their kitchen. Pete said to no one, "We all have brokenness in our lives, but God is always moving us toward new life, bearing fresh fruit. There must be power in a name after all."

Book Club Questions

Part I   Hide and Seek

1. What do you think of Pete's perception of elderly people?
2. Pete describes himself as "entangled." What do you think he means? In what ways might you be entangled?
3. How do most people try to become unentangled? How did Faith?
4. DJ says there is significance and power in a name. What do you think? (Why is no one named Judas?)
5. What do you think Pete was running from? Why?
6. What do you think about Pete's analysis of the meaning of life and the "camps" we find ourselves in?
7. What was your first reaction to James Addison, Jr.'s story? (It is based on true events.) Is it better to stand on our principles regardless of the cost?
8. When Pete first sees Faith, he draws certain conclusions. How do his conclusions compare to who she really is? What can we learn from this?
9. Why is it sometimes easier to reveal ourselves to strangers than to friends?
10. If you were to tell *your* story, where would you begin? What would be significant?
11. Is your experience like Pete's, hearing the voice of a parent throughout your life? How has that affected you?
12. Faith talks about forgiveness as healing and a struggle. What is the nature of forgiveness in your experience?
13. Why was Faith able to forgive her father?
14. What do you think of the idea that we are all somehow connected? What are the implications if that is true? How does that speak to racial divisions?
15. Can we make a future without dealing with the pain of our past, pretending nothing ever happened?
16. Character is mentioned as a desirable attribute. What is character? How is it developed, and how do you discover it in others?

17. What attribute does Faith find particularly appealing in Pete? Do you think that is important? What attributes do you look for in a friend?
18. Pete had difficulty being alone in the cabin with silence. Why do we as a culture avoid silence?
19. Pete questions whether we can change our paradigm of reality. What do you think?
20. How does the change in Lou Marks take place? What does that tell us about God's view of us?
21. How might the acceptance of death enhance life?
22. What role does God play in this book? In your life?

Part II Fire!

1. How do you react to Crystal's question, "Could I be doing more?"
2. Does activity in itself bring meaning to life?
3. To you, what is the most difficult thing about unexpected tragedies?
4. What is your impression of Faith as she returns to Kellogg?
5. Why do you think Agnes is so touched by the mine fire?
6. Do you identify with Penny in any way? How can we respond to someone who is experiencing such loss?
7. What does the fact that this event went from front page to old news when J. Edgar Hoover died tell us about our society and the press?
8. What did you learn from Hollis?
9. How does Cable teach us about the strength and resilience of children?
10. What is the significance of wind, breath, and spirit?
11. What did you learn from Larry Frost?
12. What did you learn from Emma Stone? What did you appreciate most about her?
13. What did you learn about the importance of knowing someone's story in order to understand them, not judge them, and perhaps love them?
14. What role did death play in this book, and what does death teach us about living?

Acknowledgments

John Donne was right. "No man is an island." None of us are singular, even though we may think we are. Nor does anyone write a book without help, encouragement, consoling, and assistance. Because this book was written over three decades, many people have assisted me, some giving me a secluded place and others a word of encouragement. I'd like to acknowledge the following people who have all helped make this book possible.

Louis Shaddock, who believed it was a worthwhile project.

Katie Kerns, my first proofreader, without whose enthusiasm I probably would have never finished.

Lisa Voth for her editing and helpful criticism.

Matt Green who saved me from the black hole of technology and made completion possible.

Joanna Koziol for asking hard questions. Brittan Hart for her photograph of me, and Moses Hart for his tech skill. Warren Bakes for his forever positive spirit.

My team at Lucid Books, who turned my efforts into reality, and Sue Vander Hook, my dedicated proofreader.

And finally, my family, my tech-savvy grandchildren, and especially my wife, Kathleen, for her patient encouragement.

Additional Reading

Carpenter, Cory. "The Sunshine Mine Disaster: Idaho's Worst Mining Disaster." *Spokane Historical.* https://spokanehistorical.org/items/show/461.

Lewis, C. S. *Mere Christianity.* (New York: Harper Collins, 1980).

Lukas, J. Anthony. *Big Trouble.* (New York: Simon & Schuster, 1997).

Lynch, Martin. *Mining in World History.* (London: Reaktion Books, 2002).

"Mine Disasters in the United States: Sunshine Mining Company, Sunshine Mine Fire." *United States Mine Rescue Association.* https://usminedisasters. miningquiz.com/saxsewell/sunshine.htm.

Mukherjee, Siddhartha. *The Emperor of All Maladies: A Biography of Cancer.* (New York: Scribner, a Division of Simon & Schuster, 2010).

Olsen, Gregg. *The Deep Dark: Disaster and Redemption in America's Richest Silver Mine.* (New York: Brown Publishers, 2005).

Russell, Bert. *North Fork of the Coeur d'Alene River.* (Harrison, ID: Lacon Publishers, 1984).

Schwantes, Carlos A. *In Mountain Shadows: A History of Idaho.* (Lincoln, NE: University of Nebraska Press, 1996).

Notes

1. Hemult Thielecke, in Ray S. Anderson, ed, *Theological Foundations for Ministry*, Google Books, 627.
2. Fanny Crosby, "Blessed Assurance," *The Hymnal for Music & Celebration*, 345, https://hymnary.org/hymn/HWC1986/345.
3. John 1:14 ESV.
4. Lam. 1:12 ESV.
5. Eccles. 3:1 ASV.
6. Gen. 32:28.
7. John Bunyan, *The Pilgrim's Progress*, Google Books.
8. J.R.R. Tolkien, *The Lord of the Rings Trilogy*, quoted in Goodreads, https://www.goodreads.com/quotes/7379112-where-there-s-life-there-s-hope.
9. See Gen. 29:20.
10. Joachim Neander, "Praise to the Lord, the Almighty," *Hymnary.org*, https://hymnary.org/text/praise_to_the_lord_the_almighty_the_king.
11. John 3:8.
12. Eccles. 3:4.